Leading Beyond

Leading Beyond

Biblical Leadership That Unifies Opposition

Pierre Everson Cannings

WIPF & STOCK · Eugene, Oregon

LEADING BEYOND
Biblical Leadership That Unifies Opposition

Copyright © 2024 Pierre Everson Cannings. All rights reserved. Except for brief quotations in critical publications or reviews, no part of this book may be reproduced in any manner without prior written permission from the publisher. Write: Permissions, Wipf and Stock Publishers, 199 W. 8th Ave., Suite 3, Eugene, OR 97401.

Wipf & Stock
An Imprint of Wipf and Stock Publishers
199 W. 8th Ave., Suite 3
Eugene, OR 97401

www.wipfandstock.com

PAPERBACK ISBN: 978-1-6667-8559-3
HARDCOVER ISBN: 978-1-6667-8560-9
EBOOK ISBN: 978-1-6667-8561-6

VERSION NUMBER 06/18/24

Unless otherwise noted, Scripture quotations taken from the (NASB®) New American Standard Bible®, Copyright © 2020 by The Lockman Foundation. Used by permission. All rights reserved. lockman.org

This current study is dedicated to God, who I hope takes pleasure in my labor and service to his kingdom purposes. It was only through his word, grace, strength, and wisdom that this study was possible.

Contents

Acknowledgments | ix
Abbreviations | xi

1 Introduction | 1
    Thesis   2
    Literature Review   3
    Theological Foundations   8
    History of Racism and Divide in the North American Church   14
    Twenty-First Century Challenges to Diversity in the North American Church   16
    Transformational Leadership   21
    Transformational Pastoral Leadership   26
    Justification for the Study   29
    Chapter Summaries   31

2 The Book of Acts | 33
    Background of Acts   33
    Historicity and Interpretation of Acts   34
    Geographical Review   48
    Initial Spread of the Gospel   52

viii CONTENTS

3 Peter's Transformational Leadership after Pentecost | 66
   Introduction   66
   Peter's Origin   67
   Burns's Origin   68
   Peter   72
   Conclusion   108

4 Paul's Transformational Leadership after Pentecost | 109
   Paul's Origin   109
   Conclusion   155

5 The Transformational Leadership of Peter and Paul and
   the Principles Applied to the Current Church | 157
   Comparison of Transformational Leadership and Responses
   to the Diversity of Peter and Paul   158
   Transformational Leadership Principles of Peter and Paul
   Applied to the Current Church   183
   Conclusion   204

6 Leadership Themes Summary and Conclusions | 206
   Summary of the Transformational Leadership Principles
   of Paul and Peter   206
   New Learning from Historical Analysis   209
   Future Areas of Study   209
   Conclusion   210

Bibliography | 213

Acknowledgments

To my beautiful wife, Monica, you faithfully loved, supported, encouraged, and motivated me to complete this endeavor. Without you, this feat would have been impossible. You have endured with me and prayed for me endlessly. Without your strength, I would not have finished. To my children, Natalia, Pierre II, and Carter, who supported and witnessed my toil, I pray this journey exemplified the perseverance, diligence, and dedication that is necessary to achieve your individual and God-given goals.

I am forever grateful to my father and mother for their undying and unwavering support in my life and academic pursuits. Thank you for modeling the perseverance necessary to pursue my goals. From my childhood, you taught me to pursue educational excellence, and as a man, that pursuit remains unchanged. Thank you for always lifting me in prayer. To my brother, Paul, thank you for always loving and protecting me from our childhood. To Auntie, thank you for your constant support and investment in my studies. Thank you for opening your home and wisdom to me as I journeyed this path. To all my family and friends who prayed and encouraged me, I am eternally thankful and look forward to sharing this completion with you.

To my cohort, this has been an amazing journey, and I am thankful I was able to do it with each of you. We laughed, cried, and persevered together. In the end, we became a family filled with lifelong memories. I want to acknowledge individually Kenny Comstock, my friend and classmate, whom I miss dearly. Cathy and Deborah, I am forever grateful for your grace, intelligence, flexibility, and perfectionism, which have made this current study possible. To Dr. Goodyear, thank you for your wisdom, patience, and grace as you led me through my dissertation. To Dr. Whiting, thank you for your input and correction, which helped refine the current study to its completion.

Abbreviations

ABD	*Anchor Bible Dictionary.* Edited by David Noel Freedman. 6 vols. New York: Doubleday, 1992
AThR	*Anglican Theological Review*
AYBRL	Anchor Yale Bible Reference Library
BDAG	Danker, Frederick W., et al. *Greek-English Lexicon of the New Testament and Other Early Christian Literature.* 3rd ed. Chicago: University of Chicago Press, 2000
BEB	*Baker Encyclopedia of the Bible.* Edited by Walter A. Elwell. 2 vols. Grand Rapids: Baker, 1988
BECNT	*Baker Exegetical Commentary on the New Testament*
CBQ	*Catholic Biblical Quarterly*
DPL	*Dictionary of Paul and His Letters.* Edited by Gerald F. Hawthorne and Ralph P. Martin. Downers Grove, IL: InterVarsity, 1993
EBD	*Eerdmans Bible Dictionary.* Edited by David Noel Freedman. Grand Rapids: Eerdmans, 1987
EDNT	*Exegetical Dictionary of the New Testament.* Edited by Horst Balz and Gerhard Schneider. ET. 3 vols. Grand Rapids: Eerdmans, 1990–1993
HarBD	*Harper's Bible Dictionary.* Edited by Paul J. Achtemeier. SBL 10. San Francisco: Harper & Row, 1985

ICC	International Critical Commentary
L&N	Louw, Johannes P., and Eugene A. Nida, eds. *Greek-English Lexicon of the New Testament: Based on Semantic Domains.* 2nd ed. New York: United Bible Societies, 1989
LBD	Lexham Bible Dictionary. Edited by John D. Barry. Bellingham, WA: Lexham, 2016. Ebook
*NBD*³	*New Bible Dictionary.* Edited by D. R. W. Wood et al. 3rd ed. Downers Grove, IL: InterVarsity, 1996
NDBT	New Dictionary of Biblical Theology: Exploring the Unity & Diversity of Scripture. Edited by T. Desmond Alexander et al. Downers Grove, IL: InterVarsity Press, 2000. IVP Reference Collection. Ebook
NICOT	New International Commentary
NIGTC	New International Greek Testament Commentary
SBL	Society of Biblical Literature
TDNT	*Theological Dictionary of the New Testament.* Edited by Gerhard Kittel and Gerhard Friedrich. Translated by Geoffrey W. Bromiley. 10 vols. Grand Rapids: Eerdmans, 1964–1976
TNTC	Tyndale New Testament Commentaries
WBC	Word Biblical Commentary

1

Introduction

The North American church's history with racism, slavery, and social equality is blemished and stained with silence, complicity, comfort, and inactivity. Religion and racism are rooted deeply in America's history:

> The racial problem in America is the asterisk on an otherwise respectable reputation. Whether manifesting itself overtly in conflicts between differing racial and cultural groups, or simply lurking below the surface as a suspicion camouflaging the true depth of the problem, it continues to be the one dominant area of our failure as a nation.[1]

Despite the biblical and theological mandate and understanding for diversity, the church has failed throughout history to properly address the lack of unity. The American church struggles with cultural diversity, causing persistent issues with division in the local and universal body of Christ. Martin Luther King Jr. famously stated that Sunday is the most racially segregated day of the week.[2]

The church's issue with diversity is not new, and we can see it throughout the Bible. According to Scripture, the knowledge of God and Jesus provides people of the Christian faith everything they need for life and godliness (2 Pet 1:3). The problem in the Christian church of a lack of diversity can be addressed through the principles, models, and directions of the Scriptures. A careful examination of Scripture can give the church today the necessary principles and model for unity. Particularly, the

---

1. Evans, *Oneness Embraced*, 17.
2. Emerson, *People of the Dream*, 121.

historical accounts of the early church and the leadership of the apostles in the book of Acts are a model for the twenty-first-century church.

Thesis

The thesis of this book, simply stated, is: "In the book of Acts, Paul's and Peter's responses to the diversity of Pentecost demonstrated a model of transformational leadership, which can be applied to the twenty-first-century American church." The research will exegetically investigate the leadership principles in the book of Acts during the diversification of the church during Pentecost and their influence on diversification of the church while spreading the faith around the world. The research will closely examine James MacGregor Burns's theory of transforming leadership and its application to the leadership of Peter and Paul in Acts. While acknowledging his expansive works, the examination of Burns's theory of transforming leadership will focus on his classic book, *Leadership*. Burns states that the "result of transforming leadership is a relationship of mutual stimulation and elevation that converts followers into leaders and may convert leaders into moral agents."[3]

Paul and Peter responded missionally to the diversity of Pentecost, following their calling to any people group as moral agents. Therefore, the research will seek to show Peter and Paul as moral agents, while converting more leaders from different ethnic backgrounds and how their transformational leadership principles apply to the American church in the twenty-first century. The research will examine exegetically the apostles' leadership principles during the diversification of the early church after Pentecost, while applying the definition, theories, and results of Burns's transforming leadership so that the twenty-first-century American church can pattern its leadership in response to the churches of Christianity's cultural diversity. The current study proposes that the leadership principles of Paul and Peter in the book of Acts are applicable and relevant to the current issues in church diversity.

---

3. Burns, *Leadership*, 4.

Literature Review

Defining Diversity

Race, nationality, and ethnicity have separated people for centuries. In his dissertation, "The Impact of Ethnically Diverse Leadership upon the Culture of a Historically African American Church of Christ," Ervin Jackson states that even though general use of the terminology for cultural diversity exists, researchers have varying definitions of what diversity really means. Diversity literature is broad and expansive, addressing many nuances; however, the literature is usually confined to secular and educational organizations. In "Toward a Model of Diversity Leadership: Examining Leadership's Role in Creating an Inclusive Workplace," Sheilesha Willis agrees that the increased desire of academics and practitioners for studies in diversity have increased conceptualizations and definitions.[4]

"Literature that addresses diversity is very restricted in scope," Ervin Jackson writes.[5] After review, however, Jackson adopted the definition from Johnson, Bassin, and Shaw: "Ethnic/Racial Background: Of a nation; any of the different varieties or populations of human beings distinguished by physical traits, blood types, genetic code patterns, or inherited characteristics that are unique to an isolated breeding population."[6] Jackson recognized this definition limits diversity to physical characteristics and results of socialization. However, Willis expands the definition beyond physical characteristics. Before Willis presents her definition, she provides a definition of diversity by Barak, Cherin, and Berkman in "Organizational and Personal Dimensions in Diversity Climate." The definition is "visible or non-visible differences in a specific background such as race, religion, sexual orientation, education, gender, culture, age, or function."[7]

According to this definition, diversity can be broadened to any physical or relational difference. Therefore, Willis summarizes and concludes that a broad definition was better served. Willis defines diversity as "the combination of relational or informational differences within a work unit that can lead to either positive or negative outcomes."[8] Jackson

---

4. Willis, "Model of Diversity Leadership," 4.
5. Jackson, "Ethnically Diverse Leadership," 3.
6. Family and Youth Services Bureau, *Enhancing the Cultural Competence*, 25.
7. Willis, "Model of Diversity Leadership," 3.
8. Willis, "Model of Diversity Leadership," 4.

and Willis agree on the existence of broad multiple concepts and definitions. Therefore, it is advantageous to delineate the definition of diversity into categories for this current study is advantageous.

Research has often indicated that diversity can be categorized to ethnicity, race, and culture. When addressing diversity, each definition is necessary to delineate the meaning of current research. Although culture, ethnicity, and race are distinct, some churches and research confuse or intermingle the terminology.

Some scholars and practitioners have used the terms *multiracial, multiethnic, multicultural,* and *diverse* interchangeably; it is also common to find churches with intentionality toward diversity referring to themselves as either multiracial, multiethnic, or multicultural. It is important to make a distinction between race, ethnicity, and culture, because unlike race and ethnicity, culture does not rely on traits and physical characteristics. Culture is transmissible by shared experience, social interaction, and learning.[9]

Leander's argument proposes that scholars and practitioners have not differentiated ethnicity, race, and culture. A lack of definition creates the assumption that each term is identical or similar. For the sake of clarity, therefore, it is critical that current research defines and chooses the correct terminology.[10]

Race

Race deserves definition due to its distinction from ethnicity and culture. Although ethnicity and culture have varying definitions, race is unique in its origins and limitations. Emerson and Short both agree that race is socially constructed and based on physical characteristics.[11] The social construct can be traced back to the sixteenth and seventeenth centuries.[12] Short states that race is a social construct that "generally refers to skin color and other readily observable physical characteristics."[13] Emerson agrees with Short, stating that "race is socially constructed at

---

9. Leander, "Intercultural Leadership," 2.
10. Short, "Meeting the Challenge," 31.
11. Short, "Meeting the Challenge," 31; Emerson, *People of the Dream*, 7.
12. Emerson and Smith, *Divided by Faith*, 7.
13. Short, "Meeting the Challenge," 31.

these points because selected physical characteristics are associated with selected social characteristics."[14]

According to Emerson, race is a social construct that limits a person with the assumption that physical characteristics determine social outcomes. Despite the limitations and origins, race continues to play an integral role in society. Emerson writes, "Who people marry, where people live, political struggles, objective interest, and identity, among others, are all part of the racialized character of society, and the 'structure' of racial formation."[15] Due to the limitations and assumptions in the definition of race, it is difficult to express the nuances that are included with culture and ethnicity.

Culture

Unlike race, culture includes many nuances that need to be defined. "It is important to make a distinction between race, ethnicity, and culture because unlike race and ethnicity, culture does not rely on traits and physical characteristics."[16] The definition of culture requires specificity due to numerous definitions and nuances. Short agrees that authors have applied various definitions of culture.[17] Northouse states that "Anthropologists, sociologists, and many others have debated the meaning of the word culture. Because it is an abstract term, it is hard to define, and different people often define it dissimilar ways."[18] The differences and nuances make it critical to differentiate ethnicity, race, and culture.

Northouse defines culture as "the learned beliefs, values, rules, norms, symbols, and traditions that are common to a group of people. It is these shared qualities of a group that make them unique. Culture is a dynamic that is transmitted to others."[19] Short agrees with Northouse's definition but adds that culture is not static and in flux.[20] According to the definitions, culture is fluid learned behaviors and materials shared by a group of people.

14. Emerson, *People of the Dream*, 7.
15. Emerson, *People of the Dream*, 7.
16. Leander, "Intercultural Leadership," 2.
17. Short, "Meeting the Challenge," 32.
18. Northouse, *Leadership*, 429.
19. Leander, "Intercultural Leadership," 2.
20. Short, "Meeting the Challenge," 33.

Defining culture helps differentiate the term from ethnicity. Leander states that the primary difference between culture and ethnicity is that culture does not rely on physical characteristics and traits. He adds that culture is transmissible by shared experience, social interaction, and learning.[21] Therefore, culture has noticeable differences that distinguish the use of culture and ethnicity in this current study.

Ethnicity

Ethnicity's definition is distinct because it focuses on the individual's heritage, origin, and ancestry. Chadwick Short, in "Meeting the Challenge of Diversity: Ministry and Mission in a Multicultural Milieu," summarizes ethnicity:

> Ethnicity, as used in this project, has two sides: the understanding a group of people holds about themselves, and the understanding others have about a group, whether that understanding is real or active, based on elements such as common ancestry, shared national origin, and distinctive cultural traits.[22]

This definition summarizes the commonly stated definitions of ethnicity. Ethnicity describes a group of people who hold an understanding about themselves based on their ancestry, shared nations, origin, or cultural traits. Robert Winthrop summarizes ethnicity as social markers that distinguish groups in social interactions. The "distinctions are both social and cultural including physical appearance (race), geographic origins (migration), economic specialization, language, and expressive patterns such as clothing and diet."[23]

James and Lillian Breckinridge add that a group of people's understanding about themselves comes from their childhood, "that part of cultural development occurring prior to the onset of a child's abstract intellectual powers as a result of his direct personal contacts with the people around him and with his immediate environment."[24] Due to the definitions provided, this current research will not adopt Mark DeYmaz's definition of "multiethnic" in "Building a Healthy Multi-Ethnic Church,"

---

21. Leander, "Intercultural Leadership," 2.
22. Short, "Meeting the Challenge," 32.
23. Winthrop, "Ethnicity," 94.
24. Breckinridge and Breckenridge, *What Color*, 57–58; see also Ramirez, "Pastoral Leadership Practices."

which includes educational and generational aspects.²⁵ Therefore, ethnicity broadly defines a group of people who are distinguished socially and culturally by their ancestry, geographic origins, and distinct cultural traits that are understood during one's childhood.

In agreement with DeYmaz, this research will use ethnicity to emphasize the broad definition that encompasses social and cultural differences. Compared to race, ethnicity correlates to the biblical understanding that humans are one race but multiple ethnicities. God created one human race; in God's diverse plan, however, he made humans with different physical appearances, geographic origins, languages, and ancestries. DeYmaz and Li provide biblical support: "The Bible makes it clear that there is only one race—the human race—comprised of many ethnicities (*ethne*, Greek plural, as used in Acts 17:26, for example, where we are told God 'made from one man every nation [*ethnos*, Greek singular] of mankind')."²⁶ The *New Dictionary of Biblical Theology* states, "In 64 passages *ethnos* has no specialized sense. The reference is to a people or peoples (including the Jewish people; cf. Acts 10:22; 1 Pet 2:9, *éthnos* being used interchangeably with *laós* in this regard). *Pánta éthnē* denotes all nations."²⁷

The Bible recognizes nationalities or people of all nations. People from all nations possess diverse cultures, origins, languages, and ancestries. Dennis Durst defines ethnicity as "groups of people linked by kinship, land, culture, or government; in the Bible, 'the nations' especially refers to those who are not Israelite."²⁸ The New Testament understanding of *ethnos* originates in the Abrahamic covenant. God promised to make Abraham a father to many nations:

> The NT depiction of Jews and Gentiles is largely built on two major OT themes: the Abrahamic promise (Gen. 12:1–3) and the Isaianic Servant of the Lord (42:1–4; 49:1–6; 50:4–9; 52:13–53:12; 61:1–3). Pervading the NT is the conviction that in Jesus, the promised seed of Abraham, all the nations have been blessed (Acts 3:25; Rom. 4:17–18; 15:8–12; Gal. 3:6–9, 13–14). The evangelists affirm at the very outset that Abrahamic descent is not confined to physical Israel (Matt. 3:9 par).²⁹

25. DeYmaz, *Building Healthy Multi-Ethnic Church*, 519.
26. DeYmaz and Li, *Ethnic Blends*, 39.
27. Andreas J. Köstenberger, "Nations," *NDBT* 677.
28. Dennis L. Durst, "Nations," *LBD*, para. 1.
29. Köstenberger, "Nations."

The pursuit of the Abrahamic promise to all nations was implemented throughout the New Testament. The apostle Paul spread the gospel to all the gentile nations throughout the New Testament.[30] Galatians 3:14 highlights the gospel going forward from the Abrahamic covenant to all the nations. In continuation with the New Testament, this current research will utilize the term *multiethnic* when discussing diversity in the modern-day church.

Theological Foundations

The discussion of diversity is not simply a congregational and pastoral issue. Theologians and scholars have spent countless hours debating and researching God's design for diversity and ecclesiology:

> The question of the church's response to cultural diversity has been considered not only at the level of the local congregation, but at the academic level as well. Theologians and missiologists have discussed and debated the matter at great length. While there are some areas of agreement, significant areas of disagreement remain.[31]

The church's understanding of the theological implications for the ecclesiological response to diversity is critical. "Of course, God's heart for the nations is made clear in the Bible, from the book of Genesis through the apostle John's writing in the book of Revelation."[32] The entire Bible reveals God's plan for diversity and God's desire for unification of all nations. The foundation for diversity within the church is founded in theology and biblical studies.

Understanding God's intent for diversity begins with his creation. God created all humankind in his image. From the beginning, Gen 1:26 states, men and women are created in the image of God, and God values all of his creation:

> To explore and understand the role of culture from a biblical framework, we must go all the way back to the creation story in Genesis. The idea that humanity has been given a responsibility and duty from the Creator to go forth and create culture

---

30. Köstenberger, "Nations."
31. Short, "Meeting the Challenge," 17.
32. DeYmaz and Li, *Ethnic Blends*, 40.

originates from the theological understanding that humanity was made in the image of God.[33]

In "Majority World Theology in an Urban, Multiethnic North American Church Plant," Stallard argues that the Bible defines humans as one race in God's image. Stallard specifically states, "Race is a social construct, not a biological reality. Biblically, there is only one human race, and everyone shares equally in the imago dei."[34] Despite God's creation of all humankind in God's image, human sin has created division and segregation.

Jonathan Boston, Andrew Bradstock, and David Eng, in *Public Policy: Why Ethics Matter*, argue that the core of creation is that all humanity is created equal in virtue, despite their differences in gender, ethnicity, size, or nationality. They continue by stating that people should celebrate their differences, since all are made a little lower than angels.[35] They contend that Christians cannot accept the world's view that materialism adds value to individuals.[36] In "Economic Inequality as God's Law? Considering the Nature of Economic Life," Alison Lutz writes,

> Reducing the value of human beings to the value of the goods they produce in the market system is a theologically weak proposition for another reason. One of the characteristics of God is that He is creator. God makes things. But the identity and value of God the maker of all things is not defined strictly by the value of things He creates.[37]

The comfort of riches blinds the affluent from the disadvantages of the poor, oppressed, and disenfranchised. However, Christians from all economic classes who value all humans as God's creation will seek justice for the oppressed, poor, and those affected by racial inequalities. Boston, Bradstock, and Eng write,

> God is perceived to be against systems that institutionalize the exploitation of the poor. This is most clearly seen with respect to the distribution of that most basic commodity, land. In Numbers 26, when Moses divides the land among the tribes in

---

33. Rah, *Many Colors*, 268.
34. Stallard, "Majority World Theology," 111.
35. Boston et al., *Public Policy*, 186.
36. Boston et al., *Public Policy*, 185.
37. Lutz, "Economic Inequality," 257.

proportion to their size, he does it by lot to prevent the most powerful securing for themselves the best.[38]

To take action, the church must seek to be a part of the lives and struggles of the disparaged:

> As we face this reality of a crisis in a civilization, our faith compels us to seek justice, to witness to the presence of God, and to be part of the lives and struggles of the people made weak and vulnerable by structures and cultures—women, children, people living in poverty in both urban and rural areas, indigenous people, people of African descent, racially oppressed communities, people with disabilities, forced migrant workers, refugees, and religious ethnic minorities.[39]

The Bible clearly speaks about the Christian's responsibility to defend the weak, stop oppression, stand up for the aliens, and seek justice. In *Many Colors: Cultural Intelligence for a Changing Church*, Soong-Chan Rah believes churches should expose their members to the realities of the world and the negative moral dilemmas caused by globalization.

Christianity is not limited to racial, cultural, or national identity, because according to Scripture, all children of God are made in God's image (Rom 8:16; Gen 1:27). Rah reiterates the same sentiment by stating that Christians should review the biblical framework of creation and the theological understanding that all people are created in God's image (Ps 83:3–4; Prov 13:41; Exod 23:9; Amos 5:24). Rah writes that Christians need to return to the original mandate, "which calls for believers to engage rather than categorically reject the surrounding culture, and arises out of the doctrine of the image of God. The doctrine of the image of God reveals that we bear a likeness to God in our spiritual capacity."[40] In "The Unity of the Church as the Witness of the Church," Stringfellow contends the correct understanding of God's design for diversity will change the perspective for the church. "The unity of the Church which is the witness of the Church is not necessarily a monolithic institutional unification of the several churches—a 'super church'—for the very reason that the witness requires a unity encompassing all diversities of human life."[41]

---

38. Boston et al., *Public Policy*, 10.
39. Boston et al., *Public Policy*, 185.
40. Rah, *Many Colors*, 282.
41. Stringfellow, "Unity of the Church," 525.

In addition to valuing God's creation and image, Lev 19:18 commands God's people to love their neighbors as themselves and to place everyone above themselves (cf. Phil 2:1–9). The neighbor is not limited to a person's proximity but is anyone whom one encounters anywhere in the world. David C. Carlson supports treating people as one's neighbors by stating, "The grave importance attached to treatment of the neighbor is understandable when seen as part of one's wider relationship with God and was considered something that could affect significantly the divine-human relationship."[42] God emphasizes throughout Scripture the necessity that his children love their neighbors. In Mark 12:31, when asked for the greatest commandments, Jesus reiterates the necessity to love one's neighbor. If Christians recognize their identities in Christ and their belongingness to God, they will treat all of God's creation with justice, dignity, and love.

In Acts 1:8, Jesus mandates for Christians to go to the remotest parts of the world to share the gospel. Laura Gauer concurs in *A Christian Perspective on Poverty and Social Justice: Sin Is More Than Just Flawed Character*: "Seeking justice is not limited to the national level, but justice should be persistently pursued abroad."[43] Missions is not limited to evangelism but also means helping the poor, standing for injustice, and using church resources to balance inequalities. In "The AGAPE Economy: The Church's Call to Action," Julio E. Murray agrees, saying, "We hear God calling us to live out our faith by working together to create the economy of life for the earth and all her beings, for justice and peace, for *koinonia* in the vision of God's economy."[44] All humanity should be defended, have opportunities of peace, and be a part of God's economy.

Book of Acts

In Scripture, the diversity of people is evident throughout the Bible. The book of Acts, after Pentecost, provides an example concerning diversity for the contemporary church. A careful investigation of the book of Acts can provide a model for the current church to imitate. An examination of the purpose, structure, geography, and the events of Pentecost in Acts will provide the necessary information for the study of diversity.

---

42. David C. Carlson, "Neighbor," *BEB* 2:1539.
43. Gauer, "Poverty and Social Justice," 362.
44. Murray, "AGAPE Economy," 135.

In *Eerdmans Bible Dictionary*, Allen C. Myers states that Pentecost at its root in the Old Testament means the fiftieth day as a part of the Jewish Feast of Weeks in Lev 23:15–21.[45] Freeman, in the *New Bible Dictionary*, agrees it was the fiftieth day past the offering of barley of the harvest.[46] Freeman later adds that, following the Old Testament definition, it became an "intertestamental period and later, Pentecost was regarded as the anniversary of the law-giving at Sinai."[47] Bock agrees with Freeman when he wrote that the intertestamental period included the anniversary of law giving at Sinai, which led many to believe that this day was selected for the significance to God giving his Holy Spirit.[48]

Walter A. Elwell and Philip Wesley Comfort note that in the New Testament, the required feast brought Jews from great distances to observe the festival.[49] Commentators such as Toussaint believe this was the Jews of the diaspora or the dispersion of the Jews.[50] James L. Mason, in *Baker Encyclopedia of the Bible*, defines *diaspora* as the Jewish people from Israel going to foreign lands.[51] However, it was not because of exile but for the sake of sharing the gospel to every nation (Jas 1:1; 1 Pet 1:1). Bock provides background on the people besides the Jews, who arrived from every nation and tongue to observe the feast.[52]

According to Spina, the event of Pentecost is in stark contrast to the event of the tower of Babel in Gen 11:[53]

> At Babel, God transformed a single language into many, creating confusion; at Jerusalem, the Holy Spirit made it possible for many languages to be understood as one, creating unity. At Babel, language was used to promote a human agenda ("Let us make a name for ourselves"); at Jerusalem, the "new" language was used to announce the "mighty works of God" (Acts 2:11). At Babel, God scattered the people in judgment (Gen 11:9; Gk *diespeiren*); at Jerusalem, God scattered (Acts 8:1, 4; Gk

---

45. Allen C. Myers, "Pentecost," *EBD* 811.
46. D. Freeman, "Pentecost, Feast of," *NBD*³ 898–99.
47. Freeman, *NBD*³ 898–99.
48. Bock, *Acts*, 95.
49. Elwell and Comfort, *Tyndale Bible Dictionary*, 1007.
50. Toussaint, "Acts," 2:357; Bock, *Acts*, 100.
51. James L. Mason, "Diaspora of the Jews," *BEB* 1:623.
52. Bock, *Acts*, 100.
53. Frank Anthony Spina, "Babel (Place)," *ABD* 561–62.

diesparésan; diasparentes) the people to spread the news, which would eventuate in worldwide unity.[54]

Spina uses biblical history to reconcile God's eternal plan for all nations to worship in unity. Although contrast is present, Kenneth A. Mathews reiterates that Pentecost was an integral role in God's desire to reconcile the nations from Babylon to Rev 7:9:

> The prophets speak of diverse ethnic personalities when they depict the future universal kingdom of God (e.g., Isa 2:1–4). At Pentecost, the outpouring of the Spirit upon the representative nations gathered in Jerusalem results in the spiritual union of the new church, but does not create a homogeneous language, ethnicity, or statehood. John's vision of the heavenly family includes diverse peoples from "every nation, tribe, people and language, standing before the throne and in front of the Lamb" (Rev 7:9).[55]

Mathews highlights that God did not change the diversity of tongue and ethnicity but unified every nation through the gospel. Mathews adds, "Pentecost shows that national distinctions are secondary to the union of a single people by the baptism of the Spirit in Christ. The gospel therefore is the reconciling antidote to the plurality of nations as it is preached among the world's peoples."[56] In addition, Pervo adds, "With splendid vividness, Luke has been able to intimate the coming gentile mission without prematurely inaugurating it. Jews are the missionary target, but without limit on place or language—and, it should be added, without the inconvenience of discontinuity."[57] In his vivid description and historical account, Luke lists the nations present during Pentecost:

> It begins with three countries to the east of the Roman Empire in the area known as Persia or Iran, and then (with a change of construction) moves westward to Mesopotamia, modern Iraq, and Judea. Next come various provinces and areas in Asia Minor (modern Turkey), and then Egypt and the area immediately westwards, followed by Rome. Then, we have a general statement applicable to all the peoples in mind: there was a considerable Jewish population in each of these areas, and the presence of Jews often led to the conversion of Gentiles to become

---

54. Spina, *ABD* 561–62.
55. Mathews, *Genesis 1—11:26*, 474.
56. Mathews, *Genesis 1—11:26*, 475–76.
57. Pervo, *Acts*, 71.

proselytes. Finally, and somewhat surprisingly, the list includes people from Crete and Arabia.[58]

Pentecost in Acts 2:1 is different because this is when God gave his Holy Spirit to the apostles and began the work of his church.[59]

Pervo adds, "Within the Christian tradition, the events of Pentecost, Acts 2:1–41 are viewed as the birth of the church."[60] This church was not limited to the Jews, but was the beginning of every nation having the opportunity for salvation and to take it back to their native country. Marshall states, "It must suffice to observe that the list is clearly meant to be an indication that people from all over the known world were present, and perhaps that they would return to their own countries as witnesses to what was happening."[61] This diversity of the faith is the beginning of the remainder of the book of Acts and the purpose of God's plan to save all nations.

History of Racism and Divide in the North American Church

Soong-Chan Rah states that knowing the content, larger narrative, and story of the negative aspects of racial and ethnic history of the American church helps facilitate proper diverse relationships in the church.[62] Ervin C. Jackson says that "American racism is unique because it emanates from two concepts: religion and skin-color."[63]

Despite the church's moral and theological obligations, the church often found itself on the wrong side of history against racism and social inequality. In his book *The Color of Compromise*, Jamar Tisby states, "Historically speaking, when faced with the choice between racism and equality, the American church has tended to practice a complicit Christianity rather than a courageous Christianity. They chose comfort over constructive conflict and in so doing created and maintained a status quo of injustice."[64] The church has often chosen to maintain its

---

58. Marshall, *Acts*, 75–76.
59. Walter A. Elwell, "Pentecost," *BEB* 2:1639–40.
60. Pervo, *Acts*, 70.
61. Marshall, *Acts*, 76.
62. Rah, *Many Colors*, 480.
63. Jackson, "Ethnically Diverse Leadership," 11.
64. Tisby, *Color of Compromise*, 17.

allegiance to its country and economic benefits even at the disadvantage of another ethnicity.

Even though the North American church has had a plethora of successes, increase in power, and global influence, a historical survey reveals the checkered past of failed moral stances and challenges of societal norms. Scholars, authors, and researchers have challenged the church's history by surveying the church's response to racism and racial inequalities. Tisby reviewed every era of North American church history and its complicity with racism.[65] He surveyed Christian leaders, revivals, and movements. In each era, the church failed to respond to racism and was active in constructing ideological and structural impediments during slavery, civil rights, and Jim Crow.[66] Tisby's historical survey reveals the participation of Christian leaders and churches in the defense of slavery, complicity during the Jim Crow, and compromises during the civil rights era.

In *People of the Dream*, Michael Emerson documents the historical accounts of segregation in the church. Emerson pinpoints events in history that continually advanced segregation of the church in America.[67] He documents the forced assimilation of African Americans into the American church during slavery and their eventual separation following the Civil War.[68]

In *Divide by Faith*, Emerson and Smith also address the church's role in history but focus on the church's struggle to bring races together after some Christians fought for freedom:

> In sum, through the long, arduous struggle, where religion aided racial change, it has been unidirectional: like America itself, it has occasionally helped to free people, but has been unable to bring them together or overcome racialization. The abolitionist movement worked to end slavery and free slaves, not to unite Americans in a common community. Likewise, the Civil Rights movement worked to gain rights and freedoms. Although it used the rhetoric of togetherness in its efforts, it was, to the consternation of many, unsuccessful in its realization.[69]

Emerson and Smith's survey of North American Christian history pinpoints the efforts for freedom but also highlights the struggle to provide

65. Tisby, *Color of Compromise*, 22.
66. Tisby, *Color of Compromise*, 192.
67. Emerson, *People of the Dream*, 172–382.
68. Emerson, *People of the Dream*, 254.
69. Emerson and Smith, *Divided by Faith*, 48–49.

direction in unifying ethnicities. Emerson and Smith add that throughout history, Christianity's focus on evangelism and discipleship avoided larger issues that were countercultural and remained within the larger culture, while refusing to use its influence for radical changes.[70]

Similar to Emerson and Smith, Jackson's brief historical survey concludes that "although attitudes of egalitarianism existed among some Christian abolitionists, elitist attitudes were prevalent."[71] Historians have covered the efforts of Christianity to end slavery or fight for civil rights, but they should not overlook the failures in unification and integration of ethnicities. Authors like Jackson and Smith did not omit the efforts of Christianity to end racism, but they also were willing to admit issues of equality and elitism. Tisby, Jackson, and Smith are not alone in pursuing a historical survey of the failures of the North American church and its response to diversity. The survey of North American church history is not limited to chronicling of events, but it is also evident in historical figures and architecture.

The Color of Christ, by Edward Blum and Paul Harvey, historically chronicles the persistent manipulation of the physical image of Jesus to establish racial hierarchical power. After careful review of North American church history, Blum and Harvey conclude that the white physical image of Jesus was critical to American history and a symbol of white American supremacy despite the civil rights crusades and demographic transformations.[72] The failure of the church creates the question of the change necessary for the church to correct its past actions.

Twenty-First Century Challenges to Diversity in the North American Church

The modern-day church is at a crossroads in its response to North America's increase in ethnic diversity. Diversity in North America in the twenty-first century continues to increase due to globalization and immigration:

> In large part due to globalization, immigration, and the information technology revolution—there is a more informed multicultural society that is challenging previously normative

---

70. Emerson and Smith, *Divided by Faith*, 21.
71. Jackson, "Ethnically Diverse Leadership," 12.
72. Blum and Harvey, *Color of Christ*, 22.

> but divisive social constructs related to race, ethnicity, and socio-economic class with the emergent values of diversity and inclusiveness.[73]

The increase in immigration and globalization is continually challenging the homogeneous social constructs of North America. Globalization has challenged the social constructs and the tendencies of individuals to favor their own races, ethnicities, or cultures.

Northouse refers to an individual's desire to favor his or her own group as ethnocentrism: "Ethnocentrism is the tendency for individuals to place their own group (ethnic, racial, or culture) at the center of their observations of others and their world."[74] Despite globalization's ability to spread culture, there often is an imbalance of cultural influence throughout the world. "However, the reality of globalization is that one culture, one nation, or one worldview tends to dominate the world, and there is an imbalanced flow between cultures."[75] The increase in technology and ability to transmit culture worldwide has often permitted an imbalance of influence in worldviews and cultures to permeate the world.

As in North America in general, so the church has not responded well to the increase in diversity and has often been guilty of a homogenous worship and ethnocentrism:

> The American church needs to face the inevitable and prepare for the next stage of her history—we are looking at a nonwhite majority, multiethnic American Christianity in the immediate future. Unfortunately, despite these drastic demographic changes, American evangelicalism remains enamored with an ecclesiology and a value system that reflect a dated and increasingly irrelevant cultural captivity and are disconnected from both a global and a local reality.[76]

The historical patterns of the church have failed to reflect the change in its surrounding communities, and the church should be active in changing its past.

Jackson adds an active conversation should take place for diversity and church leadership because of the increase in diversity in America:

---

73. Leander, "Intercultural Leadership," 3.
74. Northouse, *Leadership*, 428.
75. Rah, *Next Evangelicalism*, 129.
76. Rah, *Next Evangelicalism*, 12.

> Currently, most immigrants entering the United States are of non-Anglo-Saxon origin and the majority are of Asian and Hispanic ancestry. The U.S. census bureau projects that from 2000 to the year 2050 the White population will decrease from 71.4% to 52.8%; the Black population will increase from 12.2% to 13.2%; the Hispanic population will increase from 11.8% to 24.3%; the American Indian population will increase from 0.7% to 0.8%; and the Asian and Pacific Islander population will grow from 3.9% to 8.9% (U.S. Bureau of the Census, 2000).[77]

Due to the increase in diversity in the United States, churches should be active in discussing diversity and initiatives that contribute to culturally diverse churches. Brian Leander agrees that "there appears to be growing interest in the literature and across a range of organizational types of churches in diversity."[78]

Despite growing interest in diversity, many churches remain homogenous. In addition, Curtiss DeYoung, Michael Emerson, George Yancey, and Karen Kim state that church diversity has often been misrepresented:

> If we define a racially mixed congregation as one in which no one racial group is 80 percent or more of the congregation, just 7.5 percent of the more than 300,000 religious congregations in the United States are racially mixed. For Christian congregations, which form more than 90% of congregations in the United States, the share that is racially mixed drops to 5.5%. Of this small percentage, approximately half of the congregations are mixed only temporarily, during the time they are in transition from one group to another.[79]

Diversity in America continues to grow, and statistics indicate this will continue. Although America has a more diverse population, churches have fallen behind in creating a diverse church.

DeYoung et al.'s statistics illustrate the lack of diversity currently in churches. Michael Emerson agrees that those statistics evidence a multiracial church but explains his reasoning:

> More than 20 percent of the congregation must be of another racial or ethnic background for their presence to make noticeable differences. My continuous definition of a multiracial congregation is based on a measure called the general heterogeneity

---

77. Jackson, "Ethnically Diverse Leadership," 1.
78. Leander, "Intercultural Leadership," 16.
79. DeYoung et al., *United by Faith*, 2.

index. It measures the probability that two randomly selected people in a congregation will be of different racial groups.[80]

The percentages remain consistent as DeYmaz also agrees with similar statistical numbers and believes this proves the church's failure to diversify. DeYmaz states that "92.5 percent of Catholic and Protestant churches throughout the United States can be classified as 'monoracial.'"[81] Leander supports the belief that churches were behind in diversity. His research describes churches that have created mission statements for diversity and shared purpose but have rules and procedures that separate people groups.[82]

Christians within congregations are responsible for accepting, prioritizing, and integrating other cultures for the purpose of a diverse church. Jackson believes that despite societal and organizational trends to recognize the value of diversity, the church continues to lag behind.[83] According to Jackson, the issue is that churches and church research tend to focus on racial attitudes and prejudices.[84]

In *Building a Healthy Multi-Ethnic Church: Mandate, Commitments and Practices of a Diverse Congregation*, DeYmaz writes, "With this in mind, a healthy multi-ethnic church is a place in which people are comfortable being uncomfortable. In such a place, members recognize that they are part of something much bigger than themselves."[85] However, churches have tended to remain comfortable while avoiding challenging the culture or the system:

> Evangelicals usually fail to challenge the system not just out of concern for evangelism, but also because they support the American system and enjoy its fruits. They share the Protestant work ethic, support laissez-faire economics, and sometimes fail to evaluate whether the social system is consistent with their Christianity.[86]

The church's inability to disconnect from the fruits of America's culture has limited the influential capabilities of the church. As history reveals,

---

80. Emerson, *People of the Dream*, 510.
81. DeYmaz, *Building Healthy Multi-Ethnic Church*, 3.
82. Leander, "Intercultural Leadership," 17.
83. Jackson, "Ethnically Diverse Leadership," 2.
84. Jackson, "Ethnically Diverse Leadership," 3.
85. DeYmaz, *Building Healthy Multi-Ethnic Church*, 110.
86. Emerson and Smith, *Divided by Faith*, 22.

however, the church is fully capable of creating cultural and systemic change if it challenges America's social systems.

Collectively, churches can create social changes, but there must be internal change inside the lives of the people in the church. In *Planting, Transitioning, and Growing Multiethnic Churches*, Fowler believes that, despite the churches' ideologies of diversity, they have failed to reach God's design: "The United States, especially in urban areas, is becoming increasingly multiethnic, yet churches are failing to reach out to this mission field in their own communities. The ethnic representation in most churches does not reflect the diversity of ethnicity in the community."[87] Jackson's research argues that to change diversity in the church, churches have to look past the attitudes to behavioral change.[88]

In *People of the Dream: Multiracial Congregations in the United States*, Michael O. Emerson agrees that the church lacks diversity, but he adds that some churches are indifferent and apathetic to racially divided congregations.[89] Churches need to urgently seek the unity of God in the church: "Where the Church denies or rejects or perverts the gift of unity, the witness of the Church to the world is lost."[90]

In "Spiritual Formation and Multiethnic Congregations," Kevin Gushiken adds that a diverse church has to prioritize and strategize for diversity to occur. The church, he continues, cannot be confused between a culturally assimilated church and a diverse church. Gushiken addresses the failure of a racially assimilated church:

> First, there are racially diverse congregations with one ethnic group determining the organization and methodology of the church. This is referred to as the "color-blind" approach where ethnic minorities are assimilated into the church based on a faulty premise that every church operates in a similar way. This structure is attractive because it provides the appearance of multiethnicity without the discomfort of cultural blending.[91]

For a church to diversify truly, it needs a structure that incorporates all races, ethnicities, and cultural experiences into its congregation. Stallard agrees with Gushiken that North American churches need to make

---

87. Fowler, "Planting, Transitioning, and Growing," 15.
88. Jackson, "Ethnically Diverse Leadership," 4.
89. Emerson, *People of the Dream*, 135.
90. Stringfellow, "Unity of the Church," 524.
91. Gushiken, "Spiritual Formation," 186.

every effort to plant churches that are culturally relevant: "If God has created humans to be culture makers, and this manifests itself in a rich diversity of expressions, then it behooves the church to contextualize its message to correspond to this diversity."[92] Research indicates that there are applicable strategies to church diversification that can assist in creating a multiethnic church.

Transformational Leadership

The book of Acts sets the stage for the necessity of transformational leaders. Significant evidence exists of Paul's origin, purpose, calling, vision, and empowerment in the face of persecution. An in-depth definition of transformational leadership and Paul's actions in the book of Acts will affirm that Paul is the perfect model for this current study.

Study of Origins

The background of a leader can help explain his or her influence in his or her current context. Leaders should be examined not only in their time of influence but also in their background, childhood, and early experiences. In his book *Leadership*, Burns indicates that leaders' and followers' needs, personalities, and leadership behaviors can be traced back to psychological, social sources, and political leadership.[93]

Burns clearly states that the "qualities of leadership emerge out of the imitative, selective and role-taking or empathetic processes."[94] Leaders learn through imitation of others by accepting responsibilities of roles. As Burns states, "Children learn to see members of racial, caste, class, geographical, occupational, or language groups. They learn from other people not only to identify but to identify with or against."[95] One can instruct children through imitation, teaching, parenting, family, and social experiences.[96] Burns is not alone in his belief that childhood

---

92. Stallard, "Majority World Theology," 111.
93. Burns, *Leadership*, 78.
94. Burns, *Leadership*, 77.
95. Burns, *Leadership*, 83.
96. Burns, *Leadership*, 72.

and adolescent experiences can change the behavior, social role, and self-esteem of an adult.[97]

Albert Bandura became the representative for social learning theory in 1977, when he wrote his significant work, *Social Foundation of Thought and Action*. He is well regarded for his psychological contributions, especially in relation to social learning theory. His renowned and controversial Bobo doll experiment highlighted the modeling effect on an adolescent, especially with aggressive behavior.[98] His experiment supported his theory that an adolescent would imitate an adult model based on the adult's behavior. His experiment was based on his first book *Adolescent Aggression*, which applies social learning theories to adolescent aggressive behavior. Bandura's writing is consistent with his assertion that behavioral changes are based on the environment and the interaction of the presence of models. He is certain of the effects of social modeling findings and deems it as an irreplaceable theory for behavioral modification. "The provision of social models is also an indispensable means of transmitting and modifying behavior in situations where errors are likely to produce costly and fatal consequences."[99]

In addition, situations tend to produce different leaders, and qualities can emerge from childhood, political, socioeconomic, or religious experiences.[100] Burns argues that political influence begins in childhood, whether with rebellion or allegiance.[101] Schools begin training political allegiance to children at an early age. Children are made to say pledges, sing national anthems, and memorize presidents as indoctrination to allegiance to their country. Burns also stated that social influences, like religion, change future leadership.[102] With experiences like the childhood of Ghandi and Martin Luther King Jr., religion played integral roles in their adult leadership styles. Leadership is not limited to adult roles, responsibilities, and influences, but includes past situations, relationships, and experiences that shape leadership styles.

This book looks at the theories of Burns and Bandura through the lens of Scripture. A biblical understanding of a leader's origin is believed to be under the sovereignty of God and his calling. Leaders cannot lead

---

97. Burns, *Leadership*, 94.
98. Yount, *Created to Learn*, 180.
99. Bandura, "Social-Learning of Identification Processes," 213.
100. Burns, *Leadership*, 80, 85.
101. Burns, *Leadership*, 86.
102. Burns, *Leadership*, 92.

another in a calling without securing their own pursuit in Christ. A leader's calling dictates the vision, purpose, and direction of leadership.[103] A *calling* is a "term designating God's summons to a specific task or role and his special relationship to his people."[104]

God specifically designates a task for his people to accomplish. Ruth Barton adds that "being called by God is one of the most essential spiritual experiences of human existence, because it is a place where God's presence intersects with human life."[105] God's calling is a privilege given to his creation to be incorporated into his plan. God places a purpose in a Christian's heart that draws him or her to complete God's desires in the kingdom.

Defining Transformational Leadership

Observing irresponsibility and mediocrity in leadership led Burns to write *Leadership* to address the crisis of the lack of understanding and intellectual discovery of leadership. Burns wanted to differentiate between transactional and transformational leadership.[106] Transactional leadership is the exchange of power through relationships. Followers empower leaders to a position, and the leader provides the needs of the followers through his or her given power. Northouse continues Burns's thought in *Leadership: Theory and Practice* by defining transactional leadership:

> Transactional models focus on the exchanges that occur between leaders and their followers [while] . . . transformational leadership refers to the process whereby an individual engages with others and creates a connection that raises the level of motivation and morality in both the leader and the follower. This type of leader is attentive to the needs and motives of followers and tries to help followers reach their fullest potential.[107]

A transactional leader gauges the ideals, values, and wants of the follower. He or she then communicates his or her abilities to meet their desires so that they will empower him or her into the position of power.

---

103. Collins, *Christian Coaching*, 99.
104. Allen C. Myers, "Calling," *EBD* 183.
105. Barton, *Strengthening the Soul*, 204.
106. Yukl, *Leadership in Organizations*, 329.
107. Northouse, *Leadership*, 170.

In contrast, Burns states that a transformational leader seeks to satisfy the existing higher needs, demands, and motivations of the follower, while engaging the full person.[108] Bernard Bass, in *Leadership and Performance beyond Expectations*, develops further interpretation of transformational ideas. He believed transactional and transformational worked progressively in leadership. Debra Allen, in "Pastoral Transformational Leadership and Church Human Service Provision," compares the works of Bass and Burns:

> Contrary to Burns' (1978) earlier work which viewed transactional and transformational leadership as opposites, Bass (1985) described them as part of a continuum that complement each other. Bass contended that leaders could possess both transactional and transformational leadership traits and inferred that possessing both qualities made the leaders more effective. Bass named this phenomenon the augmentation effect.[109]

Although augmentation has not been studied extensively, Bass's contributions are valued in the field of transformational leadership. Leighton Ford, in *Transforming Leadership*, references Bass's transformational leadership as raising "the consciousness of people about what they want."[110]

Gary A. Yukl, in *Leadership in Organizations*, refines the definition by stating a transformational leader raises the consciousness about ethical issues to mobilize their energy and resources to reform institutions.[111] Transformational leaders need support and opposition to exchange theories, ideas, and solutions to problems. They propose solutions to change the outcome of some of the most perplexing social and political issues.

Burns focuses a portion of his writing on the study of power in leadership that is often disproportionate for coerciveness and exploitation.[112] Burns explains that the theory of power should be realigned to the dynamics of relationships.[113] Northouse agrees with Burns, stating that transformational leadership is "quite different from wielding power because it [the leader's agenda] is inseparable from the followers' needs."[114]

---

108. Burns, *Leadership*, 4.
109. D. Allen, "Pastoral Transformational Leadership," 24.
110. Ford, *Transforming Leadership*, 22.
111. Yukl, *Leadership in Organizations*, 329.
112. Burns, *Leadership*, 11.
113. Burns, *Leadership*, 12.
114. Northouse, *Leadership*, 170.

The leader is responsible to motivate the follower toward a shared purpose using the proper resources to influence the desired direction. Yukl summarizes that transformational leaders focus their attention on influencing followers' values, emotions, and attitudes to motivate them to perform beyond their expectations.[115]

In *Leadership Challenge*, Kouzes and Posner emphasize that a leader's responsibility is to influence their followers to a shared goal or aspiration. Posner and Kouzes state that leaders "mobilize others to want to struggle for shared aspirations."[116] Michael Cooper concurs in "The Transformational Leadership of the Apostle Paul: A Contextual and Biblical Leadership for Contemporary Ministry," stating that transformational leaders uplift the morale, motivation, and morals of their followers.[117] Transformational leaders are responsible to influence and empower followers to a purpose for their benefit. Kouzes and Posner add that a leader cannot lead followers toward values without deeply holding to their own values, morals, ethics, standards, and ideals.[118]

Transforming leadership is the ability to change or mobilize followers' thoughts or actions through intellect and reformation. In *Transforming Leadership*, Burns defines transformational leadership:

> We must distinguish here between the verbs "change" and "transform," using exacting definitions. To change is to substitute one thing for another, to give and take, to exchange places, to pass from one place to another. These are the kinds of changes I attribute to transactional leadership. But to transform something cuts much more profoundly. It is to cause a metamorphosis in form or structure, a change in the very condition or nature of a thing, a change into another substance, a radical change in outward form or inner character, as when a frog is transformed into a prince or a carriage maker into an auto factory. It is change of this breadth and depth that is fostered by transforming leadership.[119]

Intellectual leaders need support and opposition to exchange theories, ideas, and solutions to problems. They propose solutions to change the outcome of some of the most perplexing social and political issues. One

115. Yukl, *Leadership in Organizations*, 379.
116. Kouzes and Posner, *Leadership Challenge*, 30.
117. Cooper, "Transformational Leadership," 50.
118. Kouzes and Posner, *Leadership Challenge*, 45.
119. Burns, *Transforming Leadership*, 24.

better can define reform leadership as moral leadership. Burns states that reformed leadership uses ethical means for moral results. Transformational leaders encounter crisis and conflict, especially if they are reformers or revolutionaries. Burns cites examples of Luther, Lenin, and Mao, who led complete and pervasive change in a social or political system.[120]

Burns defines revolutions: "In broad social and political terms, transformation means basic alterations in entire systems—revolutions that replace one structure of power with another."[121] He continues his definition by stating that a revolutionary leader has a radical new ideology and leads a movement that overtakes the existing system.

Burns believes revolutionary leaders adopt a vision and push their followers forward: "Of all the stages in a transforming revolution, the birth of an idea or vision that impels a revolution and its adoption by a decisive number of persons is probably the most crucial step toward transformation."[122] However, changing people's minds and actions is not without personal suffering and sacrifice. Burns highlights that revolutionary leader, like Castro, would have to suffer imprisonment, exile, and persecution. Transforming leadership uses both intellect and morals for the means of change. It requires vision and influence that changes people's actions and possibly their social systems.

Transformational Pastoral Leadership

The study of transformational leadership and church leadership often has been connected. Tony Bush, in "Transformational Leadership: Exploring Common Conceptions," states that transformational leadership is one of the most popular models with global interest. In their writings, both Bass and Burns used leaders like Jesus, Moses, and Martin Luther as examples of transformational leaders. In *Transforming Leadership*, Leighton Ford writes at length about Jesus's transformational leadership as an example for Christian leadership.

Thomas Scarborough continues the study in "Defining Christian Transformational Leadership" by defining Christian transformational leadership as Christian leaders "seeking to influence (or transform)

---

120. Burns, *Leadership*, 201.
121. Burns, *Transforming Leadership*, 24.
122. Burns, *Leadership*, 202.

followers on the basis of his or her vision and character."[123] Additionally, Jackson believes transformational leadership in churches is beneficial; "transformational leadership has the potential to challenge members within the organization to rise above their levels of comfort and pursue organizational goals they believe are worthy."[124] Scarborough suggests that Christian transformational leadership is based on Christlikeness of the leader that influences, strategizes, is goal-oriented, persuasive, and exhibits vision.

It is advantageous for churches to study the transformational leaders presented in the Bible and apply the model to their leadership in the church. Leander believes the study of pastoral leadership is necessary to understand a leader's influence in church diversity:

> Still, researchers have infrequently studied these emerging churches and the competencies of their leaders. More research could explain, for example, the role of the senior pastor as the leader of a Christian church that is distinguishing itself from other churches by its intentionality and orientation towards diversity.[125]

However, Leander does not apply transformational leadership to the pastor's influence in diversity. Jackson agrees that "transformational leadership is a methodology that should assist religious leaders in transforming the culture of churches to be conducive to diversity."[126]

Donald Knudsen built on previous research to discuss "The Effect of Transformational Leadership on Growth in Specialized Non-Profit Organizations: Churches." Researchers have attempted to identify correlations between church leadership and church growth and attendance. But Knudsen struggles to find correlation between a leader's transformational leadership and attendance. Like other researchers, Knudsen recommends further research to discuss transformational leadership in the church. Jackson's research also fails to find significant correlation between perceived differences and a diverse leadership team. Jackson envisions future research identifying influences and behaviors that would contribute to internal diversity.[127] Research limitations should lead to a focus on pastors

---

123. Scarborough, "Defining Christian Transformational Leadership," 58.
124. Jackson, "Ethnically Diverse Leadership," 35.
125. Leander, "Intercultural Leadership," 1.
126. Leander, "Intercultural Leadership," 6.
127. Jackson, "Ethnically Diverse Leadership," 97.

and the examples from the Bible to connect transformational leadership, behavioral examples, and diverse subjects in the church.

A pastor's role in having a diverse church is critical. God has allowed a pastor to be an integral part of creating a multiethnic church. Leander agrees that a pastor plays an integral role in transforming the church into a diverse organization:

> In multicultural organizations, leadership is critical to establishing and sustaining an organizational climate that facilitates diversity and inclusion. In addition to the social and economic forces, which continue to transform organizations, the movement towards multicultural organizations and intercultural leadership appears to be influenced by individuals who are attempting to reframe their own reality and the reality of racial, ethnic, and cultural homogeneity.[128]

A pastor's leadership is unique and transformative in nature. In "Leadership Principles from Proverbs," Grunlan reports, "Church leaders do not have the authority of military leaders or the financial incentives of the corporate world; they only have leadership skills on which to rely."[129]

The Greek word used metaphorically to describe a pastor in the New Testament is *shepherd*.[130] The shepherd oversees or leads a flock; therefore, the biblical terminology indicates God's purpose for a pastor to lead or oversee the church. He is the one the congregants look to for teaching, preaching, counseling, and as a visionary. In "The Biblical Role of the Pastor," Kidder urges pastors to focus on traditional views that pastors should be "servant caregivers" and CEOs, or leaders who gather and excite people around a cause.[131] The leader's role in the church is extensive and the removal of that leader can have a dramatic effect on the health of the congregants. The absence of the pastor comparatively means the loss of a shepherd who is supposed to lead the flock according to the word of God.

While shepherding, a pastor should be a transformational leader who challenges the flock to change their lives. A pastor should challenge his congregation to seek diversity and encourage them to remove their bias for the sake of diversity:

---

128. Leander, "Intercultural Leadership," 3.
129. Grunlan, "Leadership Principles from Proverbs," 25.
130. Walter A. Elwell, "Pastor," *BEB* 2:1618.
131. Kidder, "Biblical Role of Pastor," 19.

> The Church in the United States is at a critical juncture where its future could depend on leadership that reconciles historical patterns of incongruence among the Church, the Biblical message of reconciliation, and the socially integrated lives of people in a growing number of America's communities.[132]

Jackson says, "Transformational leadership is a methodology that should assist religious leaders in transforming the culture of churches to be conducive to diversity."[133] In *The Ten Golden Rules of Leadership: Classical Wisdom for Modern Leaders*, Michael A. Soupios and Panos Mourdoukoutas agree: "Steering clear of old paths and strategies is often a difficult thing to achieve. Old habits and institutional inertia are powerful forces that distort the need for change and innovation."[134]

In *Leadership: A Communication Perspective*, Michael Z. Hackman and Craig E. Johnson believe leaders' passion needs to challenge the past or status quo and push past previous achievements and nonessential traditions.[135] Jackson questions whether leadership-imposed diversity structures would yield more positive results. He asks if the leadership-imposed diversity would encourage the congregation to be more committed over a longer period.[136] A transformational leader must be willing to see the complacency of the organization and seek ways to adjust for the betterment of organizational efficiency.[137] He has to be willing to view the status quo as a reason for improvement.

Justification for the Study

The study of history is valuable for current issues, and historical research is necessary to learn valuable lessons from the past. Traditionally, churches seek the Bible for answers, because it is "inspired by God and profitable for teaching, for reproof, for correction, and for training in righteousness" (2 Tim 3:16). The Bible provides the history of the Christian faith and is advantageous and useful for reproof, correction,

---

132. Leander, "Intercultural Leadership," 5.
133. Jackson, "Ethnically Diverse Leadership," 7.
134. Soupios and Mourdoukoutas, *Ten Golden Rules*, 469–70.
135. Hackman and Johnson, *Leadership*, 103.
136. Jackson, "Ethnically Diverse Leadership," 98.
137. Kotter, *Leading Change*, 59.

and training. Therefore, churches have an obligation to seek answers in the Bible for their most pressing problems.

One problem that has persisted in the American church is the racial divide in congregational worship. Authors have attempted to study the division in church, but it continues to be a perpetual problem for Christianity. The current church is far from the vision of Rev 7:9, with "every nation and all tribes and peoples and tongues, standing before the throne and before the lamb." The racial divide in Christianity demands continual study and research dedicated to finding the answers in the history of the Bible. That leadership in the New Testament had to respond to diversity after Pentecost is evident (Acts 2:5–11).

The book of Acts provides the historical account of the early church's cultural diversity and the apostles' leadership in spreading the gospel in the first century. Therefore, it is critical that we research the apostles' leadership, and specifically the leadership of Peter and Paul, amidst the diversity of the early church following Pentecost in the book of Acts, so we can apply those leadership principles to the modern-day church. The study of Acts examines the account of the leadership of Peter and Paul. This current research focuses on the transformational approach the apostles exhibited in their response to Pentecost. Many writings have considered the book of Acts, and particularly Pentecost, but this book examines the leadership of Paul and Peter and integrates Burns's transformational leadership principles. This will satisfy a gap in the literature by examining biblical history to answer the following question: "How did Paul and Peter model transformational leadership in response to the diversity of Pentecost in the book of Acts?"

The necessity for historical research of leadership in Acts and examination of Burns's leadership is evident for numerous reasons. First, the historical account of the diversity of Pentecost highlights the biblical relevance to the current cultural diversity issues which challenge the American church. Acts also provides a biblical definition of diversity that will create a framework for the current church to understand. An in-depth examination of the spread of Christianity around the world will increase the need to study the leadership that transformed cultures. Acts provides the historical context for Pentecost and the spreading of the gospel. The benefit of studying history is the ability to examine the entire story. The research of Acts allows for the study to extend past events of Pentecost to the results of the apostles' leadership. Acts gives the historical context of the apostles' initial response to diversity, their continuing leadership, and the results of their spreading of the gospel.

Second, Burns's examination helps us pinpoint theoretical principles that correlate with the apostles' leadership. This current research is needed after researchers like Jackson and Knudsen struggled to find correlations with transformational leadership and diversity in the church. Therefore, leaders currently seeking to respond to diversity in America can apply leadership lessons from the apostles. A church's pastor plays an integral role in establishing the vision for the church as well as the cultural environment susceptible to diversity. It is vital that a pastor to recognize an appropriate leadership style that will promote cultural diversity. The examination of Burns and the historical context of the apostles' leadership will provide biblical leadership principles one can model in the current challenge for cultural diversity in the American church. Modern-day churches and their leadership can use the history of the early church as a model for their current dilemma of cultural diversity.

Chapter Summaries

This book creates an understanding of a biblical response to the issues of diversity in the current church. It will analyze exegetically the book of Acts, specifically the responses of Paul and Peter to diversity during and after Pentecost. Additionally, the study will investigate the transformational leadership principles of Paul and Peter in the book of Acts and challenge the current church leadership to apply these leadership principles to their current issues of diversity in the local and universal churches.

Chapters 1 and 2 set the foundation for historical backgrounds and definitions. The current study will analyze exegetically the book of Acts by first introducing the thesis, justification, and literature review in chapter one. The literature review in chapter 1 will provide the definitions of diversity, and transformational leadership. Chapter 2 narrates the historical background of Acts, authorship, history, purpose, structure, Pentecost, and the initial spread of the gospel. The structure of Acts provides geographical and biographical background of the setting. Chapters 1 and 2 set the foundation for the remainder of the research by providing definitions, historical background, and structure.

Chapters 3 and 4 build upon the foundation by applying the definition of transformational leadership and biographical backgrounds to the leadership of Paul and Peter. Chapter 3 focuses specifically on Peter's transformational leadership by analyzing exegetically Peter's origin, calling, transformation, mobilization, revolution, and reformed leadership in Acts. Chapter 4 applies the same exegetical examination to Paul's leadership in Acts. The exegetical examination of the transformational leadership of both Paul and Peter will unveil leadership principles applicable to diversity challenges of the church.

Chapter 5 compares the leadership of Peter and Paul and applies their leadership principles discovered in chapters 3 and 4 to the current American church. Chapter 5 compares the transformational leadership of Paul and Peter. The current study will examine the leadership of both Paul and Peter and the results their leadership had on the diversity of the early church. Before the study applies the principles to the modern-day church, it will examine the present diversity climate of the church to begin chapter 5. That chapter concludes by applying the leadership principles of Peter and Paul to the current church and the possible outcomes to diversify the American church if leadership changes their approach.

Chapter 6 summarizes the findings, recommending future areas of study, future areas of exploration, and conclusions. Although the current study desires to answer the thesis, it is inevitable that one will discover gaps and recommendations made for future study.

2

The Book of Acts

Research into the diversity in the book of Acts requires a thorough examination of the book's background, structure, and exegesis. An analysis of the background of Acts will reveal the details of Pentecost and the geography and characters developed throughout the book. Additionally, a detailed review of Acts exposes the structure of the book, including missionary efforts to surrounding geographical areas. Therefore, the writer dedicated this chapter to an exegetical study of the geographical structure, character development, background of Pentecost, and missionary efforts in the book of Acts.

Background of Acts

The book of Acts gives the modern church the historical background of the early church, missionary journeys, and the growth of the church. "Our knowledge of early Christianity would be greatly impoverished had Luke not conceived . . . 'The Acts of the Apostles.' Acts is unique among the New Testament writings that deal with the life and mission of the Christian community in the age of the apostles."[1] Luke provides biblical accounts of the early church and apostle movement that the Epistles lack. Luke's eyewitness account and careful investigation present an accurate and organized delivery of early foundations of the church, church traditions, and missionary movements. Luke used his literary predecessors to reference the foundations of the faith and instructions

1. Polhill, *Acts* (NAC), 20.

of the Old Testament.[2] Without the book of Acts, significant gaps would exist in the background for the activities of the church and apostles.[3] One of the apostles' activities accounted for in Acts is the geographical spread of the faith and the church. One can read the book of Acts in a structurally geographical manner. Therefore, this chapter will approach the geography of the book of Acts historically, highlighting God's eternal plan for the salvation of the Jews and gentiles.

Historicity and Interpretation of Acts

According to Donald Campbell in *The Basic Bible Interpretation*, the complexity of reading Scripture creates varying techniques of interpretations or rhetoric. Campbell defines this determination of interpretation as:

> The process of determining how the *style* (particular verbal elements or ways of expression) and *form* (organizational structure) influence how it is to be understood. Rhetorical interpretation is the process of determining the literary quality of a writing by analyzing its genre (kind of composition), structure (how the material is organized), and figures of speech (colorful expressions for literary effect), and how those factors influence the meaning of the text.[4]

One area that needs to be addressed is the determination of whether Scripture is to be interpreted literally or figuratively. In the *Moody Handbook of Theology*, Paul P. Enns defines *literal interpretation* as "the words and sentences of Scripture understood in their *normal* meaning—the ways that words are understood in normal communication."[5] Campbell ties the words "literal" and "figurative" together by defining figurative as "a colorful vehicle for presenting literal truth."[6] Campbell agreed that a figurative text has literal truth, but it is not the same interpretation in the historical and grammatical sense.

Because of the historical nature of the book of Acts, with Luke's careful investigation and eyewitness accounts of recorded events, I will conduct this research from a literal interpretation of Scripture. Enns concurs

2. Polhill, *Acts* (NAC), 40.
3. Polhill, *Acts* (NAC), 21.
4. Campbell, "Foreword," 124.
5. Enns, *Moody Handbook of Theology*, 176.
6. Campbell, "Foreword," 147; emphasis original.

that "biblically there is a precedence for interpreting the New Testament literally."[7] This research will function with the belief that Luke's accounts in the book of Acts are literal, therefore allowing Pentecost, the historical account of the early church, and the missionary journeys of Paul and Peter to be applicable to the contemporary American church.

Purpose

A careful review of Luke's writings reveals his desire to provide a historical account of the continuation with the work begun by Jesus.[8] He provides the reader with a narrative, which is a story that makes a case or defense. In *The Bible Knowledge Commentary*, Stanley D. Toussaint writes, "On the one hand some say the primary purpose is a historical one; on the other hand, some say the goal is apologetic, that is, it is a written defense."[9] Pervo would agree that Luke presents a bland, but legitimate narrative by telling a story.[10] Pervo concludes that Luke made the case for the early church, unity of Jew and gentile, and ministry of Peter and Paul.

Toussaint states, "The view that the purpose of Acts is a Pauline apologetic is buttressed by the amazing set of parallels between Peter and Paul."[11] Luke's account of the ministries of Paul and Peter proves that the book of Acts is not limited to Paul's apologetic. Toussaint added that as the main characters, Paul and Peter had a distinct purpose: "It includes both Peter and Paul as prime characters, Peter the minister to the circumcised, and Paul to the uncircumcised."[12] Pervo concludes the book of Acts is not limited to the character of Paul and Peter but provides the reader with a view of God's purpose for Jew and gentile.[13]

---

7. Enns, *Moody Handbook of Theology*, 176. Even liberal theologian Paul Tillich, who championed symbolic talk about God, acknowledged that allegorical interpretation was impossible to do completely. Tillich's solution to the dilemma was to say God is Being is to make many other statements as well, since being is all encompassing, with numerous characteristics. Tillich was correct on the basic idea, namely, that a totally allegorical (symbolic) approach to God is impossible.

8. Dunn, *Acts of the Apostles*.

9. Toussaint, "Acts," 2:350.

10. Pervo, *Acts*, 21.

11. Toussaint, "Acts," 2:350.

12. Toussaint, "Acts," 2:351.

13. Pervo, *Acts*, 21–22.

The book of Acts reminds the reader of the unity provided by Jesus Christ's death and resurrection. Marshall reiterates God's purpose of reconciliation, stating that "Luke demonstrates that in the purpose of God there can be no racial discrimination within the church. The church is called to witness to all people, and salvation is offered to all on the same terms."[14] A vital part of the purpose of Acts is to bring every nation together and remind readers of God's desire to save all nations. Toussaint argues that the book of Acts includes people from every demographic: "The gospel goes to Samaritans, the Ethiopian eunuch, Cornelius, Gentiles at Antioch, poor and wealthy, educated and uneducated, women and men, the high and lofty as well as those in humble positions."[15]

Toussaint says that with a thorough investigation, the reader encounters God's persistent plan to save all nations for his millennial kingdom.[16] Bock describes the book of Acts as a "sociological, historical, and theological work explaining the roots of this community."[17] The book of Acts creates a case for God's salvific plan for Jew and gentile by using stories like the Ethiopian eunuch, Cornelius, the gentiles at Antioch, and the Samaritans.

Structure

The structure of Acts can be understood in various ways, depending on the approach of the researcher. Pervo states that scholars have approached it from different models: thematic, geographic, or literary.[18] However, Conzelmann believed one can separate Acts broadly into two major sections of the time of the earliest church and the ministry of Paul.[19] Last, in *The Acts of the Apostles*, Dunn concludes Acts is structured as a parallel between Peter and Paul.[20] However, Acts 1:8 gives the geographical approach that provides the structure for the remainder of the book. Therefore, the structure of the book is the spread of the gospel from Jerusalem to the remotest parts of the earth. In the *Tyndale Concise Bible Commentary*,

---

14. Marshall, *Acts*, 52.
15. Toussaint, "Acts," 2:350.
16. Toussaint, "Acts," 2:351.
17. Bock, *Acts*, 2.
18. Pervo, *Acts*, 20.
19. Conzelmann, *Acts of the Apostles*, xlii.
20. Dunn, *Acts of the Apostles*.

Robert B. Hughes and J. Carl Laney agree, stating, "Jerusalem (1:1–8:3), moves to Judea and Samaria (8:4–40), and concludes in the remote (from the viewpoint of Jerusalem) regions of the world (9:1–28:31)."[21] The geographical approach separates the book into three parts and maintains the prominent roles played by Peter and Paul.

Geographical Structure

Aligning with Acts 1:8, the structure of the current research sets the geographical direction of the book. Jesus commanded the disciples to go to Jerusalem, Judea, Samaria, and the remotest parts of the earth. Hughes and Laney added that the remotest parts of the earth in the books focused on Rome, the thematic goal where diverse cultures were exposed to the gospel.[22]

Jerusalem was the center of the Israelite faith and one of the priorities of God's salvific plan. According to Pervo, Acts 1:8 reveals the direction of the gospel starting in Jerusalem and to spread from there.[23] In *Exegetical Dictionary of the New Testament*, Horst Robert Balz and Gerhard Schneider state, "In OT history, Jerusalem was the royal city of the Davidic kingdom and after the division of the kingdom, as the location of the temple, a religious center."[24] Balz and Schneider conclude that Acts 1:8 confirmed God's Old Testament plan for the word of God to go from Jerusalem to the remotest parts of the world.[25]

Judea also includes God's design for the Jews. According to Donald K. Campbell, in the *Baker Encyclopedia of the Bible*, Judea is the "land of the Jews," particularly after captivity. Campbell adds that since most of the Israelites who returned from exile were from the tribe of Judah, they were called Jews and their land was referred to as Judea.[26] God's distinct plan prioritized salvation for the Jews. Matthew 15:24 and Matt 10:6 reinforce Jesus's statement in the gospels that he came to save the Jews and commanded his disciples to continue his objective to save God's covenant people (Matt 10:6; 15:24; Gen 12:3; Isa 60:3).

---

21. Hughes and Laney, *Tyndale Concise Bible Commentary*, 487.
22. Hughes and Laney, *Tyndale Concise Bible Commentary*, 486.
23. Pervo, *Acts*, 43–44.
24. "Ἱεροσόλυμα," *EDNT* 2:177.
25. "Ἱεροσόλυμα," *EDNT* 2:178.
26. Donald K. Campbell, "Judea," *BEB* 1:1242.

According to the geographical structure set in Acts 1:8, God's mission expanded to the people of Samaria and the remotest part of the earth. Samaria's historical background was difficult and tenuous since its origin. Discord between the Jews and Samaritans began with disagreement among their descendants concerning the Samaritans' origin:

> The Samaritans offer a vastly different interpretation of their origin. They claim descent from the Jewish tribes of Ephraim and Manasseh (see Jn 4:12), and hold that the exile of Israelites in 722 BC, by Assyria, was neither full-scale nor permanent. To account for the mutual hostility that developed between their group and the Jews, the Samaritan version holds that the Jews were guilty of apostasy.[27]

The Samaritans' claims of ancestry did not change the Jews' disdain for their religious practices. After Assyria's destruction of the Northern Kingdom, the Jews believed the inhabitants adopted foreign polytheist religions.

According to their religious practices, the Jews viewed the Samaritans' location in the Northern Kingdom as neither fully Jew nor fully gentile.[28] Their schism originated from their ancestry but led to further religious conflicts. Their tension grew as Jew and Samaritan disagreed about worship place and practices. According to Samaritans, the Jews worship at the temple in Jerusalem was incorrect and was supposed to take place at Mt. Gerizim.[29]

According to the Samaritans, Mt. Gerizim is where Abraham prepared the sacrifice of Isaac, thereby constituting God's intent of Israel's place of worship. The Samaritans believed the divide continued as the Jews continued to practice worship at the temple of Jerusalem. Neither Jew nor Samaritan relinquished their religious practices and the divide increased and developed into deep relational animosity. During Jesus's ministry, the divide remained and is well documented in the Gospels:

> This animosity continued in Jesus' day. Both groups excluded the other from their respective cultic centers, the Jerusalem temple and the Samaritan temple on Mt. Gerizim. The Samaritans, for example, were forbidden access to the inner courts of the temple and offerings they might give were accepted as from Gentiles.

---

27. David C. Carlson, "Samaritans," *BEB* 2:1886.
28. Allen C. Myers, "Samaritans," *EBD* 907.
29. Elwell and Comfort, *Tyndale Bible Dictionary*, 1154.

Thus, although probably more accurately defined as "schismatics," it appears Samaritans were in practice treated as Gentiles. All marriage between the groups was therefore forbidden and social intercourse was greatly restricted (Jn 4:9). With such proscribed separation, it is not surprising that any interaction between the two groups was strained. The mere term "Samaritan" was one of contempt on the lips of Jews (8:48) and among some scribes it possibly would not even be uttered (see the apparent in Lk 10:37). The disciples' reaction to the Samaritan refusal of lodging (9:51–55) is a good example of the animosity felt by Jews for Samaritans at the time.[30]

Jesus limited his ministry on earth in his interactions with the Samaritans, but his interaction with the Samaritan woman at the well was transformative and transcendent.

In John 4:7–38, Jesus corrects the woman concerning place of worship, telling her the hour is coming when it is neither mountain nor temple, but spirit and truth. "Thus, despite his loyalty to Jerusalem (cf. Matt. 23:37–38; Luke 9:52–53) and the Jews (John 4:22), Jesus laid the foundation for a transcendence of the division between the two peoples."[31] Jesus's interaction foreshadows his future direction for the disciples to direct their ministry to the Samaritans. Despite the Samaritans' reputation, Jesus specifically mentioned Samaria as a place for the disciples to go for their mission.

Samaria became the place of missionary success, and missionaries like Philip and Paul experienced stable growth with the gospel. Schreiner provides the background to Samaria as a geographic region unassociated with the Jews. Schreiner also states that Samaria plays an integral role in the spread of the gospel by providing support, infrastructure, and the beginning of evangelism to the gentiles.[32] God's plan for the gentiles was not limited to Samaria but expanded to include the remotest parts of the earth. One can interpret the definition of remotest parts of the earth two ways. Bock states that Luke interpreted remotest part of the earth to be as he had witnessed, which would be Rome and Ethiopia. In Acts 27, Rome was considered the hub of the gentile world, which Luke could have considered the spreading of the gospel to all

---

30. Elwell and Comfort, *Tyndale Bible Dictionary*, 1154.
31. Myers, *EBD* 907.
32. David B. Schreiner, "Samaria," *LBD*, para. 20.

gentile nations.³³ Horst and Schneider questioned the definition of the "ends of the earth" by stating, "The intriguing element here is the phrase 'to the ends of the earth.' As a geographical expression, the location of this limit depends on the extent of geographical knowledge and the orientation of the speaker or narrator."³⁴

The other interpretation is not limited to the author's intent but incorporates God's knowledge of the expanse of the earth. "The latter contributes to the metaphorical sense of 'far, far away.' The range of geographical options is wide."³⁵ *Tyndale Concise Bible Commentary* says that Acts 1:8 is connected to Isa 49:6, which states salvation will go to the ends of the earth.³⁶ Bock states it is not uncommon for Luke to use Isaiah, so the connection to Isa 49:6 is plausible.³⁷ If the cross-reference is accurate, then the remotest part of the earth is not limited to Rome or Ethiopia. Acts 1:8 should take into account not just Isa 49:6 but also the entirety of Scripture and biblical theology. God has always intended to use Jerusalem to save all the nations (Matt 28:19; Mark 16:15; Rom 10:18; Col 1:23).

Horst concludes that the language is not limited to the author's knowledge or narrative.³⁸ Although Luke only recorded his experience with the gospel spreading to Rome and Ethiopia, it does not limit the intent of Jesus's command to take the gospel to the remotest parts of the earth. "Acts shows, however, that the plan did not emerge as one gradually developed by the church, but as one gradually revealed and extended by God."³⁹ The geography of Acts is vital to understanding the structure and purpose of Luke's writing. The geography of Acts exposes God's salvific plan from Jerusalem and Judea to Samaria and the remotest parts of the earth.

Biographical Structure

The geographical structure of Acts indicates the spread of the gospel, but Acts also highlights the apostles who led the missionary journeys to Jerusalem and Judea to Samaria and the remotest part of the earth:

33. Bock, *Acts*, 65.
34. *EDNT* 2:178.
35. Pervo, *Acts*, 44.
36. Hughes and Laney, *Tyndale Concise Bible Commentary*, 496.
37. Bock, *Acts*, 65.
38. *EDNT* 2:178.
39. Bock, *Acts*, 67.

> The book of Acts provides biographical glimpses of a few of the early apostles as they spread the gospel first in Jerusalem and then on to the rest of the world. Peter, Philip, and a few others were responsible for the spread of the gospel to Jerusalem, Judea, and Samaria. Paul was responsible for much of the rest of the Mediterranean world.[40]

The biographical structure introduces the characters who spread the gospel geographically. The missionary journeys draw two distinct characters in Paul and Peter. As mentioned earlier, Dunn, in *The Acts of the Apostles*, concludes that Acts is structured as a parallel between Peter and Paul.[41]

John B. Polhill says that although the book of Acts is titled *Acts of the Apostles*, the book primarily focuses on Paul and Peter. To support his claim, he separates the book's chapters by the central characters: "Of the 28 chapters of Acts, Peter is central in nine chapters, Paul in sixteen, Stephen in two, and Philip in one."[42] Polhill narrows his review by outlining the book with two main characters, Peter in Jerusalem in chs. 1–12, and Paul to the gentiles in chs. 13–28. Within the geographical structure of Acts, two main characters develop throughout the entirety of the book.

Peter's leadership, exhibited in the first half of Acts, centered on his work with the Jerusalem church and beyond. Polhill separates Peter's section of Acts to the Jerusalem church and beyond: "Jerusalem portion chapters 1–5 treat the early church in Jerusalem; chapters 6–12, the outreach beyond Jerusalem."[43] Stanley Porter concurs the biographical structure is an overview of the apostles' work as they spread the gospel. "The book of Acts provides biographical glimpses of a few of the early apostles as they spread the gospel first in Jerusalem and then on to the rest of the world. Peter, Philip, and a few others were responsible for the spread of the gospel to Jerusalem, Judea, and Samaria."[44]

Chapter 1 names Peter among the eleven remaining disciples, providing leadership with the disciples in the selection of Matthias as the twelfth disciple. Being filled with the Holy Spirit, Peter continued his leadership at Pentecost in ch. 2, where three thousand souls were saved after Peter preached the gospel. Peter's leadership in chs. 3–9 consists of imprisonments, sermons, and miracles that advanced the gospel to the Jerusalem

---

40. Porter, "Acts," 1714.
41. Dunn, *Acts of the Apostles*.
42. Polhill, *Acts* (HCBC), 500.
43. Polhill, *Acts* (NAC), 72.
44. Porter, "Acts," 1714.

church, Judea, and Samaria. In ch. 10, Peter visited Cornelius and proclaimed the message that Jesus is relevant to all nations. This is pertinent because Cornelius was in Caesarea among the gentiles, and Peter verified the gospel's availability to all nations (Acts 10:34).

In ch. 15, Peter made a final appearance, along with the disciples, to confirm the gospel for the gentiles (vv. 6–12).[45] Peter's character throughout the book of Acts continued to advance the gospel from Jerusalem to Samaria. As the geographical structure develops throughout the book of Acts, Peter is the primary character in the beginning of Acts.

As Peter's bibliographical account in Acts comes to a close, Paul's story begins. Paul's introduction and Peter's missionary work overlap in the book of Acts as Paul, then known as Saul, was in objection to the spread of the gospel. However, after Saul's conversion and name change to Paul, his bibliographical account becomes the focus of the second portion of Acts. "After a period of amazing growth among Jews, the Christian message came to gentiles. Peter baptized the first gentile convert, Cornelius, but it was through the efforts of Paul that large numbers of gentiles were brought into the movement."[46]

Porter wrote that, although the book of Acts includes the work of the Holy Spirit in the apostles, Paul is central to Acts. "The book of Acts emphasizes the work of God through the Holy Spirit in the lives of people who devoted themselves to Jesus Christ, especially Paul as he led the Gentile missionary endeavor."[47] In *Eerdmans Bible Dictionary*, Allen C. Myers emphatically agrees with Porter that Paul's bibliographical accounts are dominant in the second portion of Acts.[48] Myers proceeds to list the brief character interruptions of Paul's work with Barnabas in Asia Minor in chs. 13–14, Silas in Greece in chs. 16–18, the Council at Jerusalem in ch. 15, and Apollos preaching at Ephesus in ch. 13.[49]

Despite the pivotal work of the other apostles, Luke centered his account on Paul and Peter. Specifically, Paul played a significant role in the continuation of the gospel's spread beyond Jerusalem, especially to the gentiles:

---

45. Jason Gish, "Peter the Apostle," *LBD*, para. 9.
46. "Acts of the Apostles," *HarBD* 10.
47. Porter, "Acts," 1714.
48. Allen C. Myers, "Acts of the Apostles," *EBD* 18.
49. Myers, *EBD* 18.

As Luke describes the missionary activity of Paul, he stresses Paul's habit of going first to Jewish synagogues to present the Christian message. Almost invariably, Paul has little success among Jews and is forced to preach to Gentiles, who respond favorably and in large numbers (e.g., Acts 14:1–7; 17:1–9, 10–15; 18:1–17; 19:8–20). On three occasions, Paul announces his intention not to preach to Jews any longer but rather to go only to Gentiles (Acts 13:46–47; 18:6; 28:28). Here, there is a parallel between the geographical structure of Acts and a fundamental theological theme: geographically, Christianity, which started in Jerusalem among Jews, moved out into the wider world among Gentiles; theologically, Christianity increasingly grew distinct from and independent of Judaism.[50]

Paul's missionary journeys follow the geographical structure as he continued the spread of the gospel to the remotest part of the earth.

Paul's missionary work is well documented and structured in the book of Acts. Polhill broadly summarizes Paul's biographical account: "In the Pauline portion, 13:1–21:16 relates the three major missions of Paul; 21:27–28:31 deals with Paul's defense of his ministry."[51] In *Easton's Bible Dictionary*, M. G. Easton adds that Paul's missionary journeys in chs. 13–21 give the history of the extension and planting of churches among the gentiles.[52] Manfred T. Brauch agrees with Easton but adds that Paul's missionary work with planting churches was in untouched territories that extended beyond previous missionary work.[53] Easton expands the second portion of Paul's account in Acts by stating that chs. 21–28 account for his time in Rome. Therefore, Easton does not reference chs. 21–28 as Paul's defense of his ministry, but as the continuation of his missionary journeys, entitling them "Antioch to Rome."[54]

Brauch details that the second part of Paul's work journeying to Rome was filled with arrest in Jerusalem, lengthy imprisonments in Caesarea, and finally his time in Rome. Paul's continual advancement of the gospel caused persecution with persistent defenses of the gospel before governors, councils, and cohorts. As the Lord foretold through Ananias, Paul's defense of his ministry during his imprisonments and

---

50. *HarBD* 10–11.
51. Polhill, *Acts* (NAC), 72.
52. Easton, *Easton's Bible Dictionary*, 17.
53. Manfred T. Brauch, "Acts of the Apostles," *BEB* 1:24–25.
54. Brauch, *BEB* 1:24–25.

arrest put him before rulers, leaders, and kings. Paul's missionary work can be summarized by the Lord's word to Ananias concerning Paul: "He is a chosen instrument of mine to carry my name before the Gentiles and kings and the sons of Israel" (Acts 9:15). The Lord's calling of Paul aligns with Acts' bibliographical structure to use Paul specifically to carry the gospel to the gentiles, kings, and sons of Israel.

Pentecost

Background

In *Eerdmans Bible Dictionary*, Myers states that Pentecost at its root in the Old Testament means the "fiftieth day," as a part of the Jewish Feast of Weeks in Lev 23:15–21.[55] It was the fiftieth day after the offering of the barley of the harvest:

> Each year the priest waved a sheaf of newly harvested grain before the Lord on the day after the sabbath during the Festival of Unleavened Bread (the period of 7 days following Passover). The people then counted 50 days from the offering of that first sheaf of grain until the day after the seventh sabbath to observe the Feast of Weeks (Lv 23:11). On this day 2 loaves made of 2/10 of an ephah of flour and baked with yeast were waved before the Lord (Lv 23:17) and freewill offerings were encouraged (Dt 16:10). In addition to the agricultural produce which represented thanksgiving for God's blessing, during harvest burnt offerings of various animals were prescribed (Lv 23:18; Nm 28:27). This harvest festival was a time of great rejoicing and a holy assembly when no work was to be done (Lv 23:21; Dt 16:11). Observance of the Feast of Weeks during Solomon's time (2 Chr 8:13) is the only OT reference outside of the Pentateuch.[56]

Freeman later adds that, following the Old Testament definition, it became an "intertestamental period and later, Pentecost was regarded as the anniversary of the law-giving at Sinai."[57]

Bock agrees with Freeman when he writes that the intertestamental period included the anniversary of law giving at Sinai led many to believe that this day was selected in significance to God giving his Holy

---

55. Myers, *EBD* 811.
56. Elwell, *BEB* 2:1639–40.
57. Freeman, *NBD*³ 899.

Spirit.[58] Bock's statement regarding the coming of the Holy Spirit at the law giving at Sinai is confirmed when the Holy Spirit is in Jerusalem on the day of Pentecost. The apostles met in one house when the Holy Spirit came like a mighty rushing wind, and the apostles were miraculously able to speak in foreign tongues (Acts 2:1). Soon after the Spirit came upon everyone who gathered, they were all mutually able to speak and understand each other's tongues (Acts 2:6).

Diversity of Pentecost

In the *Tyndale Bible Dictionary*, Walter A. Elwell and Philip Wesley Comfort observe that in the New Testament, the required feast brought Jews from great distances to observe the festival.[59] Commentators such as Toussaint believe this was the Jews of the diaspora or the dispersion of the Jews.[60] In the *Baker Encyclopedia of the Bible*, James L. Mason defines *diaspora* as the Jewish people from Israel going to foreign lands.[61] However, it was not because of exile, but rather for the sake of sharing the gospel to every nation (Jas 1:1; 1 Pet 1:1).

God used the Feast of Weeks as the event to bring Jews from every tongue to hear the good news. Jews from great distances and varying backgrounds came to Jerusalem to celebrate the Feast of Weeks, which provided the perfect scenario for the outpouring of the Holy Spirit and the beginning of the church. Bock provides background, stating that, in addition to the Jews, people from every nation and tongue came to observe the feast:

> Pentecost is first mentioned in the NT as the occasion for the outpouring of the Holy Spirit upon the disciples of Christ, an event that many theologians understand as marking the beginning of the church (Acts 2:1). Since this was a required festival, Jews gathered from great distances to observe Pentecost in Jerusalem, making it an appropriate time for God's work.[62]

God's work to take the gospel to the Jews began when the Jews gathered to celebrate their festival. The Jews' dedication to the Feast of Weeks

58. Bock, *Acts*, 95.
59. Elwell and Comfort, *Tyndale Bible Dictionary*, 1007.
60. Toussaint, "Acts," 2:357; and Bock, *Acts*, 100.
61. Mason, *BEB* 1:623.
62. Bock, *Acts*, 100.

provided the perfect opportunity for Jews separated to be together to hear Peter preach and receive the Holy Spirit.

According to Spina, the event of Pentecost is in stark contrast to the event of the tower of Babel in Gen 11. In contrast to Babel, Pentecost took multiple tongues and provided one tongue so everyone could understand the gospel in unity. Babel represented a human effort to reach God, but Pentecost represented God bringing people unto himself. Spina contrasts Babel and Pentecost by stating the differences in language, agenda, and results:

> At Babel, God transformed a single language into many, creating confusion; at Jerusalem, the Holy Spirit made it possible for many languages to be understood as one, creating unity. At Babel, language was used to promote a human agenda ("Let us make a name for ourselves"); at Jerusalem, the "new" language was used to announce the "mighty works of God" (Acts 2:11). At Babel, God scattered the people in judgment [Gen 11:9; Gk *diespeiren*]; at Jerusalem, God scattered [Acts 8:1, 4; Gk *diesparésan*; *diasparentes*] the people to spread the news, which would eventuate in worldwide unity.[63]

Spina uses biblical history to reconcile God's eternal plan for all nations to worship in unity.

Although contrast is present, K. A. Mathews, in the *New American Commentary*, reiterates that Pentecost played an integral role in God's desire to reconcile the nations from Babylon to Rev 7:9. Revelation 7:9 reassures God's eternal design for diversity in the kingdom of God and Pentecost represented God's initial plan to regather the nations reunified as the new church. Mathews highlights Pentecost's beginning of God's eternal plan for diversity and unity through the church:

> The prophets speak of diverse ethnic personalities when they depict the future universal kingdom of God (e.g., Isa 2:1–4). At Pentecost, the outpouring of the Spirit upon the representative nations gathered in Jerusalem results in the spiritual union of the new church, but does not create a homogeneous language, ethnicity, or statehood. John's vision of the heavenly family includes diverse peoples from "every nation, tribe, people and language, standing before the throne and in front of the Lamb" (Rev 7:9).[64]

---

63. Spina, *ABD* 561–62.
64. Mathews, *Genesis 1—11:26*, 474.

Mathews also highlights that God did not change the diversity of tongue and ethnicity but unified every nation through the gospel. Mathews adds, "Pentecost shows that national distinctions are secondary to the union of a single people by the baptism of the Spirit in Christ. The gospel therefore is the reconciling antidote to the plurality of nations as it is preached among the world's peoples."[65]

Pervo adds, "With splendid vividness, Luke has been able to intimate the coming gentile mission without prematurely inaugurating it. Jews are the missionary target, but without limit on place or language—and, it should be added, without the inconvenience of discontinuity."[66] In his vivid description and historical account, Luke lists the nations present during Pentecost:

> It begins with three countries to the east of the Roman Empire in the area known as Persia or Iran, and then (with a change of construction) moves westward to Mesopotamia, modern Iraq, and Judea. Next come various provinces and areas in Asia Minor (modern Turkey), and then Egypt and the area immediately westwards, followed by Rome. Then, we have a general statement applicable to all the peoples in mind: there was a considerable Jewish population in each of these areas, and the presence of Jews often led to the conversion of Gentiles to become proselytes. Finally, and somewhat surprisingly, the list includes people from Crete and Arabia.[67]

Pentecost in Acts 2:1 is different because this is when God gave his Holy Spirit to the apostles and began the work of his church.[68]

Mark Olson recognizes that the work of the Holy Spirit expanded the mission and gospel: "The baptism of the Spirit at Pentecost [led to] the mission and expansion of the church to people of every nation."[69] Pervo adds, "Within the Christian tradition, the events of Pentecost, Acts 2:1–41 are viewed as the birth of the church."[70] This church was not limited to the Jews, but was the beginning of every nation having the opportunity for salvation and to take it back to their native countries. Marshall states, "It must suffice to observe that the list is clearly meant

---

65. Mathews, *Genesis 1—11:26*, 475–76.
66. Pervo, *Acts*, 71.
67. Marshall, *Acts*, 75–76.
68. Elwell, *BEB* 2:1639–40.
69. Mark J. Olson, "Pentecost," *ABD* 222–23.
70. Pervo, *Acts*, 70.

to be an indication that people from all over the known world were present, and perhaps that they would return to their own countries as witnesses to what was happening."[71] This diversity of the faith is the beginning of the remainder of the book of Acts and the purpose of God's plan to save all nations.

Geographical Review

Luke clearly pictures the diversity of Pentecost in the event of Pentecost with his detailed list of "devout men from every nation under heaven" (Acts 2:5). As discussed previously, the Greek defines the term *nations* as "a body of persons united by kinship, culture, and common traditions, *nation, people*."[72] The people in attendance of Pentecost were diverse in backgrounds, culture, traditions, and tongues. "Although these are Jews, they are culturally and linguistically members of many nations; thus, even from the church's inception as an identifiable community, the Spirit proleptically moved the church into multicultural diversity under Christ's lordship."[73] Due to the diaspora of the Jews, the Feast of Weeks' devout men had to come from their distinct nations together for worship. Luke went beyond a general description of the diversity of the people present, but later documented a geographical listing.

Luke's writing and documentation of this monumental event has often intrigued scholars, especially Luke's choice to list the nationalities.[74] The Jews and Proselytes of Parthians, Medes, Elamites, Mesopotamia, Judea, Cappadocia, Pontus, Asia, Phrygia, Pamphylia, Egypt, districts of Libya, Cretans, Arabs, and visitors of Rome were all in attendance (Acts 2:9–10). Geographical patterns are difficult for scholars to pinpoint; however, it is important that we understand the diversity of people who attended Pentecost:

> It begins in what is present-day Iran (Parthia) and then proceeds across the Middle East (Mesopotamia), then southward to Judea, then north to central Turkey (Cappadocia), to northern Turkey (Pontus), eastward to the Aegean coast of Turkey (Asia), inland to Phrygia, then south to the Mediterranean coast of

---

71. Marshall, *Acts*, 76.
72. "ἔθνος," BDAG 276.
73. Keener, *New Testament*, Acts 2:9–11, "People of Pentecost," para. 4.
74. Polhill, *Acts* (NAC), 102.

Turkey (Pamphylia). To this point, with the exception of Judea, which seems strangely out of place, the progress is a more-or-less regular curve, from southeast to north to southwest. After Pamphylia, no real pattern is discernible. The catalog covers North Africa (Egypt, Libya, Cyrenaica), then north and west all the way to Rome, then southeast to the Mediterranean island of Crete, and finally much farther east and southward to Arabia.[75]

Polhill adds that geographical theories like the Davidic empire, Paulus chart, or astrological chart are all unconvincing or not all inclusive.

The geographical structure of the attendees of Pentecost may not have a pattern, but their distinct locations and nationalities are evidence of the diversity present. I. Howard Marshall agrees that the geographical locations complicate possible explanations: "It is an odd list, and nobody has been able to explain satisfactorily why it includes the particular selection of countries that it does, and why they come in this strange order."[76] Despite the lack of geographical structure each nation represented, all had extensive Jewish communities.[77]

Even without a satisfactory reason for Luke's list of nations, it is still a representation of the Jewish diaspora gathering at Pentecost. *Diaspora* is defined as a "dispersion of Jewish people from Israel to foreign lands. *Diaspora*, a Greek noun meaning a 'sowing' or 'scattering,' is extensively used in the Septuagint to mean 'exile.'"[78]

> How widely the Jews were scattered is suggested in the Book of Acts, where Luke listed Jerusalem's visitors: "Parthians and Medes and Elamites and residents of Mesopotamia, Judea and Cappadocia, Pontus and Asia, Phrygia and Pamphylia, Egypt and the parts of Libya belonging to Cyrene, and visitors from Rome ... Cretans and Arabians" (Acts 2:9–11). Those Jews of "the diaspora" were in Jerusalem to celebrate the feast of Pentecost.[79]

Luke's list highlights the extensive scattering of the Jews. A. F. Walls confirms Pentecost's role in bringing Jews together from their *diaspora* but emphasized how widespread the Jewish communities were throughout the world. "The spread of the Dispersion was not confined to the Roman empire: it was prominent in the Persian sphere of influence too, as the

---

75. Polhill, *Acts* (NAC), 102.
76. Marshall, *Acts*, 75–76.
77. Polhill, *Acts* (NAC), 102.
78. Mason, *BEB* 1:623; emphasis original.
79. Mason, *BEB* 1:624.

account of the Pentecost crowd illustrates (Acts 2:9–11)."[80] The Jewish communities were not limited to one demographic but spread from Rome to Persia.[81] The recognition of widespread communities around the world emphasizes the diversity of the attendees at Pentecost.

Another important aspect of the biblical text was the inclusion of Jews and converted gentiles. Acts 2:10 states both Jews and proselytes were present. In the Old Testament, a *proselyte* is someone "who resided in the land, thereby lacking the protection and privileges associated with blood relationship and native birth."[82] However, in Acts the proselytes were gentiles converted to Judaism. The New Testament uses the term for gentiles who were aliens to the Jewish tradition but were adopted or converted into Judaism:

> The LXX translated Heb *gēr* with Gk *prosēlytos* 77 times, but only in those cases where the context suggested a religious meaning, employing the terms *xenos* and *paroikos* elsewhere. This narrowing of the definition was a result of the Jews' altered circumstances in the Diaspora. The translators of the LXX appropriated the OT concern for resident aliens on behalf of the gentiles who adopted the religion and customs of Judaism, thereby providing a biblical basis for a practical reality.[83]

Former gentiles who accepted Judaism practiced Jewish customs and religious practices. The proselyte presence at the Feast of Weeks evidences the Jewish influence in their surrounding community. Due to increasing influence of the Jewish communities, the gentiles were being converted into the Jewish community and were increasing the population of their communities.

Instead of the diverse Jewish communities segregating themselves, then, this account suggests that they were assimilating into their surrounding communities. Marshall adds that after the extensive list, a broad generalized statement includes all people: "Then we have a general statement applicable to all the peoples in mind: there was a considerable Jewish population in each of these areas, and the presence of Jews often led to the conversion of Gentiles to become proselytes."[84]

---

80. A. F. Walls, "Dispersion," *NBD*³ 278.
81. Polhill, *Acts* (NAC), 101–4.
82. Paul F. Stuehrenberg, "Proselyte," *ABD* 503.
83. Stuehrenberg, *ABD* 503.
84. Marshall, *Acts*, 76.

The presence of proselytes at Pentecost adds to the diversity because their background before assimilation to the Jewish religion was different from that of a natural-born Jew.

Geographical diversity is evident with the multiplicity of tongues present at Pentecost. Luke's writing gave evidence that the nationalities present did not share a common language. "Finally, the long list of nations in vv. 9–11 is sandwiched between references to people who marvel at hearing the Christians in their own language (vv. 8, 11b). The list obviously illustrates the breadth of the languages that were spoken."[85] Each nationality present shared their own common tongue. Although scholars debate the definition of tongue, the definition of language in v. 6 is unambiguous:

> The word "tongue" may be ambiguous in v. 4, but the word "dialect," or "language" [*dialektos*], in vv. 6, 8 is not. It can only refer to a known language or dialect. Luke used the expression "to speak in other [*heteros*, "different"] tongues [languages]" in v. 4, thus making a distinction from tongue-speaking (which he did know and referred to in 10:46).[86]

That would explain why in Acts 2:6, Luke stated the crowd was bewildered that each ethnicity present was able to hear in their own languages. The language that appeared in Act 2:6 confirms that each ethnicity heard Peter's message in their own dialects:

> Some MSS made the verb agree with the singular subject [ἤκουεν, or ἤκουσεν], but the noun of multitude, πλῆθος, naturally treated as a singular in συνῆλθεν and συνεχύθη, is equally naturally differentiated into individuals when the point is that *each one* [on εἷς ἕκαστος see on v. 3] heard in his own language. διάλεκτος is a local or national language.[87]

This statement verifies that nationalities presented shared languages common with their own ethnicities, but through the work of the Holy Spirit were able to hear in their native tongues. However, the work of the Holy Spirit provides more evidence that the diaspora led Jew and proselyte to adopt the native tongues of each of their communities:

---

85. Polhill, *Acts* (NAC), 100.
86. Polhill, *Acts* (NAC), 99–100.
87. Barrett, *Commentary on Acts*, 119.

> The miracle was a demonstration of the Spirit's power and presence: these Diaspora Jews heard their own tongue spoken (not Aramaic or Greek) and realized that this should have been impossible for the "Galileans." This "sign" prepared them for Peter's speech, which probably was in Aramaic and which they indeed understood. The note that they represented "every nation under heaven" is perhaps a bit of poetic license but a not altogether inaccurate description of the extent of the Jewish Diaspora.[88]

Despite their inability to understand Peter's speech in Aramaic, the Holy Spirit allowed the gospel to be heard. Although the miracle that occurred through the Holy Spirit was done for everyone to hear Peter's message, it still provided evidence for the diversity of devout men coming from all over the world. God used Pentecost to draw the Jews from their diaspora to the Feast of Weeks to hear the gospel through the work of the Holy Spirit.

In addition, the diversity of the Jewish communities is directly correlated to the wide spread of the gospel. "It must suffice to observe that the list is clearly meant to be an indication that people from all over the known world were present, and perhaps that they would return to their own countries as witnesses to what was happening."[89] After gathering from their local communities to Pentecost, they returned home, spreading the gospel to their own demographics. "The purpose of this catalogue is patent: to symbolize—in fact, to achieve—the universal mission of the church."[90] The mission and growth of church all over the world began when a diverse group returned home to their communities with the gospel.

Initial Spread of the Gospel

Although the people who returned from Pentecost brought back the gospel to their communities, the apostles began missionary journeys to spread the gospel in accordance with the geographical structure of Acts. Apostles followed Pentecost with journeys from Jerusalem, Judea, Samaria, and to the remotest parts of the earth. Therefore, it is critical to discuss the initial missionary journeys and the cultures the apostles encountered in their visits.

---

88. Polhill, *Acts* (NAC), 101.
89. Polhill, *Acts* (NAC), 101.
90. Pervo, *Acts*, 66.

Jerusalem

The first five chapters of Acts center on the missionary efforts to the Jews in Jerusalem. Acts 1:8 sets the stage for the first portion of the book when it states the missionary work should begin in Jerusalem and Judea. "Much of Acts concerns the Christian witness to the Jews. The first five chapters center in Jerusalem and are preoccupied with the preaching to the Jews of the city. Four of the major speeches of Acts are addressed to Jewish audiences (chaps. 2; 3; 7; 13)."[91]

Following Acts 1:8, the success of the gospel began at Pentecost when God converted three thousand people through the preaching of the gospel (Acts 2:41). Acts 2:5 states Jews were living in Jerusalem to hear Peter's sermon. In ch. 3, Peter again addresses Jews in Jerusalem immediately after healing the lame beggar. Peter was in Jerusalem at the temple for the ninth hour of prayer when approached by a lame beggar. "Apparently there were several times for prayer at the Jerusalem temple—9 a.m., 12 noon, and 3 p.m."[92] After Peter's having healed the lame beggar, the crowd arrived, presenting Peter with the opportunity to share the message of the gospel. Peter's message centered on Jesus as the Messiah and the need for Jews to have faith and ask for forgiveness. However, in ch. 4, the priests, the captain of the temple guard, and the Sadducees met Peter and John's message with apprehension and threats (Acts 4:21).

Despite being jailed and beaten, more than five thousand believed the message. "The Sadducees tried their best to stop the witness of the apostles. They did not succeed. The Christian message was finding too much acceptance with the people. The rulers raged, but it was all in vain (4:25)."[93] The opposition continued, however, and Peter and John were questioned not only by the priest and temple guard but also by the Jewish leadership. Stunned by the miracle, elders and rulers of the people gathered at the council to question the authority of the miracle performed. The council, or Sanhedrin, the "supreme court and administrative body of the Jews, consisted of seventy-one members, including the high priest. Most of them were Sadducees. In Acts this was the first of four times some of Jesus's followers were brought before the Sanhedrin (cf. Peter and the apostles, 5:27; Stephen, 6:12; and Paul, 22:30)."[94] The

---

91. Pervo, *Acts*, 66.
92. Toussaint, "Acts," 2:360.
93. Polhill, *Acts* (NAC), 140.
94. Toussaint, "Acts," 2:363.

council recognized Peter and John as being with Jesus but still referred to them as untrained men; they had to leave the council. Although they were amazed by the lame man who was healed, they decided to command Peter and John to stop speaking about Jesus's name.

Chapters 3 and 4 introduce the Jewish leadership's opposition to the spread of the gospel. Despite the miracles at Pentecost and with the lame beggar, Jewish leadership was not ready to accept the gospel of Jesus Christ. The same pattern continued in ch. 5 as more miracles took place. People who were sick, afflicted, and possessed unclean spirits were traveling from the surrounding vicinities of Jerusalem (Acts 5:16). In addition, the story of Ananias and Sapphira struck fear in the church and all who heard (Acts 5:11). Although miracles attracted people to come, the news of Ananias and Sapphira demanded a healthy fear within the church:

> Nevertheless, they held the Christians in the highest regard. Luke was working with a paradox here. It is the same two-sidedness of the Spirit's power that had just been demonstrated in Ananias and Sapphira. The power of the miracles attracts. The awesome power of the Spirit that judges also demands commitment and responsibility. Before that power, the crowd kept its distance with healthy respect, unless they were willing to fully submit to that power and make a commitment.[95]

The spread of the gospel continued as the apostles performed miracles and authority increased within the church. News traveled to surrounding communities of the empowerment and authority of the apostles as people began to travel to see them:

> In any event, crowds came from all the surrounding villages to Jerusalem to be healed by the apostles. One is reminded of Jesus' own healing ministry as recorded in Mark 6:53–56 and the similar response of the people. At this point the apostles were still confined to Jerusalem. The people came to them from the outlying villages. Only later would they go forth from Jerusalem and take their gospel and their healing ministry into the villages of Judea (cf. 9:32–43).[96]

The healing ministry of the apostles strengthened the message of the gospel but heightened the opposition of the Jewish leadership. The increased attention to the apostles and the growth of the church created

---

95. Polhill, *Acts* (NAC), 163–64.
96. Polhill, *Acts* (NAC), 164.

jealousy with the high priest and the Sadducees. Again, as in ch. 4, the high priest rose up against the apostles, beat them, and imprisoned them. "The whole passage, with its focus on the healing ministry and the growing acclaim of the people, prepares for the renewed concern of the Sadducees and their arrest of the apostles, just as the healing of the lame man (3:1–10) led to the first arrest (4:1–22)."[97]

The opposition increased as the apostles expanded their influence and added more leadership to the church. Acts 6 introduces the complaint among the Grecian Jews with the service to the widows as well as the need to add disciples to meet the needs of the growing church. "The early church evidently felt the problem of the unintentional neglect of Grecian Jewish widows would be best solved by the Hellenistic Jews; certainly, they would not neglect the Aramaic-speaking widows."[98] Stephen was among the disciples chosen to be a leader; he helped with the responsibilities of the church and defense of the gospel. In ch. 6, however, Stephen was opposed in the synagogue, and the leaders conspired to stir up the people against him. Despite Stephen's defense in ch. 7, the council stoned Stephen to death. Later, ch. 8 introduces Paul as a participant who hearty agreed with Stephen's stoning. Luke marked the day of Stephen's stoning as a momentous day of persecution for the church (Acts 8:1):

> The reference to "that day" in v. 1b means that at that very time, following the death of Stephen, a great persecution arose against the Christians. The opposition to the Christians had been gaining momentum throughout chaps. 4–6. It came first from the Jewish officials in the arrest of the apostles and the two hearings before the Sanhedrin. The first resulted in a warning (4:21); the second, in a flogging (5:40). With the Hellenist Stephen came a third Sanhedrin trial, and this one resulted in death for the Christian witness (7:58–60). The new factor was that this time the officials had the backing of the people (6:12).[99]

Stephen's death at the hands of the council cemented the immense opposition the church leadership was facing. The opposition did not end with Stephen's death. The Sanhedrin's opposition to church leadership and the egregious act of stoning Stephen was the pinnacle of opposition in Jerusalem:

---

97. Polhill, *Acts* (NAC), 162–63.
98. Toussaint, "Acts," 2:367.
99. Polhill, *Acts* (NAC), 211.

If anything, his bold witness in both his Sanhedrin testimony and his death only served to fuel the flames. A violent persecution erupted, and the Christians were forced to flee Jerusalem—i.e., "all except the apostles." This note probably indicates that the real opposition was against Stephen's fellow Hellenists. The resistance began in the Hellenist synagogue (6:9).[100]

Although the Jews left Jerusalem after Stephen's death, some remained and continued to build the Jerusalem church. Stanley D. Toussaint believes that the Greek-speaking Jews fled because they were easily identifiable for their association to Stephen.[101]

David G. Peterson agrees that the Hellenists in the church, which Stephen led, were the main target of the attack and led them to leave Jerusalem.[102] Although members of the church left in fear of persecution, the Jerusalem church remained. Chapters 3–7 highlight the juxtaposition of church growth and opposition between the disciples and Jewish leadership in Jerusalem. Although the Jewish leadership's response to the widespread growth of the church in Jerusalem provides insight into the religious environment in Jerusalem, the mission had to continue to Samaria and the remotest parts of the earth.

Judea and Samaria

Following the geographical structure, Jerusalem was first in the spread of the church, but in ch. 8, the expansion of the gospel began due to the persecution of the church. "The fact that all the Jerusalem believers except the apostles were scattered throughout Judea and Samaria was God's method of fulfilling the mandate of 1:8."[103] Chapter 8 is the "introduction to the witness of the Christians who were dispersed from Jerusalem as a result of the persecution following Stephen's death."[104]

> Luke observes the extent to which *those who had been scattered* [*hoi diasparentes*; cf. 8:1] were involved in the task of evangelism (cf. 11:19). The cognate noun of the verb used here [*diaspora*] was a technical term for the worldwide dispersion of the Jews

---

100. Polhill, *Acts* (NAC), 211.
101. Toussaint, "Acts," 2:372.
102. Peterson, *Acts of the Apostles*, 276.
103. Toussaint, "Acts," 2:372.
104. Polhill, *Acts* (NAC), 210.

among the Gentiles (cf. Jn. 7:35). Here another sort of dispersion begins, involving the Jewish disciples of Christ but soon to include believing Samaritans and Gentiles.[105]

Hellenistic Jews scattered to Judea and Samaria in fear for their lives in the day of persecution; however, the persecution did not stop the spread of the gospel (Acts 8:4). Following the day of persecution, Philip traveled to Samaria proclaiming the good news and performing signs as crowds gathered and rejoiced. Despite the evil of the persecution by the Sanhedrin, the diaspora confirmed God's design for the geographical spread of the gospel.[106]

The intensification of the spread of the gospel in Samaria drew the attention of the apostles, causing them to send Peter and John so that they would receive the Holy Spirit. "The reference to the apostles evangelizing the Samaritan villages is significant. Not only did they endorse the Samaritan mission, but they also enthusiastically participated in it. A new stage in the Christian mission had been reached—the witness to Samaria."[107] Peter and John's visit to Samaria confirms God's intent for the Holy Spirit to empower the apostles to be witnesses of the gospel in Samaria (Acts 1:8).

Samaria's reception of the gospel not only confirms the geographical structure, but also God's purpose to save all his people through Jesus Christ. The Samaritans' historical hostility is well documented in the Bible and historical literature. "The relationship between Jews and Samaritans, which was rocky during the Persian period, grew more hostile during the Hellenistic era (late third century)."[108] Their hostility continued to increase during the Maccabean revolt, when the Samaritans contested the centralization of religion in Jerusalem. "The Samaritans' religious practices were similar to the Jews with a few major exceptions—mainly, the Samaritans thought of Mount Gerizim, not Jerusalem, as the proper place of worship."[109]

Another significant difference is their belief in the coming Messiah. According to Deut 18:18, they believed the coming Messiah would be a

---

105. Peterson, *Acts of the Apostles*, 279; emphasis original.
106. Brian Maiers, "Samaritans," *LBD* 227.
107. Polhill, *Acts* (NAC), 221.
108. Maiers, *LBD* 227.
109. Maiers, *LBD* 227.

first-century Samaritan.[110] Their religious differences continued into the New Testament as Jewish leaders expressed their disdain for Samaritan ethnicity. Balz and Schneider summarize the Samaritans' negative portrayal (or absence) within the Gospels:

> Mark never mentions the Samaritans, and Matthew mentions them only once (and negatively, at that: 10:5), but the Lukan writings (Luke 9:51–56; 10:30–37; 17:11–19; Acts 1:8; 8:1–25; 9:31; 15:3) and John (4:4–42) are greatly interested in them. In general, the Gospels reflect the hostility between Jews and Samaritans. On the Jewish side the word Σαμαρίτης is used as an insult and equated with "possessed person" (John 8:48). The Jewish scribe in Luke 10:37 avoids uttering the word "Samaritan" and instead uses a circumlocution.[111]

Even Jesus recognized the divide when he healed the leper who returned to give him thanks for healing. Jesus questioned whether he, the foreigner, was the only one to come back to give gratitude. However, Jesus did not maintain the divide but sought to reconcile it. Despite the historical hostility, Jesus exemplified the mission to the Samaritans during his encounter with Samaritan woman at the well (John 4:4–42).

His encounter with the woman at the well dispelled previous notions of ethnic avoidance and affirmed the universality of forgiveness. Jesus's missionary work while on earth prepared the groundwork for the gospel at his departure in Acts 1. The similarities with waiting for the Messiah primed the Samaritans to be open to Jesus, despite his Jewish heritage. This became evident in the scriptural occurrences in the New Testament. Luke provides evidence to their receptivity in Acts 8 when he states that the Samaritans received the gospel with excitement. "Luke taking place in Samaria is exclusive to this Gospel and reflects its interest in despised and rejected persons."[112] The inclusion of the Samaritans not only confirmed the geographical structure but also highlighted God's intentionality of including ethnicities that once were excluded and despised.

---

110. Maiers, *LBD* 227.
111. "Σαμάρεια," *EDNT* 3:226–27.
112. Maiers, *LBD* 227.

Samaria

Samaria's hostility to the Jews is well documented, but it is highlighted in ch. 8 to emphasize the gospel's indiscrimination to those who believe and the universality of the gospel. Following the Samaritans' inclusion, Luke continues to document the spread to the remotest parts of the earth:

> The inclusion of Samaria also presents God's purpose to present the gospel to every nation. . . . The focus is now on the founding of Christian communities outside Jerusalem, in active fellowship with that first community of believers. Special attention is drawn to the gift of the Spirit to the Samaritans (8:14–17). As in later narratives about Cornelius and his household (10:44–46; 11:15–17), this gift verifies God's true people, "regardless of their past ethnic or cultural hostility to Jews."[113]

After a successful missionary journey to Samaria, they began to return to Jerusalem. On their return journey, the gospel continued to spread to more ethnicities later in ch. 8, when God led Philip to share the gospel with an Ethiopian eunuch. The ethnicity of the eunuch is evidence of God's purpose to spread the gospel to those whose past ethnicities were unwelcome in the community of believers.

Ethiopia, also rendered as Cush, was in the region of the upper Nile and south of Egypt. In the Old Testament, Ethiopia was a country known to be culturally opposed to the Israelites. Despite mention in Num 12:1 of intermarriage, Ethiopians were a people worthy of the wrath of God:

> Aware of that country's commercial enterprise (Isa. 45:14) as well as political and military involvements (e.g., Ezek. 30:5–9; Nah. 3:9; cf. Ezek. 38:5), the Israelite prophets held up Ethiopia as the example of a sinful kingdom (Amos 9:7). Not only would Ethiopia fall to the kingdoms of the earth (Isa. 20:3–5), it would also experience the wrath of God (Zeph. 2:12). With Ethiopia, as with Egypt and Seba, would ransom exiled Israel (Isa. 43:3).[114]

In the New Testament, however, the distance between Ethiopia and Jerusalem created a sense of intrigue and mystery. Ethiopians were viewed as remote and removed from the descriptions in the Old Testament. Greek writers had shown curiosity in Ethiopians and Luke's audience

---

113. Peterson, *Acts of the Apostles*, 277.
114. Allen C. Myers, "Ethiopia," *EBD* 355.

would have perceived the eunuch as a positive mystery character from a distant homeland.[115]

Luke's description included the eunuch as a court official of Candace, queen of Ethiopia, which also confirms intrigue for the remote culture (Acts 8:27).

> The geographical name "Ethiopian" would signal to Luke's audience that the eunuch was from territories south of Egypt. Since he is also identified as an official of Candace, 1st-century readers would connect him specifically with the kingdom of Meroe, the queens of which traditionally were called "Candace."[116]

Luke's inclusion of his office confirms not only his geographical location but also Luke's possible interest in and appreciation for Ethiopian culture:

> Eunuchs frequently held places of respect and trust in Eastern courts, as does this one, and the identification of this figure as a eunuch may simply reinforce the reader's impression that he is an unusual person, a person who has come from the "end of the world"—at least from the end of Luke's world.[117]

Most importantly, Luke's inclusion of the eunuch was a purposeful signaling to the audience of the universality of the gospel. The mystique of the character and the distance of the traveler's homeland would have intrigued Luke's audience.[118]

The inclusion of such a foreign character draws the attention of the audience and exaggerates Jesus's intent for the gospel to reach the remotest parts of the world:

> Indeed, Philip's witness to the eunuch may be considered the first conversion of a Gentile and in many ways parallels the story of Cornelius in chapter 10. Ethiopia was considered "the end of the earth" by the Greeks and Romans, and Philip's witness to the Samaritans and the Ethiopian comprises a "foretaste" of the completion of Christ's commission (1:8) by the whole church in the subsequent chapters of Acts.[119]

---

115. Beverly Roberts Gaventa, "Ethiopian Eunuch," *ABD* 2:667.
116. Gretchen Ellis and T. Michael W. Halcomb, "Kush," *LBD*.
117. Gaventa, *ABD* 2:667.
118. Gaventa, *ABD* 2:667.
119. Polhill, *Acts* (NAC), 222.

Even with the intrigue with Ethiopians and the good news of the spread of the gospel, this story still highlights the lack of inclusion of the eunuch. Despite his long travels, his gentile background would have separated him from the Jewish temple worship. However, the Ethiopian's lack of inclusion into the Jewish community did not hinder his familiarity with Jewish traditions since the Old Testament.[120]

"Ethiopian's actions underscore this portrayal of him as an intriguing, romantic, even exotic personage. Luke initially explains that the Ethiopian had been to Jerusalem to worship and was in the process of returning home."[121] The eunuch recognized the need to worship at the temple and was willing to travel long distances. Also, on his return, he was reading from the book of Isaiah. The readiness of the Ethiopian eunuch to receive the gospel only confirms God's plan and activity in spreading the good news to the remotest parts of the earth. "It shows that even the most remote persons (viewing "Ethiopia" in its broadest ancient usage) and those least acceptable to the stringent tenets of Jewish practice might receive and respond to the gospel."[122] One cannot understate the inclusion of the Ethiopian eunuch, and the purposeful inclusion by Luke introduces the widespread of the gospel.

Remotest Part of the Earth

The Ethiopian eunuch parallels the story of Peter's first conversion of a gentile named Cornelius. Acts 10 introduces Cornelius from Caesarea, a centurion of the Italian cohort. As with the Ethiopian eunuch, Cornelius's background is critical to understanding the geographical spread of the gospel:

> The importance of this event is seen in the fact that Luke recounts it three times—here in Acts 10, again in chapter 11, and finally in 15:6–9. The geographic extension of the gospel in Acts is an initial fulfillment of Jesus' words in Matthew 8:11: "Many will come from the east and the west, and will take their places . . . in the kingdom of heaven."[123]

---

120. Myers, *EBD* 355.
121. Gaventa, *ABD* 2:667.
122. Myers, *EBD* 355.
123. Toussaint, "Acts," 2:379.

Cornelius was enlisted as a centurion in Roman military in Caesarea, which is located in Palestine. Cornelius's location in Caesarea confirms his gentile background. Caesarea was a part of the Roman empire valued for its harbors.[124] "A seaport city built by Herod the Great at Strato's Tower in honor of Caesar Augustus, Caesarea became the residence of the Roman procurator."[125]

The gospel's spread continued to the gentile-Roman world, where Caesarea played a pivotal role in reaching the gentiles. "Through the change of scene from Jerusalem to Caesarea, Luke indicates the transition of the Pauline witness to Christ from the Jewish to the Gentile-Roman world, which has its goal in the imperial metropolis of Rome."[126] Cornelius's profession adds more support to his gentile-Roman background. His position as a centurion in the Roman army solidified his command over one hundred.[127] His position and location support the geographical movement of the gospel.

Luke, however, decided to include Cornelius's religious background to provide further insight into his previous religious affiliation. According to Luke, Cornelius was "one who feared God with all his household, and gave many alms to the *Jewish* people and prayed to God continually" (Acts 10:2). Although Cornelius was a gentile, he was known as a "God-fearer" because of his ardent participation to Jewish practices like alms and prayer.[128] Toussaint adds that Cornelius was also a participant at the synagogues: "Evidently he attended the synagogue and to the best of his knowledge and ability followed the Old Testament Scriptures. Nevertheless, he had not entered into New Testament salvation."[129]

Luke's detailed encounter of Cornelius's story is a critical introduction to the missionary efforts to the gentiles. Peter's participation in the gentiles' salvation provides evidence and solidification of God's plan for the inclusion of gentiles all over the world:

> Luke not only repeats the story at some length but further underlines the importance that he sees in the event by putting into Peter's mouth a significant reference to it in 15:7–9, where it is represented as the beginning, under God's decision and choice,

---

124. Robert L. Hohlfelder, "Caesarea (Place)," *ABD* 800.
125. Maiers, *LBD* 236.
126. Maiers, *LBD* 236.
127. "ἑκατοντάρχης," BDAG 299.
128. F. F. Bruce, "Cornelius," *NBD*³ 228.
129. Toussaint, "Acts," 2:379.

of the evangelization of Gentiles. Divine participation and control are made clear in the elaborate construction of the story with its complementary visions carefully fitted together, angelic messengers, and finally the spontaneous gift of the Spirit. The importance of the story for Luke and for Luke's book is thus unmistakable. It marks the final critical stage in the extension of the Gospel and the expansion of the church.[130]

Luke's details and repetition in this story highlight the importance of the expansion and inclusion of the gospel. Peter reported back to Jerusalem after all of Judea heard what happened at Cornelius's house, and they concluded that they believed Peter's report of God's desire for the gentiles to receive the gospel. Luke reported that they said, "God has granted to the Gentiles also the repentance *that leads* to life" (Acts 11:18b).

The spread of the gospel continues as Luke records the missionary journey at the church of Antioch. "Christianity was brought to Antioch ca. A.D. 40 by Hellenists who fled from Jerusalem after the martyrdom of Stephen (Acts 11:19–20). Thus began the first Christian generation at Antioch (A.D. 40–70)."[131] The diaspora continued in connection to the persecution in connection to Stephen. Men from Cyprus and Cyrene came to Antioch and began "preaching the Lord Jesus" to the Greeks (Acts 11:20).

The term *Greeks* is significant because it distinguishes them from the Jews and provides background of Luke's Greek reference. "Βy Ἕλληνες, though with no particular emphasis, it means a. Greeks or Hellenised inhabitants of Syria and Asia Minor, and b. inhabitants of Hellas and Macedonia."[132] Hellenistic Syrians were targets of the gospel in Antioch:

> Anonymous Jewish Christians from Cyprus and Cyrene, and therefore baptized Jews of Greek language and civilization, were the first, in Antioch (11:20), to speak πρὸς τοὺς Ἕλληνας, i.e., to non-Jewish, Greek-speaking inhabitants of this former capital of the Seleucid kingdom and the contemporary capital of the Roman province of Syria, whose population in its upper strata consisted of descendants of true Greeks and Macedonians, and especially of Hellenistic Syrians.[133]

---

130. Barrett, *Commentary on Acts*, 491.
131. "Antioch," *HarBD* 33.
132. Hans Windisch, "Ἕλλην," *TDNT* 2:510.
133. Windisch, *TDNT* 2:510.

The Lord caused a substantial number in Antioch to believe, and after the church of Jerusalem heard about the large numbers of people who believed, they sent Barnabas. The choice is no accident, due to his background as a Levite and a diaspora Jew.[134]

The leadership and trust that Barnabas developed among the people of Antioch are fitting, due to his Jewish background and his familiarity of the current diaspora. "The Jerusalem church sought to control this new development by sending Barnabas, a fellow Cypriote, to guide the Antiochene community. To aid him in teaching this 'large company' of believers, Barnabas brought Saul."[135] Barnabas's arrival and work as a man of faith resulted in a significant increase in number. After his initial work, Barnabas left for Saul and when they returned, they remained a year, where they gathered with the church; this is the first use of the term *church* to mean Jewish and gentile believers gathering together.

The church of Antioch is unique, the beginning of a new mutual gathering of Jew and gentile:

> The Jerusalem believers had no exclusive claim on the term *ekklēsia*, despite its OT associations, and the mixed assemblage of Jewish and Gentile believers which was formed at Antioch on the Orontes was without ceremony also called "the church" there (Acts 11:26; 13:1). Moreover Antioch, not Jerusalem, was the model of the "new church" which was to appear all over the world. It was founded by Hellenist Jews. Here believers were first dubbed Christians, or "Christites," by their Gentile neighbors (Acts 11:26). Antioch became the springboard for the expansion of the gospel throughout the Levant.[136]

The church of Antioch introduced the term *Christians* and the beginning of Jew and gentile assembling and worshiping together. However, the church of Antioch was groundbreaking for the Christian faith as the church made a conscious decision not to make gentiles proselytes:

> At Antioch Hellenists from Cyprus and Cyrene made the momentous decision to begin, as a matter of policy, to convert Gentiles without circumcision. This striking difference from Jewish proselytism set these believers apart, and so it was at Antioch that they received a new name, "Christians" (Acts 11:26).[137]

---

134. Jon B. Daniels, "Barnabas (Person)," *ABD* 610.
135. *HarBD* 33.
136. D. W. B. Robinson, "Church," *NBD*³ 201.
137. *HarBD* 33.

Antioch was the model for the "new" gathering of believers that came from gentile and Jewish backgrounds. This new model of the church initiated the expansion of the gospel throughout the world and challenged the previous understanding of gentile conversion.[138]

The new model of Jew and gentile challenged the Council of Jerusalem in ch. 15 to examine and clarify a gentile's position in the church without circumcision.[139] The influence of the church of Antioch is evident throughout the book of Acts and became the establishment for gentile ministry. "Antioch was the perfect gateway to gentile ministry and served as the headquarters for Paul's missionary travels (Acts 13:1–3; 14:26–28; 18:22–23)."[140] Acts 13 details Saul and Barnabas being sent on the first missions from the church of Antioch.[141] Antioch's formation became the model, gateway, and foundation for future ministry, including the influential journeys of Paul.

---

138. Phillips, "Geographic Importance of Antioch," 276.
139. Walter A. Elwell, "Antioch of Pisidia," *BEB* 1:121.
140. Phillips, "Geographic Importance of Antioch," 276.
141. Elwell, *BEB* 1:121.

3

Peter's Transformational Leadership after Pentecost

Introduction

The diversity of the church in the book of Acts revealed the importance of Pentecost, geography, and biographical characters. The spread of the gospel to the many nations highlighted the biographical development of Paul and Peter. As noted in chapter 2, Paul and Peter played an integral role in beginning the spread from Jerusalem to the remotest parts of the earth. An in-depth analysis of both Paul's and Peter's leadership is important. The analysis will use the framework of Burns's transformational leadership. First, the biographical study of Peter in Acts will analyze the definition of transformational leadership Peter exhibited that contributed to diversity in the church.

Peter's leadership is well documented throughout the Gospels. The authors recorded his faith as well as his undeniable flaws. Peter is the disciple who walked on water with Jesus but also the one who denied Jesus. However, after Peter's denial, Jesus commissioned Peter to shepherd his sheep and be the rock of the church. Despite Peter's flaws, Jesus still entrusted him with leadership among the disciples.

Gish highlights the transformation of Peter from his denials to a bold proclaimer to the church:

> Simon Peter is one of Jesus' first disciples and later becomes the spokesman of the Twelve. Although Jesus gives Simon the name "Peter" ("rock"; Πέτρος, *Petros*; in Matt 16:18; Mark 3:16;

Κηφᾶς, *Kēphas*; in John 1:42), his ability to live up to it is often in doubt in the Gospels. Peter's rebuke of the Lord (Matt 16:22–23; Mark 8:32–33), his falling asleep in the garden (Matt 26:40; Mark 14:37), his attack on Malchus (Mark 14:47; John 18:10–11), and his denial of Jesus (Matt 26:69–75; Mark 14:66–72; Luke 22:55–61; John 18:15–27) all support this perception. However, Jesus' reinstatement of Peter in John 21:15–17 ("Do you love Me . . . feed My sheep") communicates His confidence in and selection of him as the head of the early church. Luke demonstrates this in the book of Acts, which portrays Peter as a bold proclaimer of the gospel (Acts 2:14–41; 3:12–26; 4:8–21), a miracle worker (Acts 3:1–11; 9:32–35, 38–42), and an authoritative figure in the early church.[1]

The evidence of Peter's strengths and weaknesses throughout the Gospels is clear. However, Peter's leadership after Jesus's charge merits analysis, especially as the church grew and diversified. It is worthwhile to study Peter's leadership development throughout the Gospels and his leadership throughout the book of Acts.

Peter's Origin

Knowing the origin of a transformational leader is vital to understanding the behaviors and decisions of the leader. The dissection of a leader's origins can pinpoint their personal transformation as they developed biographically. Thorough research can provide insight into the leader's current motivations, values, and decisions. This current research will apply Burns's origin model to suggest that personal transformation is indicative of future transformational leadership. According to Burns, one should analyze transformational leadership origins through psychological, social, and political beginnings.[2] Therefore, understanding Peter's leadership after Pentecost and in the church begins with an understanding of Peter's psychological, social, and political beginnings written in the Gospels.

Understanding Peter's psychological matrix of leadership will be difficult. The lack of data can hinder the pursuit of a full understanding of the character. Burns acknowledges, "Our knowledge of the early psychological experiences of famous leaders also is limited by the paucity

---

1. Gish, *LBD*, para. 2.
2. Burns, *Leadership*, 53.

of data."[3] Also, attempting to complete psychological analysis of historical characters is personally and culturally biased.[4] Personal bias can include beliefs of a "great" person is limited to a person of power or influence.[5] Therefore, it is critical in studying origins that the researcher analyzes only the information available and not allow bias or inference in his or her study.

Burns's Origin

Regardless of the limitations of psychological analysis, opportunities exist to review biographical data to understand a person's leadership: "Despite its limitations, psychobiography, which depends on a psychoanalytic approach to biographical data, can be an indispensable tool in analyzing the shaping influences on leadership."[6] Burns believes that psychological analysis can reveal the development of personality, wants, needs, and values.

Reviewing the leader's formative years to discover motivations that determine personality requires a cumulative and comparative analysis to form a strong hypothesis. Burns presents brief reviews of Hitler, Ghandi, Nixon, and Roosevelt to highlight the possible childhood determinants that could have affected their leadership personalities: "Cumulative and comparative analysis of a large number of leaders should eventually provide stronger foundations for generalizations and hypotheses. We may come to understand better the powerful influences of family, school, and adolescent experience."[7] The cumulative and comparative analysis explores the motivations created by family, school, and adolescent experience that allow the psychological work of proposing new sources in leadership.[8] Understanding personality development is critical to analyzing the leader and follower relationship. A leader's personality development will determine their interaction with their followers and reciprocal relationship.

3. Burns, *Leadership*, 51.
4. Burns, *Leadership*, 50.
5. Burns, *Leadership*, 51.
6. Burns, *Leadership*, 53.
7. Burns, *Leadership*, 60–61.
8. Burns, *Leadership*, 61.

Wellspring of Wants

Burns continued, stating that the psychological review of the origins of a leader reveals their wellspring of wants. He defines wants as "palpable tissue demands in their simplest and most powerful state, expressed in the phenomena of persons directly and consciously."[9] It is vital to understand the wants of leaders because this is their guide to action and serves as motivator and energizer for their purposes. Burns differentiates between wants and needs. He states that needs are socially influenced, versus wants, which consist of self-conscious action that satisfies one's desires.[10] In addition, Burns says that wants are a biographical requirement of the human system.

Before a leader is even born, his biographical makeup determines his personality. Burns summarizes: "The genetic inheritance initiates the series of openings and closures of life chances—mechanisms powerful enough to have a direct impact on evolving personality."[11] The biographical makeup does not determine the totality of the leader's wants, but it also interlocks with psychological factors. In addition to a leader's biographical inheritance, their wants begin the moment they are born and progress throughout childhood:

> At the moment infants are expelled from the calm warmth and dependence of the uterus into the shocking, bewildering world of light and sound, of touching and prodding, of deprivation and fulfillment, they begin the lifelong process of stimulus and response that will culminate for some in skills and motivations for leadership.[12]

In each moment in a child's life, the child develops tendencies to stimuli. A child's psychological upbringing will include social, political, and cultural stimuli that will determine the development of wants and needs. Burns provides an example: "This powerful need for affection and belongingness, combined with the effect of social influences and political forces, helps produce a variety of forms of leadership. A passion for affection and acceptance could manifest itself in leadership."[13]

---

9. Burns, *Leadership*, 63.
10. Burns, *Leadership*, 64.
11. Burns, *Leadership*, 61.
12. Burns, *Leadership*, 61.
13. Burns, *Leadership*, 67.

A leader's biographical and social backgrounds and the stimuli he may have experienced all exert a significant effect on the leader's future wants, which affect motivations and interactions. In addition to psychological factors, no factor is more impactful than the learning of a leader: "Learning from experience, learning from people, learning from successes and failures, learning from leaders and followers: personality is formed in these reactions to stimuli in social environments."[14] Burns cites Albert Bandura and Richard Walters as examples of theorists who state learning is not limited to conditioning but imitation of identifiable persons. A leader's learning from imitation conditions one's wants and personality development. The wellspring of wants first develops biologically and then interlocks with psychological developments of social, political, and cultural stimuli that determine their future motivations and interactions. The study of a leader's wants is critical to understanding their present motivations that guide their actions.

Transmutation of Need

While wants represent longing due to biological and psychological factors that determine self-conscious decisions and motivations, needs are determined by social and environmental shifts and influences; therefore, "if wants are drives experienced as feelings of longing, needs are wants influenced by the environment. When environments change because of longtime shifts in the climate, for example, wants must yield to the new circumstances or the wanting creature will yield to biological imperatives."[15] Long-term shifts in the climate or circumstances can change one's biological wants. Burns explains:

> It is the act of deliberate and selective "socializing"—the influencing in terms of group values of another person's wants—that brings the conscious leadership process into play. The leader—parent, teacher, doctor, priest, schoolmate—chooses to encourage certain wants and discourage others. Drives and wants remain the basic energizers, the main "pushers," but the targets toward which the wants are directed become more focused as wants give way to needs.[16]

14. Burns, *Leadership*, 63.
15. Burns, *Leadership*, 68.
16. Burns, *Leadership*, 69.

Deliberate and consistent socialization redirect the target toward the needs, rather than the wants, of the leader.

Although wants drive the energy and motivations through socialization and environmental shifts, the leader can yield wants for needs and push for the fulfillment of needs. According to Burns, a leader has to have the ability to make decisions not based on simple biological wants but on wants that transform into needs.[17] If a leader is willing to meet the lower needs of the followers, then the higher needs will become more apparent.[18] Therefore, for leaders to understand social and environmental changes so that they can meet emerging needs is critical. A leader's ability to decipher biological wants and socially developed needs gives one the opportunity to lead followers toward higher needs.

Burns expands this idea by addressing the development of needs to the hierarchies and values: "Children progress from the received morality of the cave, the herd, the tribe, the family, to the broader, more consciously conceived values that will guide and strengthen them in wider collectivities."[19] Personal development of needs from childhood helps formulate future social and political values. He defines values as "desirable or preferred end-states or collective goals or explicit purposes, and values are standards in terms of which specific criteria may be established and choices made among alternatives."[20]

Values can be end states that are intrinsically the goal or end states that are instrumental in achieving future ends.[21] One must internalize values deeply, such that they can change personalities and behaviors. Once the value is implanted deeply, whether consciously or unconsciously, it will dictate a leader's direction despite incentives, sanctions, or witnesses.[22] At this stage of values, a leader requires the capability to communicate and balance meeting the needs of followers, while maintaining their own goals, purposes, and principles. Therefore, it is important that leaders understand their values to mediate the needs of the follower, while leading the follower to higher purpose.

Burns's progression from wants and needs to values includes the transformation of biological wants by climate and social needs and then

17. Burns, *Leadership*, 68.
18. Burns, *Leadership*, 70.
19. Burns, *Leadership*, 72.
20. Burns, *Leadership*, 74.
21. Burns, *Leadership*, 75.
22. Burns, *Leadership*, 75.

formulating values. The psychological analysis of leadership should include the progression from wants to values. However, Burns admits this progress is not always cohesive or conscious: "It is still in many ways a mystery how the child or adolescent is propelled from one level to another. As we have seen, some do not change; they remain indefinitely in a stage of deference, of conformity, of simplistic norm-observance, of a literal following of rules."[23] While recognizing the levels of needs, wants, and values, it is important to understand that not all leaders or followers progress; some may remain stagnant or indifferent. Understanding a leader's development from their origins to their current state of leadership allows a thorough analysis of the leader's goals, decisions, and purposes.

Peter

A historical review of Peter's biographical data reveals his geographical, religious, family, and occupational origins. This review will help create an analysis of Peter's personality developments, wants, needs, and values. Applying Burns's development of wants, needs, and values, this current research will evaluate Peter's biographical progression.

Peter's Wellspring of Wants

Peter was raised in Bethsaida, which Scripture later states to be in Galilee.[24] Research in Galilee has conflicting reports religiously and culturally, but in the New Testament a distinct Jewish culture was present: "In OT times, Galilee was not significant in Israelite life, but in NT times it was a prominent Jewish population center."[25] Even without archaeological evidence of synagogues, Galileans historically maintained a strict following of the sabbath and Jerusalem pilgrimage.[26] In addition, the Gospels reveal that the Galileans played an integral role in the life of Jesus and his disciples:

> The Galileans of the gospels are enthusiastic about Jesus' healing activity, whereas his teaching appears to have been directed to a more intimate band of traveling companions/disciples. The

---

23. Burns, *Leadership*, 78.
24. Grant R. Osborne, "Peter, the Apostle," *BEB* 2:1659–60.
25. Henry W. Holloman, "Galilee, Galileans," *BEB* 1:834.
26. Seán Freyne, "Galileans," *ABD* 878.

fourth Gospel generalizes this picture by declaring that the Galileans received (that is, accepted) Jesus in a way that the inhabitants of Judea did not (John 4:3, 43–45).[27]

Jesus's life and ministry were well received by the Galileans and explain Peter's willingness to receive Jesus's discipleship. His wellspring of wanting a messiah is related to his upbringing in Bethsaida.

Peter's family background is also important to understanding his psychological analysis. For Peter's family background, however, "the New Testament provides limited information on Peter's life and background before his call to discipleship. His Hebrew name is Simon or Simeon (see Acts 15:14). His father's name is John, and his brother's name is Andrew (the disciple of Jesus)."[28]

MacDonald explains that the inclusion of Andrew as a disciple helps confirm Peter's family religious background and acceptance of Jesus.[29] Despite the New Testament's lack of interest in Andrew, the Gospel of John adds that Andrew brought Peter to the Messiah (John 1:41–42). Andrew readily accepted Jesus as the Messiah and brought Peter to Jesus. This minute biographical fact confirms that Peter and his family readily received Jesus.

Also, according to Mark 1:29–31, Jesus healed Peter's mother-in-law. This implies that Peter was married, and he either would break from missionary journeys or his wife was accompanying him.[30] His sacrifice to follow Jesus was not just occupational but also separated him from his family. His time away from his family helps explain his questioning of Jesus about the possibility of a reward (Matt 19:27). Jesus understood their sacrifice and responded to Peter, stating that the twelve disciples will sit on twelve thrones in heaven. Despite this reassurance, Peter again asked Jesus about their sacrifice when he wondered about salvation (Mark 10:28–31). Jesus acknowledged the disciples' leaving their families and told them that they would receive a hundred times as much in eternal

---

27. Burns, *Leadership*, 78.

28. Gish, *LBD*, para. 3. According to John 1:44, Peter had a brother named Andrew, and they were both referenced as coming from Bethsaida.

29. Dennis R. MacDonald, "Andrew (Person)," *ABD* 242. "The NT shows little interest in Andrew. His name occurs only twelve times, four of these merely in lists of apostles (Mark 3:18; Matt 10:2; Luke 6:14; and Acts 1:13). According to Mark, Jesus called Andrew and his brother Peter to leave their nets to 'become fishers of men' (1:16–18)."

30. Osborne, *BEB* 2:1660.

life. Peter's willingness to lose time with his family is clearly creating a psychological need for reward or motivation.

Peter's occupation also contributes to the psychological analysis. He was a fisherman by trade and met Jesus while he was at work (Luke 5:1–11). His trade is not a surprise, but rather completely normal, due to his geographical upbringing. Gish provides background: "Peter grew up in Bethsaida (Βηθσαϊδά, Bēthsaida), a fishing village on the shore of the Sea of Galilee. He operated a fishing business in partnership with the Zebedee brothers, James and John (also disciples of Jesus)."[31] This common occupation in Bethsaida led Peter to his initial encounter with Jesus (Matt 4:18–22). Further belief is that he continued the fishing intermittently while Jesus discipled him.[32] Scholars often note his willingness to leave his occupation behind as a part of the disciple's sacrifice to follow Jesus (Matt 19:27). Peter's biographical analysis of his occupation is similar with that of his family. His willingness to leave everything, including his trade, factors into his dependency on Jesus and his finding unfathomable that someone would crucify Jesus. Like leaving his family, his occupational sacrifice also contributes to his wellspring of wants for temporal and earthly kingdom rewards.

Peter's Transmutation of Needs

As noted, Peter's cultural background matches his receptivity to Jesus's ministry. However, his strong belief in Jesus became his disbelief that Jesus would die and leave him. His wellspring of wants had to change to Jesus's teaching and socialization with his messiah. Jesus's deliberate, consistent teaching transformed Peter's biographical wants of acceptance and targeted them toward his needs. In Matt 16:21, Jesus harshly rebuked Peter for his denial of Jesus's death. Jesus's ministry was taking place primarily in Galilee, but he foreknew that his travels to Jerusalem and Judea would encounter opposition.[33] Blomberg expounds, "Most of his ministry had taken place in and around Galilee; but now he had to go to Judea and to Jerusalem, the capital city of Israel, the heart of the

---

31. Gish, *LBD*, para. 3.
32. Elwell and Comfort, *Tyndale Bible Dictionary*, 1021.
33. W. Allen, *Gospel According to St. Matthew*, 180.

power of the Jewish authorities, where hostility against him increased to the point of execution."[34]

Peter's experience with Jesus's ministry in his surrounding community was well received, but he could not foresee the Jewish people rejecting him as they traveled. Morris highlights Peter's bewilderment: "For Peter it is unthinkable that the one he has just pronounced 'the Messiah, the Son of the living God' should be rejected and killed. How could the Jewish nation reject the Jewish Messiah?"[35] Peter could not fathom the Jesus he just proclaimed to be the Messiah being rejected by the Jewish people. Peter's wellspring of wants became evident at the thought of the Jewish messiah suffering at the hand of his people. "Peter had his view that Jesus was the Messiah confirmed; in the light of that he found it incredible that this would entail rejection and suffering and death."[36]

The disciples were focused on the triumphant aspects of Jesus the Messiah.[37] The disciples' misperception of the messianic kingdom is Jesus's earthly reign, while Peter and the disciples would lead by his side. Peter's subconscious wants are also evident in his perceived authority to challenge the authority of Jesus. His confidence is linked to Jesus's previous proclamation that Jesus will give Peter authority and make him the rock on which Jesus will build the church. "Perhaps emboldened by the promise that the gates of hades will not prevail against the church, the apostle did not yet recognize that the way to life is through death."[38] Peter's newfound authority revealed his wellspring of wants to lead with Jesus, and he could not grapple with that coming to an end.

Even after Jesus's life on earth, Peter's upbringing remained clear. In Jesus's absence, Peter maintained his Galilean and Jewish traditions, which strongly influenced his leadership. In Burns's terms, Peter's wellspring of wants transitioning to the transmutation of needs becomes evident later in his leadership in the church in the book of Acts. Luke's account in the book of Acts highlights his internal conflict with his religious upbringing and his leadership in the Christian church:

> Yet the stance of James, the brother of the Lord, on issues such as the dietary laws (Gal 2:10), and even the vacillation of Peter on

---

34. Blomberg, *Matthew*, 258–59.
35. Morris, *Gospel According to Matthew*, 429.
36. Morris, *Gospel According to Matthew*, 430.
37. Hagner, *Matthew 14–28*, 478–81.
38. Davies and Allison, *Matthew 8–18*, 661–62.

such matters, indicates that not all Galileans were automatically open to a more liberal understanding of their faith as proposed by Jesus, especially in regard to relations with gentiles.[39]

Acts 11 addresses Peter's concern for Jewish dietary restrictions and relationship with the gentiles.

He had to receive a vision to change his belief in dietary restrictions, and Paul confronted him on his treatment of gentile believers (Gal 2:11–14). Acts 11 highlights Peter's report at Jerusalem about God's vision to him concerning eating food once deemed unclean. In that vision, Peter's initial response was to reject the permission to eat four-footed animals of the earth and the wild beasts and the crawling creatures and the birds of the air (v. 6). A voice from heaven spoke to Peter three times: "What God has cleansed, no longer consider unholy" (Acts 11:9).

Peter's apprehension argues his staunch Jewish upbringing. Polhill confirms Peter's struggle: "In Lev 20:24b–26 the laws of clean and unclean are linked precisely to Israel's separation from the rest of the nations."[40] His Jewish background is evident within his internal struggles to relinquish his upbringing despite his new learnings with Jesus. Peter's religious biographical background becomes fundamental to understand his transformation in the leadership of the church. According to Burns, Peter's wellspring of wants transformed to needs through Jesus's teaching and religious climate changes.

Values

The progression from wants to values is evident throughout Peter's leadership in the church. As Burns notes about values, Peter progressed from his perceived childhood morality to more consciously perceived values.[41] It begins in the upper room and continues throughout the book of Acts. Polhill adds, "Peter assumed leadership among the apostles and convened the assembly. Throughout Acts, he played this role. He was the spokesman, the representative apostle. The other apostles were present and active, but Peter was their mouthpiece."[42] Luke's historical approach to the book of Acts documents Peter's distinct leadership in the church. Barrett

39. Freyne, *ABD* 878.
40. Polhill, *Acts* (NAC), 255.
41. Burns, *Leadership*, 72.
42. Polhill, *Acts* (NAC), 91.

summarizes Peter's early decisions, preaching, and leadership, which set the foundation in the formation of the New Testament church:

> His prominence continues until the beginning of Paul's first journey (chapter 13), is resumed in chapter 15, and is then dropped. Peter is also prominent in the gospels and in the tradition of the post-apostolic age (cf. 1 Clem. 5:4; Ignatius, *Romans* 4:3; *Smyrnaeans* 3:2). That he played a leading part in the early church is hardly to be doubted.[43]

Peter standing up among the disciples was not a rare occurrence but evidence of Peter's willingness to accept his appointed role.

Acts 1 highlights the beginning of the transformation of Peter's leadership. Peter first assumed his role as he stood and spoke among his brethren regarding the replacement of Judas as a disciple (Matt 16:16–18). Peter's leadership in the upper room signifies his full understanding of Scripture in Judas's role in Jesus's death and resurrection. Peter did not understand the necessity for Jesus's death, resurrection, and ascension; however, now he understood the need for the disciples to continue in the work prescribed by Jesus in his absence. "For Peter the recollection of Judas's gruesome end must have been a grim reminder of his own denial of his Lord as he now sought to lead the assembly to fill the abandoned post."[44] He progressed from denying Jesus to leading his fellow apostles to the selection of a new disciple to replace Judas. His past wants and needs distracted him from the proper understanding of Jesus's purpose and Old Testament prophecy, but now Jesus's resurrected life changed Peter's values.

The transformation of Peter continued in the following chapter as he stood to preach the gospel at Pentecost. He recognized the value of sharing the gospel with all the people at Pentecost. Polhill documents Peter as the spokesperson of the disciples to deliver the message of Jesus's death and resurrection:

> Peter stood up along with the eleven other apostles. The eleven are not incidental to the narrative. As the Twelve, the apostles were the witnesses to the resurrection, which would be the central subject of Peter's sermon. As always in the early chapters

---

43. Barrett, *Commentary on Acts*, 95.
44. Polhill, *Acts* (NAC), 92–93.

of Acts, Peter was their representative, the spokesman for the testimony of all Twelve.[45]

The sermon clearly illustrated the gospel message. Peter detailed Jesus's fulfillment of Old Testament prophecy of a messiah of Davidic lineage that conquered death through resurrection (Acts 2:14–36).

Peter's leadership as the spokesperson for the apostles communicated the necessity of the death and resurrection. His message was the beginning of the New Testament church and the outpouring of the Holy Spirit as over three thousand people were saved.[46] Despite his past resistance to Jesus's death, he was now the primary messenger. His shift of values changed his leadership and allowed him to lead others to a higher value in the gospel message. His understanding of Scripture, experience of following Jesus, and witnessing of Jesus's death and resurrection transformed his purpose and direction.

The value of the gospel and continual shift in leadership in the spread of the news of Jesus's death and resurrection were not Peter's only transformation. He also had to let go of his own origins of customs and cultural upbringing to adopt correct values for the growth of the church of both Jew and gentile. This required that he relinquish his Jewish customs as a necessity to reach the gentile nations. Upon his meeting with a gentile named Cornelius, Peter had a vision releasing two possible apprehensions of dining with a gentile. First, according to Lev 20: 24–26, Peter was not to be associated with the gentiles. Also, Lev 11:2–47 details the clean diet of the Israelite nation. Polhill elaborates on the connection between Leviticus and the Jew and gentile food restrictions:

> Yet the cleansing of food is not wholly parabolic: there is a connection between the abrogation of the levitical food restrictions and the removal of the barrier between believing Jews and Gentiles, for it was in large measure the Gentiles' eating of food which was "unclean" (not *kosher*) by Jewish law that made association with them a source of "defilement" for Jews (cf. v. 28).[47]

Peter's acknowledging of and abiding by both Scriptures were objectives of the heavenly voice. His rejection only confirmed Peter's dedication to his upbringing. Three times he needed reassurance that

---

45. Polhill, *Acts* (NAC), 108.
46. Polhill, *Acts* (HCBC), 503.
47. Bruce, *Book of the Acts*, 206.

God made the food clean despite his objections. Polhill summarizes Peter's objections:

> A voice from heaven commanded Peter to rise, kill from among the animals, and satisfy his hunger. Peter was perplexed by the vision and protested vigorously. What the voice requested was strictly against the law. Never had he eaten anything defiled and unclean. The voice ignored his protest, reissuing the command and adding, "Do not call anything impure that God has made clean." The command came three times; each time Peter objected and fell into further confusion.[48]

Despite his confusion, Peter submitted to the voice of the Lord. His submission to the values of God helped merge the division among the Jew and gentile. Peter's transition in leadership was necessity for unity of the church of Jew and gentile and for outreach to the gentile nations. Although it may seem simple, according to Polhill, the removal of food laws created genuine opportunity for Jew and gentile fellowship:

> The Jewish food laws presented a real problem for Jewish Christians in the outreach to the Gentiles. One simply could not dine in a Gentile's home without inevitably transgressing those laws either by the consumption of unclean flesh or of flesh that had not been prepared in a kosher, i.e., ritually proper, fashion (cf. Acts 15:20).[49]

Peter's vision and compliance opened the door for unification of Jew and gentile. God entrusted Peter with the vision due to the call on Peter to lead the church. Peter followed the direction and purpose of the Lord and soon after the vision the gentiles received the gospel message (Acts 10:45). Similar to Peter's change of eating and social interaction with gentiles, another hurdle to the unification of Jew and gentile was present. Shortly after the gentiles received the gospel and the Holy Spirit, the circumcised confronted Peter about his interaction with the gentiles (Acts 11:1–4).

Peter reported all that happened from the vision with the gentiles receiving salvation, and the crowd quieted and praised God for what he had done. Peter's leadership shift in values transformed the Jews' views of gentile repentance and acceptance of the gospel. But Bruce highlights monumental hurdles that still required Peter's leadership:

---

48. Polhill, *Acts* (NAC), 255.
49. Polhill, *Acts* (NAC), 255.

> The rapid progress of Gentile evangelization in Antioch and farther afield presented the more conservative Jewish believers with a serious problem. The apostles had acquiesced in Peter's action in the house of Cornelius because it was attended by such evident marks of divine approval; but now a new situation confronted them.[50]

After evangelical success in the church of Antioch, many Hellenistic Jews demanded male circumcision. Acts 15 highlights the continual divide between Jew and gentile concerning the gentiles' observance of the Mosaic law. Again, Bruce pinpoints the division that existed:

> The vast majority, including such a Hellenized Jew as Philo of Alexandria, insisted on circumcision as indispensable for all males in the commonwealth of Israel, whether they entered it by birth or by proselytization. This was probably the attitude of the rank and file in the Jerusalem church—"zealots for the law," as they are called on a later occasion (21:20).[51]

Although a minority of Jews understood the spiritual significance of the gentiles' inward spiritual change, Jewish leadership and zealots of the law viewed the church as an extension of Judaism. However, Peter stood up again among the elders and apostles at the Council of Jerusalem to address concerns from the Pharisees, zealots, and Hellenized Jews. "Peter, as leader of the apostles, spoke out unambiguously in the interests of gospel liberty. He had maintained these interests with purpose of heart ever since his visit to Cornelius in Caesarea."[52] Although Peter's experience with Cornelius was years previous, it dramatically changed his defense of God's witness to the gentiles.[53]

Peter's calling to the gentiles exposed him to God's acceptance of the gentiles through the cleansing of the heart without physical changes. Peter's willingness to reevaluate his wants and needs came as he experienced God's calling to the gentiles. Peter's leadership in the book of Acts changed his custom wants and needs on social interaction, food, and circumcision. His leadership adjustments helped lead to the unification of the church between the Jew and gentile. His willingness to stand

---

50. Bruce, *Book of the Acts*, 286.
51. Bruce, *Book of the Acts*, 286–87.
52. Bruce, *Book of the Acts*, 290.
53. Polhill, *Acts* (NAC), 326.

among his peers and pronounce God's message and value changed the landscape of the church.

Peter's origins revealed his deep conviction to Jewish upbringing and customs. His wants and needs became evident in his discipleship with Jesus Christ. After Jesus's death and resurrection, however, Peter's wants transitioned to the values necessary for him to fulfill his calling as the leader of the church.

Peter's Purpose

Peter's values revealed his explicit purpose. As noted, "values indicate desirable or preferred end-states or collective goals or explicit purposes, and values are standards in terms of which specific criteria may be established and choices made among alternatives."[54] However, Jesus designated Peter's purpose by transforming his values. As Peter's teacher, Jesus shaped and declared Peter's future end goals. Burns states that a teacher through "formal preachings and moralizings—helped to draw students up through the levels of moral development."[55] Jesus's direct moralizing and preaching to Peter shaped his values and therefore shaped his moral obligations.

With Burns's terminology in view, we see that the biblical viewpoint needs to redefine the terms of values. Burns's viewpoint of values shifting one's morality and purpose in biblical theology includes calling or election.[56] *Calling* or *election* is "a term designating God's summons to a specific task or role and his special relationship to his people."[57] In slight contrast to Burns, scripturally, God designates a person's purpose and not just preaching or moralizing. I. Howard Marshall explains calling as "God also chose their leaders, such as Saul and David (1 Sam 10:24; 2 Sam 6:21), apart from any popular vote by the people. The Word thus indicates God's prerogative in deciding what shall happen, independently of human choice."[58]

Unacknowledged by Burns, God is solely responsible for the summoning of specific individuals for their designated purpose. Another

---

54. Burns, *Leadership*, 74.
55. Burns, *Leadership*, 78.
56. Mathew, "Apostle Peter's Cross-Cultural Leadership," 107.
57. Myers, *EBD* 183.
58. I. Howard Marshall, "Elect, Election," *BEB* 1:682.

contrast is God's foresight and predetermined plan for the individuals called to certain tasks (Jer 1:1–10). Elwell continues in defining calling:

> God's choices not only arise from within his own eternal being and are consistent with what he is, but they are also based on his own divinely chosen plan. This renders them purposeful rather than arbitrary. They are not a randomly chosen collection of acts or decisions that have no inner coherence. Rather, according to an eternal plan, based on God's goodness, grace, and love, He weaves his will into the fabric of fallen human history and there He triumphs (Eph 1:9–12).[59]

Jesus was more than Peter's teacher; he was God on earth, delivering his purpose as divine and predetermined with futuristic ramifications. Jesus selected Peter as one of his disciples purposefully and with foreknowledge.

Nolland explains that calling is not independent of the empowerment of Jesus: "Jesus calls the fishermen in 4:18–22 to fish for people, but though they leave everything to follow Jesus they seem to do nothing that could be called fishing for people until Jesus empowers them and gives them specific mission instructions in chap. 10."[60] Each disciple was elected to fulfill his role while Jesus was on earth and upon his departure. Elwell and Comfort conclude that calling is not limited to the disciples:

> "Election" can also be used of God's choice of people to serve him. Jesus chose the 12 disciples out of the larger company of those who followed him (Lk 6:13; Acts 1:2). The same thought reappears in John's Gospel; Jesus commented that although he chose the Twelve, one of them turned out to be a devil (Jn 6:70; 13:18). When a replacement was needed for Judas, the church prayed to Jesus and asked him to show them which of the two available candidates he would choose to fill the gap in the Twelve (Acts 1:24). Peter attributes his evangelism among the Gentiles to God's election of him for that purpose (15:7). Similarly, Paul was an elected instrument for God's mission to the Gentiles (9:15). The initiative in Christian mission rests with God, who elects people to serve him in particular ways.[61]

While on earth, Jesus communicated to Peter his future role in the church and reinforced it following Peter's denial (Matt 26:69–75). On

---

59. Walter A. Elwell, "Elect, Election," *BEB* 1:200.
60. Nolland, *Gospel of Matthew*, 670.
61. Elwell and Comfort, *Tyndale Bible Dictionary*, 418.

two separate occasions, Jesus spoke directly to Peter calling Peter to his elect purpose.[62]

Jesus's first direct call to Peter came when he designated Peter's future designation as the "rock of the church" (Matt 16:18–19). Jesus's mention of the church is only the second reference to the coming age of the church.[63] This deserves attention, especially in his designation of leadership. After his admission of Jesus Christ as the Messiah, the church elected Peter to be its leader. Balz and Schneider discuss Jesus's decision to call Peter the stone of the church:

> Jesus refers to Peter as the stone foundation of the edifice of the eschatological people of salvation (composed of Jews and Gentiles), as the decisive mediator of the revelation tradition. This pronouncement from the Easter epiphany tradition in Jesus' words of promise concerning the construction of his Church "on this *rock*" (= the noble rock "Peter") has been set by Matthew into the portrayal of Peter's messianic confession.[64]

Before Jesus proclaimed Peter as the rock of the church, Peter professed Jesus as "the Christ, the Son of the living God" (Matt 16:16). Upon his confession, Jesus details Peter's future role in the church even to minute details of Peter's name.[65]

Jesus's use of Peter is purposeful and intentional, according to God's predetermined role for Peter. Nolland addresses the purposefulness of Jesus's naming of Peter:

> "Peter" to Simon not as an affectionate nickname nor even in the first instance as an alternative name, but rather as a means of marking destiny in some manner. "Peter" is not used to address Simon during Jesus' ministry, but it becomes the name by which he is called when this destiny is being worked out in the early life of the church. Mt. 16:18 gives concrete expression to the form of destiny to which Jesus has appointed Simon Peter; it interprets the impulse that lay behind the giving of the name "Peter."[66]

---

62. Mathew, "Apostle Peter's Cross-Cultural Leadership," 107.
63. Davies and Allison, *Matthew 8–18*, 623–41.
64. "πέτρα," *EDNT* 3:81; emphasis original.
65. Hagner, *Matthew 14–28*, 469–74.
66. Nolland, *Gospel of Matthew*, 668.

Peter's name was an indication of his God-elected destiny. The name, meaning "rock," symbolized Jesus's choice to elect him to lead in the build of the early church.

Peter's name is directly correlated to Peter's future functionality and responsibility. Jesus's election was not limited to his name but to his service to the church and reconciliation of Jew and gentile. Hagner confirms that Peter's name is not only his role but his authority to function within his call with the other apostles:

> At the same time, the thrust of the present passage (like that of 18:18) has more to do with the establishment of the authority of Peter (the apostles and the church) in his mission to the world. The judgment of Peter, and by implication that of the church, reflects what is in accord with what is settled in heaven as the fully determined will of God.[67]

Peter's role not only was fundamental but also authoritative in the foundation of the church. However, Jesus had to elect Peter for him to have the authority with the apostles and in the early church. Jesus declared, "I will give you the keys of the kingdom of heaven and whatever you bind on earth shall have been bound in heaven, and whatever you loose on earth shall have been loosed in heaven" (Matt 18:18).

Jesus alone had the authority to give Peter the keys and ability to loosen and bind. The keys symbolize the power given to Peter to exercise as a leader of the early church and among his apostles. Hagner addresses the authority of Peter by stating,

> Peter, as the leader of the twelve, is the "rock" upon which the new community will be built. With this commissioning of Peter comes the authority symbolized by his possession of τὰς κλεῖδας τῆς βασιλείας τῶν οὐρανῶν, "the keys of the kingdom of heaven." Peter, as the leader of the twelve, is the "rock" upon which the new community will be built. With this commissioning of Peter comes the authority symbolized by his possession of τὰς κλεῖδας τῆς βασιλείας τῶν οὐρανῶν, "the keys of the kingdom of heaven." For "kingdom of heaven," see Comment on 3:2. "Keys" are above all a symbol of authority and, hence, a symbol of power over something.[68]

---

67. Hagner, *Matthew 14–28*, 474.
68. Hagner, *Matthew 14–28*, 472.

Under Peter's possession of the keys, God gave him the ability to bind and loose permanently under the kingdom of heaven. Although each apostle holds distinct leadership in the church, Peter played an integral role in the early church as he helped lead the unity of Jew and gentile into the gospel of Jesus Christ.

As evidenced in the book of Acts, Peter had the authority to interpret the Torah and judge conduct in relation to God. Hagner clarifies and defines Peter's authority:

> In its primary meaning, the phrase "binding and loosing" refers to the allowing and disallowing of certain conduct, based on an interpretation of the commandments of the Torah, and thus it concerns the issue of whether or not one is in proper relationship to the will of God (contrast the reference to the Pharisees' misuse of their authority [note implied keys!] in 23:13). In Matthew, Jesus is the true interpreter of Torah. His disciples will pass on that interpretation and extend it. Thus, Matthew may have in mind the teaching office of Peter and the apostles (for whom the power of binding and loosing is also assumed in the plural verbs of 18:18 in the discourse on "church discipline").[69]

The book of Acts reveals Peter's fulfillment of Jesus's predestined elected plan. Peter's leadership contrasted the Pharisees who incorrectly judged people, according to their interpretation of the Torah.[70] Peter displayed the God-given purpose during the upper room, at Pentecost, with Ananias and Sapphira, at the house of Cornelius, and with the Council of Jerusalem. Notably, however, his leadership was not exclusive of the other apostles, as evidenced in involvement and agreement in the Council of Jerusalem.

The eternal election of Peter's purpose was undeterred, despite Peter's denial before Jesus's crucifixion. After the resurrection, Jesus approached Peter after breakfast and John recorded this interaction:

> "Simon, *son* of John, do you love Me more than these?" He said to Him, "Yes, Lord; You know that I love You." He said to him, "Tend My lambs." He said to him again a second time, "Simon, *son* of John, do you love Me?" He said to Him, "Yes, Lord; You know that I love You." He said to him, "Shepherd My sheep." He said to him the third time, "Simon, *son* of John, do you love Me?" Peter was grieved because He said to him the third time,

---

69. Hagner, *Matthew 14–28*, 473.
70. W. Allen, *Gospel According to St. Matthew*, 176–80.

"Do you love Me?" And he said to Him, "Lord, You know all things; You know that I love You." Jesus said to him, "Tend My sheep." (John 21:15–17)

Peter's response to Jesus's questioning is unique, beginning with a threefold response to Peter's denials. Jesus was intentional with his repetition, and each part of the interaction deserves attention. Blum confirms Jesus's intentionality: "Jesus' threefold question and threefold commission of apostolic mission contrast directly with Peter's three denials."[71] He does not seek comparison with other disciples but only Jesus's knowledge of his love for him.[72]

Peter knew that Jesus's knowledge of his love was all that mattered. Despite Peter's denial of Jesus, Jesus did not remove his elect purpose but reaffirmed it after questioning Peter's love. Three times Jesus addressed Peter's love and then directed him to his eternal purpose. For each of Peter's denials, Jesus affirmed his election of his pastoral care of the early church.[73] Borchert explains Jesus's reaffirmation of Peter:

> It was Peter who needed to be sifted by the penetrating questioning of Jesus in order to do the work of the risen Lord and be reinstated after his devastating fall. God/Jesus does not bless human beings primarily to provide them with status but to carry out the divine purposes in the world. Thus, mission is inseparably linked to the calling and blessing of God.[74]

Jesus resolidified Peter's mission to pastoral care of the early church. Despite his failure, Jesus charged Peter with tending and shepherding his sheep. However, this verse is not aligned explicitly with Matt 16:18–19. Jesus is not asserting Peter's authority above the apostles but rather realigning him to his role after his failure.[75]

Only Jesus could validate Peter's role and commission him for his role in the church after he denied Jesus. However, tending and shepherding are not authoritative terms placing Peter over the other apostles as the only shepherd.[76] This statement requires emphasis and clarification: despite Peter's role in the early church, he did not assume supremacy to

---

71. Edwin Blum, "John," 345.
72. Carson, *Gospel According to John*, 675–79.
73. Carson, *Gospel According to John*, 675–79.
74. Borchert, *John 12–21*, 337.
75. Carson, *Gospel According to John*, 675–79.
76. Bernard, *Gospel According to St. John*, 701–8.

the other disciples. Beasley-Murray clarifies Peter's authority by defining Peter's role of tending the flock:

> A similar charge by Paul to the elders of Ephesus is recorded in Acts 20:28: "Keep watch over yourselves and over all the flock (ποίμνιον) of which the Holy Spirit has made you guardians (ἐπισκόπους) to shepherd the Church of the Lord" (ποιμαίνειν τὴν ἐκκλησίαν τοῦ κυρίου). Both passages speak in the same manner as the risen Lord spoke to Peter on restoring him to fellowship and to the service of pastor. The verbs are the same, ποιμαίνω or variants of it; the scope of the ministry is the same—"my lambs, my sheep . . . the flock of God, the Church of the Lord." There is no formal difference of meaning in the language by which the risen Lord confirmed Peter in his calling to be a shepherd of his sheep from that by which Peter and Paul exhorted the pastor-elders to fulfill their calling as shepherds of the flock of God in 1 Pet 5:1–3 and Acts 20:28. This applies also to the representative nature of the shepherd's office and the authority which it carries.[77]

Peter's commission was not an addition to his authority but a shift from his original calling to be a fisher of men.

Despite assertions of Peter's primacy of leadership, limited evidence exists to support additional authority in the Scripture in this passage. According to Bernard, Peter was progressing from being a fisher of men to a shepherd, who tended to God's sheep: "Henceforth the ministry consists not only of 'catching' men, but of guiding and guarding them in their new spiritual environment. And so the image now used at Peter's second 'call' is not that of the *fisher*, but of the *shepherd*."[78]

Peter needed affirmation that his future role was to nurture the sheep of God along with the disciples. The shepherding role is a call designated by Jesus for Peter to fulfill upon Jesus's ascension. Jesus as the teacher transformed Peter's values and end states through his teachings, moralizing, and preaching. Jesus was specific each time he called Peter to a designated task. He shifted Peter from being a fisher of men to a shepherd and gave him his role as the rock of the church. Jesus designated Peter's purpose, which shifted Peter's end state and values.

---

77. Beasley-Murray, *John*, 406–7.
78. Bernard, *Gospel According to St. John*, 705; emphasis original.

Peter's Evidence of Transformational Leadership throughout Acts

Although it seems clear that Peter shifted his values and end state from his origins, continual proof exists of his transformational leadership throughout the book of Acts. The book of Acts reveals that Peter's transformation leadership dramatically changed the trajectory of the spread of the Christian faith. However, influence of Peter's leadership is inadequate without the stimulation and conversion of followers to the same goals. Burns states, "I define leadership as leaders inducing followers to act for certain goals that represent the values and the motivations—the wants and needs, the aspirations and expectations—of both leaders and followers."[79] The exploration of Peter's transformational leadership will reveal his abilities to satisfy wants, motives, and needs, and engage the full person as a follower for real change. To evaluate the real change of goals and values of the followers to determine the effectiveness of Peter's transformational leadership is critical.

Mobilization

At a basic level, Burns states that "in no society are there leaders without followers or followers without leaders."[80] The relationship between a leader and follower will determine the success of the goals, values, and end states. Transformational leadership is noted as the ability to raise the level of morality and motivation. "Transforming values lies at the heart of transforming leadership, determining whether leadership indeed can be transforming."[81] A follower's real change is determined by his/her active participation in shared goals, values, and motives with the leader. Burns states, "The result of transforming leadership is a relationship of mutual stimulation and elevation that converts followers into leaders and may convert leaders into moral agents."[82] Therefore, a leader's role is to activate and mobilize followers to a higher end state, morality, and goals. Burns again confirms, "Leaders have a special role as activators, initiators, mobilizers."[83]

79. Burns, *Leadership*, 19.
80. Burns, *Leadership*, 134.
81. Burns, *Transforming Leadership*, 30.
82. Burns, *Transforming Leadership*, 4.
83. Burns, *Transforming Leadership*, 134.

A transformational leader awakens followers to be active participants in pursuit of shared morality, goals, values, and real change. A leader's effectiveness is determined by one's ability to move followers from their original states to a shared working experience to achieve stated goals. Burns defines mobilization:

> Leaders take the initiative in mobilizing people for participation in the processes of change, encouraging a sense of collective identity and collective efficacy, which in turn brings stronger feelings of self-worth and self-efficacy, described by Bernard Bass as an enhanced "sense of 'meaningfulness' in their work and lives." By pursuing transformational change, people can transform themselves.[84]

He again expands the idea of mobilization by explaining that "exceptional leadership may also make a difference in transforming dormant into active followers."[85] An evaluation of Peter's ability to awaken Jew and gentile to a shared faith and goal to spread the gospel will determine his effectiveness as a transformational leader. The mobilization of the Christian faith is determined by followers being active in their pursuit of real change and shared morality, goals, and values.

A review of Peter's leadership indicates a substantial transformation within the early church. Peter's leadership in the book of Acts indicates transformational leadership that dramatically affected real change and significant mobilization. The first evidence of mobilization occurs at Pentecost when three thousand people were saved after Peter stood and preached the gospel (Acts 2:41). Thousands of people transformed their beliefs, converting their faith to Jesus Christ as their Messiah. This conversion of their faith is the beginning of the transformation of the followers. Peter first had critically to defend Jesus Christ as the Messiah, utilizing prophecy and history to persuade the diverse listeners.

The first step to transformational leadership is the adoption of a new vision or ideology. "Of all the stages in a transforming revolution, the birth of the idea or vision that impels the revolution and its adoption by a decisive number of persons are probably the most crucial steps toward transformation."[86] During Pentecost, a decisive number of people adopted a new belief that dramatically changed the spread of

---

84. Burns, *Transforming Leadership*, 25–26.
85. Burns, *Transforming Leadership*, 137.
86. Burns, *Leadership*, 202.

Christianity. However, the initial adoption of the faith is not the totality of transformation but the beginning of the mobilization of the followers. Total transformation requires the full participation of the adoption of the new belief. Peter's next challenge would be reshaping former ideologies, beliefs, and traditions that hindered the growth of new faith.

Within the same chapter after the conversion, new believers began to gather and form a community (Acts 2:37–47). At the end of ch. 2, directly following Pentecost, Luke gives a glimpse of new converts incorporated into a believing community.[87] Within the community, new believers were praying, sharing resources, creating genuine relationships, and reading teachings. This gathering evidenced the beginning of the formulation of similar ideologies and vision. Burns states that "leaders and followers are engaged in a common enterprise; they are dependent on each other, their fortunes rise and fall together, they share the results of planned change together."[88]

This first gathering of believers represented a group of people dependent on each other, that were willing to sacrifice for their common interests. Luke's description of the first gathering included terminology that capitulates unity, dependency, and togetherness. His use of "everything in common" in v. 44 "seems to depict the gathered community, with a strong emphasis on their unity. This unity is further expressed by their holding 'everything in common' (which is described in verse 45 as selling their goods for the benefit of others whenever a need arose)."[89] Additionally, in the phrase "with one mind or accord" in v. 46, "the word translated 'with one accord' (*homothymadon*) is commonly used in Acts to express unity of purpose and particularly applies to the 'one heart and mind' (4:32) of Christian fellowship (cf. 1:14; 2:1; 4:24; 5:12; 15:25)."[90]

Another applied connotation of "one mind" is that the gathering of believers had one impulse.[91] They were directed and attracted to the same beliefs and ideologies. The first gathering in Acts 2 reflected new converts' common enterprise that created dependence and unity for their rise and fall. The group continued to grow in number as people were getting saved

---

87. Polhill, *Acts* (NAC), 118–22.
88. Burns, *Leadership*, 426.
89. Polhill, *Acts* (NAC), 120.
90. Polhill, *Acts* (NAC), 121.
91. "ὁμοθυμαδόν," BDAG 4.

(Acts 2:47). The mobilization continued as more people were being saved and transforming their ideologies and vision.[92]

Conflict

After the initial gathering, however, conflict often presents opportunities for the testing of shared values, vision, and goals. According to Burns, conflict is a natural part of human relations that causes growth and health, as well as destruction: "The potential for conflict permeates the relations of humankind and that potential is a force for health and growth as well as for destruction and barbarism. No group can be wholly harmonious."[93] Burn elaborates:

> The word for this process is empowerment. Instead of exercising power over people, transforming leaders champion and inspire followers. Tension can develop in this process. As leaders encourage followers to rise above narrow interests and work together for transcending goals, leaders can come into conflict with followers' rising sense of efficacy and purpose.[94]

Leader and follower can encounter conflict as they attempt to raise their sense of purpose and goals. Conflict is necessary to identify shared values as followers become active in common goals and vision.

While seeking common values and goals, it is pertinent to conclude that varying backgrounds and cultures will be susceptible to conflict. However, conflict can lead to growth if leadership engages followers to a higher shared goal. The leader's motivation is for followers to have shared values or goals that lead them to conflict with a higher value against other institutions or ideologies. Burns states that conflict is a part of leadership as followers seek to be engaged, satisfied, and aroused toward the shared values and goals. He states, "Leadership over human beings is exercised when persons with certain motives and purposes mobilize in competition or conflict with others, institutional, political, psychological, and other resources so as to arouse, engage, and satisfy the motives of followers."[95] Conflict is inevitable as humans transform and as institutions are challenged to meet the needs or motives of the followers.

92. Burns, *Leadership*, 202.
93. Burns, *Leadership*, 37.
94. Burns, *Leadership*, 26.
95. Burns, *Leadership*, 18.

Conflict is necessary if directed at growth between leaders and followers to a higher call. The new shared value motivates them to mobilize in conflict with other institutional, political, and psychological values for a larger transformation. Peter's leadership in the book of Acts was full of conflict. The unification of Jew and gentile was not without conflict, as both parties had to find a shared goal of the gospel message. Mathew addresses the persistent threat dominant cultures will present due to their power and influence:

> Dominant cultures pose a threat, intimidation, and challenge to other cultures because of their power and influence. The dominant culture rhetoric includes a conscious or subconscious superior attitude (e.g., opinions and analysis from a Western framework are the only ones considered), which may not always be obvious to those who are part of the dominant culture but clearly recognizable by those outside of the dominant culture.[96]

The Jews continually present conflict as Jew and gentile are being unified in the church. As noted previously, within Peter's individual conflict and transformation, people from the Jewish community engaged in the same conflict.

Jews struggled with the gentiles' dietary and circumcision practices. Jews' initial acceptance of the gentiles was contingent upon their assimilation to Jewish practices and traditions. In Acts 11, Jews who took issue with Peter's association with the gentiles confronted him. They questioned Peter's decision to eat with the gentiles at Cornelius's house.[97] Barrett summarizes the transition from conflict between Jew and gentile to a resolution of acceptance:

> The interplay of these questions, which it must often have been very difficult to keep separate from each other, complicates the story of the Gentile mission as this unfolded in Acts; the complication appears in the fact that at v. 18 the dispute, which began with the complaint that a Jew had had dealings with a Gentile, ends with the recognition that Gentiles are to be accepted as recipients of God's gift of life.[98]

The Jews were conflicted in their acceptance of gentile association, but they came to accept that God granted the gentiles' repentance. Despite

---

96. Mathew, "Apostle Peter's Cross-Cultural Leadership," 121.
97. Barrett, *Commentary on Acts*, 533.
98. Barrett, *Commentary on Acts*, 533.

their resolution, they persistently struggled with the gentile traditions and practices.

Bruce highlighted the correlation between the evangelization of the gentiles with increasing conflict:

> The rapid progress of Gentile evangelization in Antioch and farther afield presented the more conservative Jewish believers with a serious problem. The apostles had acquiesced in Peter's action in the house of Cornelius because it was attended by such evident marks of divine approval; but now a new situation confronted them.[99]

The integration of Jew and gentile was bound for continual conflict due to their opposing cultures and backgrounds. The integration of Jew and gentile desperately needed leadership to reconcile differences, especially surrounding the issue of circumcision. Another conflict occurred in Acts 15, when men from Judea were teaching that gentiles needed circumcision for conversion: "But those Gentiles should be admitted on terms similar to those required of proselytes to Judaism: they must be circumcised and assume the obligation to observe the Mosaic law."[100]

At the Council of Jerusalem, Peter declared that the gentiles received salvation through faith and were given the Holy Spirit. James also stated to the brethren not to trouble the gentiles turning to God (Acts 15:19). However, James, the apostles, and brethren agreed that the gentiles refrain from "things contaminated by idols and from fornication and from what is strangled and from blood" (Acts 15:20). In agreement with Peter, James played an integral role in leading the conversation with elders and apostles in the dealings with the gentiles. Although Peter stood among the apostles, the agreement, leadership, and involvement of the other apostles confirms that the decisions were not exclusively Peter's to make.

This standard was accepted and written so that gentiles would understand the standard for their conversion. The conflict that persisted between Jew and gentile is evidence of Burns's assertion:

> Conflict is evidence for reformed leadership as two parties from previous predispositions find commonality for continual growth and shared goals. How to mobilize persons of reform instincts but of diverse and volatile predispositions behind a

---

99. Bruce, *Book of the Acts*, 286.
100. Bruce, *Book of the Acts*, 286.

considered reform effort; how to connect one reform cause with related but seemingly separate ones.[101]

The diverse disposition as the gospel spread created an inevitable conflict that would result in reformation. Peter's mobilization of Jew and gentile connects them through their new cause of the gospel and the spread to gentile nations.

Leader Transformation

As followers increase, the probability for conflict is concurrent with the increased followership. The evidence of a transformational leader is the ability to mobilize followers to the point of them leading in the proposed value, moral, and principle. Burns classifies this as transcending leadership: "Transcending leadership is dynamic leadership in the sense that the leaders throw themselves into a relationship with followers who will feel 'elevated' by it and often become more active themselves, thereby creating new cadres of leaders."[102]

An element of an effecter leader is one's ability to transform one's followers into increased activity and the opportunity for new leadership mobilization. Burns adds, "Followers might outstrip leaders. They might become leaders themselves. That is what makes transforming leadership participatory and democratic."[103] Peter's ability to mobilize leaders is indicative of his own transformation. Acts 6 highlights the need to select more leaders. As followership increased, conflict increased as well in the church of Jerusalem. The disciple wisely concluded that there should be a selection and approval of seven new disciples. The Jerusalem Christian community had witnessed considerable growth; and as is often the case with rapid increase, administrative problems developed.[104]

The problem included the distribution of charity left in the hands of the apostles. The growth of the church coincided with needs of serving the community, especially the widows of the Hellenistic Jews. Following the recognition of the expansion, the Jews selected disciples under certain criteria to help further growth of the church and community.[105]

---

101. Burns, *Leadership*, 190.
102. Burns, *Leadership*, 20.
103. Burns, *Transforming Leadership*, 26.
104. Polhill, *Acts* (NAC), 178.
105. Burns, *Leadership*, 181.

The apostles, including Peter, exemplified transcending leadership that elevated other leaders to meet the needs of the growing community. Due to the growing community and arising conflict, followers recognized the need for growth of leadership.

Peter's Evidence of Reformed Leadership

Within transformational leadership, Burns defines four diverse types of leadership. Each leadership style has its own definition and qualities that help categorize transformational leadership. Peter displayed reformed and revolutionary leadership. Burns defines reformed leadership: "Reform leadership by definition usually implies moral leadership, and this imposes a special burden. It means that reformers must not follow improper means in trying to achieve moral ends, on the grounds that the means can taint and pervert the ends."[106] Reformed leadership comprises moral and ethical burdens that require the leader to maintain proper means to attain their end goals. The leader must be willing to modify current goals and morals while maintaining harmony and ethics. Burns adds, "The reformer seeks modifications harmonious with existing trends and consistent with prevailing principles and movements."[107]

Amidst seeking prevailing principles and movements with harmony, the leader can fall victim to compromise. According to Burns, compromise can inhibit significant change and fall into transactional patterns:

> The other tendency is the failure of reform leadership to achieve the actual (real) social change proportionate to the transformations that the leader promised, and in the name of which reform was promised. Reform leaders may act on the benevolent notion that true politics is simply morals applied to public affairs, but they find in the heat of battle that true politics is the everyday scuffling and swapping in governmental and political marketplaces. Because reform leaders typically accept the political and social structures within which they act, their reform efforts are inevitably compromised and usually inhibited by the tenacious inertia of existing institutions. Far-reaching change in the end is carried through less by reform leaders, vital though their role is, than by politicians who see their political ambitions entangled in the reform effort. Reform is ever poised between the

---

106. Burns, *Leadership*, 170.
107. Burns, *Leadership*, 170.

transforming and the transactional—transforming in spirit and posture, transactional in process and results.[108]

A reformed leader often adds morals to current affairs, which can lead to the possibility of transactions to produce the end goals. A reformed leader has the potential to accept social structures as long as they achieve the ethical and moral goals.

Peter's leadership is critical in transforming the morality and ethics of the early church. Throughout the book of Acts, Peter often had to lead the Jews into the new morality. Peter led the reformation of morality issues of dietary restrictions in Acts 11 and circumcision in Acts 15. In both instances, he was in the heat of battle with social structures that were staunch preexisting institutions. Each battle was handled within the religious structure speaking with other apostles, brethren, and council. Acts 15 provides the formality of the Council of Jerusalem. Cousar provides background, stating, "This conference (also called 'the Apostolic Council') designates the meeting at Jerusalem of leaders of the early Church to discuss the implications of preaching a gospel of grace among the gentiles."[109] Peter's formality and use of social structure for the achievement of moral goals aligns with Burns's reformed leadership.

Within Peter's moral pursuit, Gal 2:11 revealed a lack of tenacity in the heat of battle between Jew and gentile. He conformed to religious pressures and compromised his own convictions at the helm of existing Jewish traditions. Scholars believe Gal 2:11–21 to be Paul's parallel and account for the events before the Acts 15 Council of Jerusalem.[110] The book of Galatians adds details to the conflict within leadership over circumcision of the gentiles and their salvation (Gal 2).

Paul details the account of his confrontation with Peter and his rebuke of Peter's behavior at Antioch. Paul opposed Peter physically and directly, emphasized by the wording of "opposed him to his face." Longenecker says that "the idiom 'κατὰ πρόσωπον (to the face)' does not of itself necessarily imply hostility, but only direct encounter."[111] Paul did address Peter from afar but expressed his opposition directly to Peter. Paul's strong language in v. 11 pointed to the adverse reaction to Peter. Paul's use of the words "stood condemned" highlights Paul's opposition

---

108. Burns, *Leadership*, 199–200.
109. Charles B. Cousar, "Jerusalem, Council of," *ABD* 766.
110. Allen C. Myers, "Apostolic Council," *EBD* 68.
111. Longenecker, *Galatians*, 71; see also Barrett, *Commentary on Acts*, 697.

to Peter. Longenecker provides more detail to the confrontation, saying, "Paul's judgment on Cephas's conduct is exceedingly severe: 'he stood condemned.'"[112] Paul's opposition was warranted as he reviewed the outside influences that directly manipulated the pure fellowship of Peter and the converted gentiles.

Peter's swift shift in fellowship with the gentiles directly connects to the arrival of "certain men" and the "party of the circumcision." The "certain men" were a Jewish delegation or messengers from James that were possibly carrying the message of disdain for Peter's continual dining with gentiles.[113] According to the evidence, Longenecker concludes:

> All that the evidence warrants is that a delegation from the Jerusalem church arrived at Antioch, probably sent by James to express certain practical concerns of Jerusalem believers regarding the expression of the Christian faith at Antioch, and that the arrival of these men and their statement of the Jerusalem church's concerns served to trigger Peter's withdrawal from table fellowship with Gentile believers at Antioch.[114]

Paul's terminology for the "party of the circumcision" further clarifies the delegation that had arrived (Gal 2:12). The "party of the circumcision" were Jews more concerned with nationalism and anyone who sympathized with gentiles.[115]

The party invaded the church of Galatia and forced the practical nature of circumcision to the theological forefront, in turn, forcing the Council of Jerusalem.[116] Paul was appalled that Peter would allow the influence of the party to force his withdrawal. The pressures from a Jewish delegation and their disapproval of Peter's fellowship directly correlated to Peter's following actions. Ernest De Witt Burton states, "Under their domination illustrates both his own instability and the extent to which the legalistic party had developed and acquired influence in the Jerusalem church and Jewish Christianity generally."[117] The party's arrival revealed that the conviction Peter previously displayed was unstable and penetrable.

---

112. Longenecker, *Galatians*, 71.
113. Bruce, *Epistle to the Galatians*, 130.
114. Longenecker, *Galatians*, 73.
115. Longenecker, *Galatians*, 74.
116. Longenecker, *Galatians*.
117. Burton, *Epistle to the Galatians*, 107–8.

Peter feared the ridicule of his fellowship with uncircumcised gentile believers and the party of the circumcision so much that it changed the scope of ministry.[118] Paul's use of the word "feared" suggests that Peter was terribly frightened.[119] Robertson sets forth, "It was not that Peter had changed his views from the Jerusalem resolutions. It was pure fear of trouble to himself as in the denials at the trial of Christ" (Gal 2:12).[120]

Peter was not just apprehensive or passive, but he also allowed pressure and judgment to cripple his decision-making. Bruce describes in detail Peter's interaction with the gentiles:

> He was not confining himself to missionary work among the Jews of the city; he was enjoying table-fellowship with Gentiles—Gentile Christians, presumably. The Jerusalem agreement was flexible enough to accommodate such friendly fellowship as this. It was Cephas's *volte-face* that made Paul speak out so bluntly, "because he was in the wrong"—literally "condemned" (κατεγνωσμένος), not by any external authority but (as Paul saw it) by the inconsistency of his own conduct.[121]

Paul observed Peter's gradual change in behavior, progressively folding to the ideologies of delegation. Burton highlights the verb tense that pinpointed Peter's behavior: "The imperfect tense is very expressive, indicating that Peter took this step not at once, immediately on the arrival of the men from James, but gradually, under the pressure, as the next phrase implies, of their criticism."[122]

Peter did not disappear instantly but gradually removed himself from the place in which he continually fellowshipped as the pressure mounted.[123] Therefore, the tense of the verb indicates Peter habitually or repeatedly ate with the gentiles but removed himself despite his consistent practices.[124] Paul noticed his pretense or insincerity and called out his hypocrisy.[125]

---

118. Hansen, *Galatians*, Gal 2:12–14, paras. 4–6.
119. "φοβέω," BDAG 1060.
120. Robertson, *Word Pictures*, Gal 2:12.
121. Bruce, *Epistle to the Galatians*, 129.
122. Bruce, *Epistle to the Galatians*, 107.
123. George, *Galatians*, 173.
124. Longenecker, *Galatians*, 73.
125. George, *Galatians*, 177.

Hypocrisy generally means concealing one's feelings under a guise or even a mask, like an actor.[126] Longenecker clearly describes Peter's hypocrisy:

> Hypocrisy, consisting essentially in the concealment of one's real character, feelings, etc., under the guise of conduct implying something different (ὑποκρίνεσθαι is "to answer from under," i.e., from under a mask as the actor did, playing a part; cf. Lk. 20:20), usually takes the form of concealing wrong feelings, character, etc., under pretense of better ones. In the present case, however, the knowledge, judgment, and feelings which were concealed were worse only from the point of view of the Jews of whom Peter and those who joined with him were afraid. From Paul's point of view, it was their better knowledge which they cloaked under a mask of worse, the usual type of hypocrisy which proceeds from fear. By the characterization of this conduct as hypocrisy Paul implies that there had been no real change of conviction on the part of Peter and the rest, but only conduct which belied their real convictions.[127]

Under the premise of fear, Peter's behavior did not reflect his true convictions. Despite Peter's previous convictions occurring during his interactions with Cornelius, he still chose not to lead amid pressure. George agrees that "Peter had donned a mask of pretense; he was shamefully acting a part contrary to his own true convictions. What Paul rebuked was the inconsistency of his conduct."[128]

According to his internal convictions, Peter's lack of leadership was hypocritical and led others to commit the same mistake. Paul noted the influence of Peter's decision on the other Jews and even on Barnabas. The phrase "rest of the Jews" indicates Jews who were of the same belief as Peter in Antioch.[129] Longenecker provides details to the hypocritical encounter and the influence it had on the rest of the Jews:

> Furthermore, as Jewish believers in Jesus, their practice, like that of Cephas, had been to fellowship with Gentile believers on a nonrestrictive basis. Now, however, with Cephas responding to the issues raised by the Jerusalem delegation as he did, they followed suit. They seem, like him, to have held proper

---

126. Longenecker, *Galatians*, 76.
127. Burton, *Epistle to the Galatians*, 108–9.
128. George, *Galatians*, 177.
129. Longenecker, *Galatians*, 75.

convictions, but without having thought them out to any great extent, and so to have been confused with respect to the matters raised by the delegation from James. Thus, they conformed to Cephas's course of action and "joined him in playing the hypocrite."[130]

Other Jews were joining in fellowship and creating the unity of Jew and gentile that were continually withdrawing. Hypocrisy created a divide between Jew and gentile in Antioch that had once been healed. However, Paul was even more disheartened that the withdrawal was not just by Peter and the Jews but also by Barnabas.

Paul called out Barnabas's hypocritical behavior. Burton pinpoints Barnabas's behavior in his statement: "That even Barnabas, who shared with Paul the apostleship to the Gentiles, yielded to the pressure exerted by the brethren from Jerusalem shows again how strong was the influence exerted by the latter."[131] Paul included Barnabas in addressing the influence Peter's decision had—not only on the Jews but also on a fellow leader. Longenecker agrees in his summarization of Paul's inclusion of Barnabas:

> The conjunction ὥστε ("so that") introduces a result of what went on at Antioch that was particularly painful to Paul personally: "even Barnabas" became confused and took the same course of action. The pathos that reverberates in the expression καὶ Βαρναβᾶς ("even Barnabas") is gripping, for Barnabas had been Paul's advocate at Jerusalem (cf. Acts 9:26–28), mentor at Antioch (cf. Acts 11:25–30), and esteemed colleague in the evangelization of Cyprus and southern Galatia (cf. Acts 13:2–14:26). Barnabas, in fact, was the last person of whom such action would have been expected (on Barnabas, see Comment at 2:1; also 2:9). He certainly was in favor of the gospel going directly to Gentiles apart from any Jewish restrictions, as his past ministry clearly demonstrates. And on the basis of such a track record, who could doubt that he would stand with Paul on the matter raised at Syrian Antioch? Yet it seems somehow, he too became confused, being torn between what he knew to be right and his sympathies for the plight of the Jerusalem church under Jewish nationalistic pressures. Thus, Barnabas too capitulated, being "led astray by their hypocrisy."[132]

---

130. Longenecker, *Galatians*, 75–76.
131. Burton, *Epistle to the Galatians*, 109.
132. Longenecker, *Galatians*, 76.

The confusion of Barnabas reveals Peter's leadership influence.

Despite Barnabas's leadership among the gentiles and his active role in the mission, he still withdrew. Paul's verb tense illustrates his belief that Peter bore responsibility for Barnabas's decision. Longenecker used the verb tense to highlight Paul holding Peter responsible:

> The aorist passive συναπήχθη ("was led astray"), the instrumental dative τῇ ὑποκρίσει ("by hypocrisy"), and the possessive pronoun αὐτῶν ("their") all point to the fact that Paul credited Cephas and the other Jewish believers with being the agents of Barnabas' defection, and that he viewed Barnabas as only following along.[133]

Peter's lack of proper leadership was instrumental in the religious confusion at Antioch. His inability to stand against the pressure and his conformity to previous religious institutions harmed the relational progress between Jew and gentile.

Peter's leadership was fundamental in the change of morality of Jew and gentile. His leadership was reformational as he spread the gospel and changed religious structures relating to dietary and circumcision. Peter's willingness to challenge preexisting institutions in Acts 11 and Acts 15 is evidence of reformed leadership. He often had to stand in front of his fellow apostles, brethren, and council to cause change in morality. However, Peter's inability to withstand continual pressure momentarily diminished his influence. His failure clearly matches the definition of a reformed leader who is more vulnerable to compromising and accepting preexisting structures.[134]

Reformed leaders often fail by attempting to balance transactional and transformative leadership characteristics. Burns delineates reformed and revolutionary leadership, saying, "The reformer seeks modifications harmonious with existing trends and consistent with prevailing principles and movements. The revolutionist seeks redirections, arrest or reversal of movements, and mutation of principles."[135] Peter's reformed leadership was not permanent, and he displayed numerous characteristics of a revolutionary leadership.

---

133. Longenecker, *Galatians*, 76.
134. Burns, *Leadership*, 199–200.
135. Burns, *Leadership*, 170.

Peter's Revolutionary Leadership

Peter's temporary failure in leadership does not summarize the totality of his transformational leadership in the book of Acts. It was a momentary lapse as he attempted to modify rather than redirect and reverse principles. However, sufficient existent evidence supports Peter's revolutionary transformational leadership. Revolution "in its broadest meaning is a complete and pervasive transformation of an entire social system. It means the birth of a radical new ideology; the rise of a movement bent on transforming society on the basis of that ideology."[136]

The transformation of a society demands a revolutionary leader who is characteristically willing to be different. Burns highlights a successful revolutionary leader's dedication, ability to address needs, pursue conflict, and be missional:

> But we know some of the requirements for success. The leaders must be absolutely dedicated to the cause and able to demonstrate that commitment by giving time and effort to it, risking their lives, undergoing imprisonment, exile, persecution, and continual hardship. Thus, Castro and his small band experienced constant privation. This commitment, which may end in martyrdom, must survive all defeats and setbacks. Too, the revolution, like all genuine leadership, must address the wants and needs and aspirations of the populace—motives that may not be felt by followers at the time but can be mobilized through propaganda and political action. Further, a revolution requires conflict, as does all leadership. But revolutionary conflict is more extreme; it is dramatized in the characters of saints and devils, heroes, and villains. As the lines become more sharply drawn between the establishment or elite and the poor and the rebelling, doctrine and purpose are hardened in the crucible. Finally, there must be a powerful sense of mission, of end-values, of transcending purpose. These processes can be summarized in a phrase: the raising of social and political consciousness on the part of both leaders and followers.[137]

Although the characteristics are similar, revolutionary leaders are extreme, resolute in their purpose, undauntedly committed to the cause, and immovable in mobilization. It's important to survey Peter's leadership in the book of Acts and his tireless and sacrificial pursuit of mobilization

---

136. Burns, *Leadership*, 202.
137. Burns, *Leadership*, 202–3.

to the purpose of the gospel. Evidential support affirms that Peter was instrumental in the transformation of a society with his dedication to the cause, mobilization, conflict, and sense of mission.

Peter was influential in the rise of the early church movement that transformed the entirety of Christian society based on the gospel. Peter's leadership in Pentecost after Jesus's ascension was the communication of the new ideology. Burns agrees that a revolution is the birth of an idea or vision communicated to a number of people who decide to adopt the new ideology:

> Of all the stages in a transforming revolution, the birth of the idea or vision that impels the revolution and its adoption by a decisive number of persons are probably the most crucial steps toward transformation, save perhaps for the actual physical capture of state power. The source of that idea or that vision in a leader, or in a small group of leaders, may be as mysterious as the origin of the sparks of creativity in an artist or writer. The spread of the new gospel—like that by the small band of persecuted Christians is equally mysterious.[138]

Burns categorizes the spread of the "new gospel" as a mark of a revolution. Peter's leadership was a crucial part of the spread of the gospel. It began with Peter's sermon at Pentecost and continued as he was persecuted in the movement of Christianity. Peter's message communicated the ideology as Christ the Messiah and outpouring of the Holy Spirit.[139]

Achtemeier provides background on the fulfillment of the prophecy of Jesus: "Within the literary context of Acts, the events associated with Pentecost constitute the fulfillment not only of the prophecy of Joel but also of the promise of Jesus."[140] Quoting Joel 2:28–32, Peter confirmed the pouring of the Spirit was occurring right there at Pentecost. It was the fulfillment of the promise of the Holy Spirit empowering the apostles to accomplish the work of the gospel and the building of the church.

Elwell states that "Pentecost is first mentioned in the NT as the occasion for the outpouring of the Holy Spirit upon the disciples of Christ, an event which many theologians understand as marking the beginning of the church (Acts 2:1)."[141] At Pentecost, a decisive number of people adopted the new ideology by believing in the gospel and becoming a

---

138. Burns, *Leadership*, 202.
139. Polhill, *Acts* (NAC), 111.
140. "Pentecost," *HarBD* 769.
141. Elwell, *BEB* 2:1640.

part of the church. Barrett confirms, "There is no reason to doubt that considerable numbers adopted the Christian position, convinced at least that something out of the ordinary had occurred and willing to accept the latest messianic claimant."[142]

In Acts 2:41, Luke gives an exact amount of three thousand people from diverse regions and languages who adopted the faith and were baptized.[143] The birth of the church is monumental in the spread of the gospel and new ideology of the new community of the church. Beginning with Pentecost, Myers addresses two factors:

> Two factors involved in the interpretation of the Pentecost event of Acts 2 are Jesus' promise of the giving of the Holy Spirit (Luke 12:12; Acts 1:8) and the prophetic view of the future age of the Spirit and of salvation (represented by the quotation of Joel 2:28-32 MT 3:1-5] at Acts 2:17-21). Another important factor that shapes the report of this event is the understanding of it as the initiation of the Church's worldwide preaching of the gospel.[144]

Peter led the revolution by pushing the vision of the outpouring of the Holy Spirit and salvation through the Messiah Jesus. His communication led a significant number of people at Pentecost to believe, which resulted in the birth of the church. As Burns states, the birth of a vision that impels the revolution and its adoption by a decisive number of people is a crucial step of transformation.

Peter's revolutionary leadership continued after Pentecost. He not only shared the vision and pushed it forward but he was also willing to sacrifice his life for the cause of the gospel. Burns clearly states that revolutionary transformation cannot occur without "risking lives, undergoing imprisonment, exile, persecution, and continual hardship."[145] Consistently, in the book of Acts, Peter was imprisoned, persecuted, and suffered hardship. Polhill addresses the growing opposition to the surging church:

> With the growing success of the Christian witness, there is a heightened reaction on the part of the Jewish authorities—at first only a hearing, warning, and release (4:5-22). Now those

---

142. Barrett, *Commentary on Acts*, 162.
143. Bruce, *Book of the Acts*, 73.
144. Myers, *EBD* 811.
145. Burns, *Leadership*, 202.

PETER'S TRANSFORMATIONAL LEADERSHIP AFTER PENTECOST   105

on the Council would impose the death penalty (5:33) and were only thwarted in their intentions by the sage advice of a Pharisee (5:34–39). The apostles were again released, but this time the Council had them whipped before so doing (5:40).... The conflict became even stronger with the killing of Stephen (6:8–8:2) and the resulting persecution of Christians in Jerusalem (8:1); and it reached its apex in chap. 12, where the execution of James and the attempt to do the same to Peter found the support not only of the Jewish officials but the populace as well (12:3).[146]

Christian growth continued to threaten the Jewish leadership. In accordance with Burns's evaluation, Peter simultaneously became the villain to Jewish leadership and the leader to new believers.[147]

In chs. 4 and beginning of 5, they used beating, imprisonment, hearings, and threats to diminish the growing faith. Beginning in ch. 4, Peter was persecuted and imprisoned due to his preaching of Jesus's resurrection from the dead (Acts 4:2). Peter greatly disturbed the Priest, Sadducees, and captain of the temple guard with his declaration of Jesus as the Messiah. Peter's doctrinal insistence confirms Burns's assumption, that "as the lines become more sharply drawn between the establishment or elite and the poor and the rebelling, doctrine and purpose are hardened in the crucible."[148] The teaching of Peter was challenging the Sadducees who rejected the resurrection.[149] They beat him and imprisoned him overnight. Polhill summarizes Peter's experience:

> Up until this point in Acts, there had been no resistance to the Christians on the part of the Jews. Indeed, the picture had been that of the general acceptance and favor accorded them by the people (cf. 2:47). In chap. 4 the picture changes. Not, however, with the people. They still were responding favorably to the message of the apostles, indeed, in an overwhelming way (cf. 4:4). It was the officials who turned against the apostles, and not even all of them. The primary enemy was the priestly Sadducean aristocracy for whom the Christians were a serious threat to the status quo. Twice they arrested the apostles. The first time occurred here, as they descended upon Peter and John in the course of their witness in the temple square.[150]

146. Polhill, *Acts* (NAC), 164–65.
147. Burns, *Leadership*, 202–3.
148. Burns, *Leadership*, 202–3.
149. Barrett, *Commentary on Acts*, 220.
150. Polhill, *Acts* (NAC), 137.

Although people were receptive to the adoption of the gospel, the social and religious system rejected the apostles to the point of persecution.

Peter willingly went to prison on behalf of the mission, end values, and transcending purpose. His willingness to suffer for the gospel amid opposition led others to believe in the gospel as the number increased to five thousand.[151] After his overnight stay in prison, he stood before the Sanhedrin for his persistent affirmation of Jesus's resurrection. Despite the opposition, Peter, filled with the Holy Spirit, continued to proclaim the vision (Acts 4:6–12). His persistence created questions among the opposing leaders, who were uncertain how to handle Peter. Therefore, they decided to threaten Peter to quiet his claims; but Peter boldly refused to be silenced (Acts 14:13–18). His continuation after his imprisonment provides more evidence for his revolutionary leadership and the effect it had on the spread of the mission.

In the following chapter, Peter again encountered threats and opposition. Polhill details Peter's second experience of suffering: "This second encounter with the Sanhedrin can be divided into three main parts: the initial arrest and its almost ludicrous result (5:17–26), the hearing before the Sanhedrin (5:27–40), and the release of the apostles with their continued witness (5:41–42)."[152] In ch. 5, however, the Pharisees were filled with jealousy because the people were coming to the apostles with their ailments, sickness, and unclean spirits for healing (Acts 5:16). Their jealousy led them to beat them and place them in jail again. But when Peter and the apostles refused to stop teaching, the council had them flogged and released, with the warning not to continue to teach about Jesus (Acts 5:40). Instead of becoming disheartened after the appearance at the council and flogging, they left joyous that they were worthy to suffer for Jesus (Acts 5:41). Again, the apostles continued to teach despite the threat to their lives and the numbers of people who believed significantly grew.

The cycle continued as Peter progressively advanced the vision. Acts 12 addresses another instance of Peter's arrest and deliverance. This time at the command of Herod, Peter was arrested as a leader of the church. Barrett provides the background of Herod: "Examples of Herod's attack follow in the stories of James and Peter; Herod (to judge from this account) thought it best to attack the Christian society through its

---

151. Bruce, *Book of the Acts*, 90.
152. Polhill, *Acts* (NAC), 164–65.

leaders. This is reinforced by the use of τινας—not the whole church, but some of its members."[153] Herod desired to please the Jews to maintain control of his power. His popularity among the Jews increased as he led the persecution of the leaders of the church. Polhill confirms Herod's need to retain his popularity: "It became all the more important for him to win the loyalty of his Jewish subjects in order to give him at least a firm footing at home."[154] Herod's selfish intent to retain power created a consistent threat to the church and its leaders.

Herod first had James the brother of John killed by the sword and then turned his attention to Peter (Acts 12:2). While awaiting the same fate as James, the church prayed for his release. Despite being shackled and bracketed between soldiers, an angel led Peter out of the prison. Upon his escape, he went to Mary's house to describe the miracle of his escape and directed them to tell James and the brethren. After describing to the people of the church who were praying, he left that night and went to another place (Acts 12:17). Peter again exhibited his willingness even to die on behalf of the mobilization of the vision and gospel. Peter's sacrifice and suffering throughout the book of Acts is continual evidence of his revolutionary leadership that helped transform an entire religious society and ethnic inclusion.

Despite Peter's reformed leadership in moments of societal pressure, he still displayed a consistent willingness to suffer and sacrifice for the mobilization of the faith. As Burns presented, a revolutionary leader must be willing to demonstrate dedication and demonstrate commitment with time, risking life, imprisonment, exile, persecution, and continual hardship.[155] As documented in the book of Acts, Peter's dedication and commitment led to his imprisonment, risking of his life, exile, and continual hardship for the doctrine and transcending purpose. Peter willingly entered conflict, becoming a villain to the Jews and a hero to the Christians. Additionally, just like Burns's definition, Peter's sacrifice mobilized a decisive number of people who believed and were willing to be active in their newfound beliefs.[156] Peter raised social consciousness and changed the religious landscape through his dedication to the transcending purpose of the gospel and led others to become active followers of the mission.

153. Barrett, *Commentary on Acts*, 574.
154. Polhill, *Acts* (NAC), 277–83.
155. Burns, *Leadership*, 202–3.
156. Burns, *Leadership*, 202.

Conclusion

The totality of Peter's life in Acts merits comprehensive examination in comparison with Burns's definition of transformational leadership. Burns's definition aligns with Peter's leadership within the diversity of the birth of the church in the book of Acts. Peter's origin revealed the wellspring of wants, purpose, and values, and exposed his complete individual transformation of purpose. His personal transformation explained his leadership failure as a reformed leader and unwillingness to disappoint his origin as a Jew. In a lapse of leadership, Peter folded under mounting pressure to conform the Jewish pressure of total unity with the gentiles. His lack of leadership caused a disruption to the mobilization of the church and unity between Jew and gentile.

However, his origin also explains his personal transformation and willingness to sacrifice as a revolutionary leader so others would experience the same transformation. The survey of the book of Acts provides ample evidence to support Peter's immense impact on the birth of Christianity and his revolutionary role in its mobilization leading both Jew and gentile. The book of Acts revealed persistent threats and risks to Peter's life as he withstood an insurmountable amount of pressure to stop his disruption to the cultural and religious norms of Jews. Without his revolutionary leadership, the success of the birth of the church would have fragmented and divided.

The "pure" form of revolution is rare in practice. Also rare is the revolutionary leader who helps initiate a revolution; endures throughout the entire revolutionary cycle of struggle, victory, and consolidation of power; and directs the process of social transformation.

4

Paul's Transformational Leadership after Pentecost

God's mission for the church is not dependent on one human transformational leader. God's plan includes using multiple human leaders to accomplish the mobilization of the gospel. The book of Acts focuses on two main characters in the birth and growth of the church. Toussaint states, "The view that the purpose of Acts is a Pauline apologetic is buttressed by the amazing set of parallels between Peter and Paul."[1] The last chapter addressed Peter's transformational leadership that revolutionized the church, society, and the world. Paul's transformational leadership deserves the same attention to analyze his significant impact on the revolution of the church, society, and world. This chapter examines Paul's origin, vision, transformation, and evidence of revolutionary leadership to confirm his transformational leadership in the book of Acts.

Paul's Origin

The beginning of Paul's life is critical to understanding his complete individual transformation. Paul's dramatic individual transformation is examined after a complete review of his background.

---

1. Toussaint, "Acts," 2:350.

Wellspring of Wants

Before a leader is even born, his biographical makeup determines his personality. Burns defines origins: "The genetic inheritance initiates the series of openings and closures of life chances—mechanisms powerful enough to have a direct impact on evolving personality."[2] Burns states clearly the advantages of reviewing biographical data to understand the evolution of the leader:

> At the moment infants are expelled from the calm warmth and dependence of the uterus into the shocking, bewildering world of light and sound, of touching and prodding, of deprivation and fulfillment, they begin the lifelong process of stimulus and response that will culminate for some in skills and motivations for leadership.[3]

From birth, Paul began to develop his personality through stimuli starting from his birthplace to childhood upbringing.

Before Paul's conversion, he went by the name Saul. That name provides background to his birthplace, citizenship, and tribe. Betz confirms the relevance of Saul's name: "While his Jewish name corresponds to his being a Benjaminite (Phil 3:5; Rom 11:1; cf. Acts 13:21), his Greco-Roman name may have been given to him in connection with his citizenship in Tarsus, a city in Cilicia, where he was born and raised (Acts 9:11; 21:39; 22:3; cf. 9:30; 11:25)."[4] Paul's birthplace helps us formulate possible influences of religious tradition and education.

Silva summarizes Paul's description of his birthplace and upbringing: "He describes himself as one 'circumcised on the eighth day, of the people of Israel, of the tribe of Benjamin, a Hebrew born of Hebrews' (Phil 3:5)."[5] Paul's Jewish upbringing is well supported in Scripture, by his own account. Paul distinguishes himself in his description of his circumcision, tribe, and Hebrew heritage. Vincent expounds on Paul's claims: "The grounds of this last, general statement are now given in the enumeration of Paul's advantages as a Jew, beginning with his inherited privileges. First is circumcision, the main point in a Jew's eyes, and that by which the whole nation was named."[6]

2. Burns, *Leadership*, 61.
3. Burns, *Leadership*, 61.
4. Hans Dieter Betz, "Paul (Person)," *ABD* 187.
5. Moises Silva, "Paul, the Apostle," *BEB* 2:1621–23.
6. Vincent, *Philippians and Philemon*, 95–96.

Paul's precise description of his circumcision was purposeful and deliberate. Hawthorne provides distinct background for Paul's circumcision:

> Together the words describe one who was circumcised on the eighth day of his life. With only two words, then, the apostle has made for himself the proudest claim any Jew could make, namely, that in strict conformity with the law he was circumcised on precisely the right day (Gen 17:12; Lev 12:3; cf. Luke 1:59; 2:21). Unlike Ishmael, who was circumcised when he was thirteen years old (Gen 17:25; contrast Gen 21:4), as were his descendants and unlike heathen proselytes to Judaism who were circumcised as adults, Paul was circumcised on the eighth day by parents who were meticulous in fulfilling the prescriptions of the law. He was a true Jew, a Jew by birth. He was no proselyte converted to Judaism in later life, no "Johnny-come-lately," we may say.[7]

The precision of the day of his circumcision proves Paul's assertion of his strict Jewish upbringing. It highlights not only his upbringing but also his direct Israelite birth. He was not a proselyte but was Jewish, according to his Israelite descent from patriarch Jacob.[8] He was from the nation of Israel and, more specifically, the tribe of Benjamin.

Paul's mention of his Israelite tribe again highlights his pride in his heritage and the historical significance of the tribe of Benjamin.[9] Paul continued his claim by stating that he was a Hebrew of Hebrews. Not only was he a descendant, but he also continued his tradition as a Hebrew speaker. Vincent addresses the background of Paul's statement:

> He might have been an Israelite and not a Hebrew speaker; but he emphasizes the fact that he was both a true Israelite and one who used the language of his forefathers. He was trained under a Hebrew teacher at Jerusalem (Acts 22:3); he spoke Hebrew, *i.e.*, Aramaic (Acts 21:40, 22:2); and he quotes often from the Hebrew Scriptures.[10]

Paul not only pinpointed his ability to carry the heritage of the Hebrew language, but he also used the terminology to distinguish himself from the gentile nations.

---

7. Hawthorne, *Philippians*, 184.
8. Vincent, *Philippians and Philemon*, 96.
9. Hawthorne, *Philippians*, 184.
10. Vincent, *Philippians and Philemon*, 97.

Vincent elaborates on the term *Hebrew*: "In the O.T., 'Hebrew' was used habitually and consistently to denote the descendants of Abraham as designated by foreigners, or as applied by the Hebrews themselves when addressing foreigners, or when speaking of themselves in contrast with other nations."[11] Paul's background proved he is distinct among those who should have confidence in his flesh and staunch Jewish heritage. Melick concluded, "In any case, the stress on the correct pedigree removed a potential question about Paul's credentials when he confronted the Jewish teachers."[12] While proving his point, Paul provided clear background and support for his Jewish origin.

Paul was not just born with Jewish rights but was also raised accordingly. In Acts 22:3, after Paul says we was born in Tarsus, he states he was reared in Jerusalem. Silva says, "Moreover, according to Acts 22:3, he was actually brought up in Jerusalem (possibly in his sister's house, Acts 23:16), and some scholars infer from that statement that Paul was brought up in a totally Jewish environment from earliest childhood."[13] Paul's Jewish environment directly impacted his beliefs and helped formulate his religious thinking.

Paul's staunch beliefs are not limited to the location of his upbringing but also include the education that took place while in Jerusalem. Paul describes his own education in Acts 22:3, "I am a Jew, born in Tarsus of Cilicia, but brought up in this city, educated under Gamaliel, strictly according to the law of our fathers, being zealous for God just as you all are today." Paul's own account of his upbringing credits his teacher Gamaliel and the strict instruction he received. Gamaliel was "a Pharisaic member of the Sanhedrin in Jerusalem who was widely respected for his learning in Torah (Acts 5:34)."[14] Silva provides details on Paul's upbringing in Jerusalem:

> Although born in Tarsus, Paul testified to the Jews in Jerusalem that he had been brought up in this city and studied under Gamaliel (Acts 22:3). It is not clear when Paul was first brought to Jerusalem, but it is likely that sometime between the ages of 13 and 20 he began his formal rabbinical studies. His teacher, Gamaliel was the grandson of Hillel, founder of a Pharisaic school whose teachings run through the Talmudic writings to

11. Vincent, *Philippians and Philemon*, 96.
12. Melick, *Philippians, Colossians, Philemon*, 129.
13. Silva, *BEB* 2:1621–23.
14. Bruce Chilton, "Gamaliel (Person)," *ABD* 904.

this day. This is the same Gamaliel whose wisdom persuaded the Sanhedrin to spare the lives of Peter and the apostles (5:33–40). No doubt, it was while studying under Gamaliel in Hillel's school that Paul began to advance in Judaism beyond many Jews of his own age and became extremely zealous for the traditions of his fathers (Gal 1:14).[15]

Gamaliel's reputation and influence within the Pharisaic school and Judaism are well documented.

The first issue will be dealt with briefly. Paul's identification of his teacher's name indicates his expectation that his audience will recognize the reputation and teaching of Gamaliel. According to Paul's account in Gal 1:14, he not only received formal rabbinical studies but also excelled and advanced past his peers. "I was advancing in Judaism beyond many of my contemporaries among my countrymen, being more extremely zealous for my ancestral traditions." Paul's zeal for his ancestral traditions pushed him to become a strict follower of a law. Silva provides clarity and definition for Paul's claim:

> The first issue may be dealt with briefly. Paul's own statement in Galatians 1:14 provides an important key, namely, his reference to "the traditions of my fathers." That phrase is equivalent to "the traditions of the elders," used by the Pharisees to criticize Jesus' conduct (Mk 7:5). It refers to the rabbinic "oral law," a body of legal biblical interpretation that played an authoritative role among the Pharisees.[16]

Paul again attested to his own righteousness as a follower of the law, "as to the righteousness under the law blameless" (Phil 3:6).

Paul's wellspring of wants began instantly after his birth. He was circumcised with strict precision in timing, confirming his family as stringent followers of the law. Paul's family's precise adherence to the law provides evidence of his pride in his heritage and uncompromising views of the law.

Transmutation of Needs

As Burns states, "If wants are drives experienced as feelings of longing, needs are wants influenced by the environment. When environments

---

15. Elwell and Comfort, *Tyndale Bible Dictionary*, 996–97.
16. Silva, *BEB* 2:1622.

change because of longtime shifts in the climate, for example, wants must yield to the new circumstances or the wanting creature will yield to biological imperatives."[17] The transmutation of needs becomes more focused when socializing refines their wants into needs.[18]

Paul's biological upbringing in Jerusalem was reinforced by his education, and involvement in the Sanhedrin. Growing up in Jerusalem surrounded him with the environment to cement his beliefs and behavior. His education further solidified his staunch obedience to the law. Based on Paul's claims, he took pride in his heritage, tribe, and education, which supports the social analysis of extreme rejection of the Christian faith. Paul's entire identity was formed according to his Jewish birth and upbringing.

Paul's strict training was not in vain as he grew past his peers. His wellspring of want led him to want to surpass his peers in his desire to excel in the law. His zeal for the law's traditions did not go unnoticed as he progressed in his influence among the Pharisees and opposition to Christianity. His zeal and strict education led his membership in the Pharisaic sect and desire to extinguish the apostasy of Christianity. Betz recounts:

> Before his conversion Paul actively preserved and protected the religious traditions of his forefathers. Considering himself an "orthodox" Jew, he was zealously committed to eradicating apostasy. Going further than his peers, he became a member of the Pharisaic sect (see Saldarini 1988: 134–43) and took it upon himself to persecute the Christian church (Gal 1:13, 23; Phil 3:6; 1 Cor 15:9).[19]

Not only was Paul knowledgeable about the law, but he also implemented the tradition of his heritage to the point of his active role in the persecution of the church.[20]

Paul's strict upbringing and education led to his extreme opposition to the Christian faith. Silva summarizes Paul's strict view against the gospel before conversion:

> With regard to Paul's pre-Christian attitude to the gospel, one thing is certain—he was opposed to it with his whole heart.

---

17. Burns, *Leadership*, 68.
18. Previously defined in ch. 3.
19. Betz, *ABD* 187.
20. Silva, *BEB* 2:1622.

In his apostolic letters he speaks of his previous hatred for the church (e.g., 21, Gal 1:13; Phil 3:6). Paul does not say explicitly why he felt this way, but there are some hints. In 1 Corinthians 1:23, for example, he speaks of the crucifixion of Christ as a stumbling block to the Jews; in Galatians 3:13, he quotes Deuteronomy 21:23 ("Cursed is everyone who is hung on a tree") as evidence that Christ, by dying on the cross, became a curse for us. It seems reasonable to infer that Paul, along with many other Jews, viewed the preaching of the gospel as blasphemy. How could these Christians regard as Messiah (God's anointed) a lowly man who suffered a criminal's death and received the divine curse itself? Not surprisingly, this theme would become a basic one in Paul's own proclamation of the gospel.[21]

His extreme behavior surfaced in the book of Acts as Paul (then named Saul) was the proponent of the persecution of the church. Acts 7:58 is Paul's first appearance in Acts, as a young man leading the stoning of Stephen.

Paul as a young man, unmarried, and educated is now active in the defense of his heritage.[22] Bruce gives background to Paul's influence in the book of Acts:

> The young man called Saul, who guarded the clothes of the chief executioners, will play an increasingly important part in the record of Acts, as a leading champion of the cause which he was now opposing. Saul was his family name as an Israelite; he is better known in history by his Roman cognomen Paullus (Paul). It may be regarded as an undesigned coincidence that while Luke alone informs us that his Jewish name was Saul, he himself claims to have belonged to the tribe of Benjamin. His parents thus gave him the name of the most illustrious member of that tribe in the nation's history—the name of Israel's first king, Saul.[23]

Paul's appearance at the stoning was not an accident but a culmination of his birth and upbringing. Paul's presence was an agreement of the death of Stephen.

He witnessed the death of Stephen and stood in approval of the appropriate action taken against Stephen's bold witness of Jesus Christ. Polhill reviews Paul's attendance at Stephen's stoning:

21. Silva, *BEB* 2:1623.
22. Barrett, *Commentary on Acts*, 386.
23. Bruce, *Book of the Acts*, 158–59.

Luke introduced Saul for the first time at the stoning of Stephen. He was the young man who watched over the garments of the witnesses as they stoned Stephen (v. 58). There is no indication that Paul himself actually lifted a stone, but he was in total agreement with the action (8:1). Paul likely had a deeper involvement with the whole incident than appears in these brief references. He was himself a Greek-speaking Jew, a Cilician, who perhaps had argued with Stephen in the Hellenist synagogue in Jerusalem.[24]

Stephen's defense of the Christian faith enraged the Sanhedrin and, as expected, Paul stood in agreement with the sentencing of Stephen to death by stoning.

"A young theologue named Saul agreed that Stephen should be stoned. The witnesses laid their clothes at his feet. This meant Saul was giving his approval by guarding their clothes (Acts 8:1; 22:20)."[25] Acts 8:1 also clearly states that Saul was in hearty agreement with putting him to death. Paul's level of involvement in the stoning is speculation, but his approval and witness were confirmed when the garments were laid at his feet. Paul's persecution of the church continued to intensify as the attacks caused the church in Jerusalem to scatter (Acts 8:1). "The opposition did not end with Stephen's death. If anything, his bold witness in both his Sanhedrin testimony and his death only served to fuel the flames."[26]

Acts 8:3 states Paul began ravaging the church, entering house after house dragging men and women to prison. The Greek word *ravaging* is defined as "to cause harm to, injure, damage, spoil, ruin, destroy."[27] Undignified in his attempts to take Christians to prison, Paul harmed and injured many people through his efforts. Polhill provides an account of Paul's vehement opposition to the church:

> Luke now turned his attention to Saul (v. 3), the third reference to him in six verses. The "escalation" of his opposition to the Christians is interesting. First, he was presented as a bystander at Stephen's martyrdom (7:58). Then we are informed that he gave full mental assent to the stoning of Stephen (8:1a). Then his consent led to full involvement. He became the church's worst enemy (v. 3). Indeed, he is portrayed as the persecution

---

24. Polhill, *Acts* (NAC), 210.
25. Toussaint, "Acts," 2:371.
26. Polhill, *Acts* (NAC), 211.
27. "λυμαίνω," BDAG 604.

personified. He is described as attempting to "ravage" the church ("destroy"). The Greek word is *lymainō*, a strong expression that is used in the Septuagint for wild beasts, such as lions, bears, and leopards tearing at raw flesh. He is said to have gone "from house to house," possibly a reference to his breaking into their "house church" assemblies. In any event, his fury stopped at nothing. He turned against women as well as men, dragging them to court, throwing them in prison. The picture is totally consistent with his own testimony elsewhere in Acts (22:4f.; 26:10f.) and in his epistles (1 Cor 15:9; Gal 1:13, 23; Phil 3:6; 1 Tim 1:13). So much did he embody the persecution in his own person that the church is described as experiencing "peace" upon his conversion (9:31).[28]

Emboldened by his witness of Peter, Paul transformed from approved witness to active persecutor. His aggression is scripturally documented, even in Paul's own account of his ruthlessness. The culmination of Paul's upbringing and strict education led to his extreme tactics and disregard for humanity in his efforts to cleanse false teaching in the church.

The wellspring of wants is first developed biologically and then interlocks with social developments of educational, political, and cultural stimuli that determine their future motivations and interactions. Paul's education, combined with his religious party affiliation and Jewish cultural stimuli, led to an extreme strict behavior and zeal for the law. The development of Paul's transmutation of needs was evidenced by his fierce opposition to the church and their teachings.

Paul's Purpose

Unlike Peter, Paul had a complete alteration from his wellspring of want and transmutation of needs to purpose. As noted previously, *purpose* is a "term designating God's summons to a specific task or role and his special relationship to his people."[29] Unlike Burns, God is solely responsible for the summoning of specific individuals for their designated purpose.[30] Another contrast is God's foresight and predetermined plan for the individuals called to certain tasks (Jer 1:1–10).

---

28. Polhill, *Acts* (NAC), 212.
29. Myers, *EBD* 183; previously defined in ch. 3.
30. Previously defined in ch. 2.

Paul's shift from his biological and sociological upbringing completely differed from the purpose that transformed the church he once vehemently opposed. Matheson, in *Spiritual Development of St. Paul*, remarks "that a man trained under such influences must, on every side, have been repelled by the spectacle of the cross of Jesus. He was required to accept him precisely at the point where his national characteristics were assailed."[31] God's use of Paul dramatically shifts the history of Christianity and highlights the grace of God to the gentiles to which Paul was sent.[32]

Paul's transition from his wants to purpose took a drastic conversion. God's necessary intimate interaction with Paul shifted his values from persecutor of the church to missionary to the gentiles.[33] Polhill details Paul's radical conversion:

> For Luke and for Paul (cf. 1 Cor 15:9f.) there was no more certain evidence of God's power and grace than in his transformation of the church's persecutor into its greatest witness. Paul's was a radical conversion experience, a total turnabout accomplished by Christ himself. Its importance for Luke is evidenced by the fact that he told the story in some detail three times in Acts— here in 9:1–30, then in Paul's speech before a Jewish crowd in the temple area (22:3–21), and finally in Paul's defense before the Jewish King Agrippa (26:2–23).[34]

After his persistent persecution of the church, Jesus confronted Paul in a dramatic fashion on the road to Damascus. Acts 9:1–2 highlights Paul's continual threats and pursuits against Christians, working with the Jewish leadership to bring disciples and any followers of "the way" to their punishment.

Paul was discontent with scattering Christians, but he now wanted to pursue them in their places of refuge.[35] Polhill details the contrast in Paul's life before his conversion:

> More significantly, they picture the preconversion Paul, which contrasts radically with the picture of Paul after the encounter on the Damascus Road. Verse 1 picks up the picture in 8:3. Paul was still the church's number one enemy, still raging against it, "breathing out murderous threats." Paul's role was

31. Matheson, *Spiritual Development*, 36–37.
32. Polhill, *Acts* (NAC), 231.
33. Peterson, *Acts of the Apostles*, 298–99.
34. Polhill, *Acts* (NAC), 231.
35. Bruce, *Book of the Acts*, 180.

not one of executioner but of arresting officer. His intent was to stamp out the new movement; and when it did come to a question of execution of Christians, he did not hesitate to vote for the death penalty (cf. 26:10). Originally, Paul's activity had primarily been directed at the Christians in and around Jerusalem (8:3; 26:10). Evidently, some had fled the city and taken refuge in Damascus.[36]

Along the road to Damascus, Jesus stopped him suddenly with a light from heaven, questioning Paul's actions against him. The light was not ordinary; rather, it was the divine glory of Christ.[37]

Paul understood the event as a revelation of Jesus Christ (Gal 1:12, 15). "His own references to his conversion imply incidentally that he heard the voice of Christ but emphasize above all that he saw him as the risen and glorified one."[38] Ananias confirmed Paul's experience with the appearance of Jesus on the road (Acts 9:17). Paul's experience with Jesus was vitally important to Paul's future apostleship in the church and the authority.[39] In order for Paul to be a disciple of Jesus Christ the experience of Jesus's glory was necessary.

Jesus questioned Paul's persecution of the church while confronting his disbelief is his resurrection. "The question has the effect not only of initiating conversation but of throwing Paul's actions and life into question."[40] Jesus's interrogation contradicted Paul's current position due to his upbringing, education, and staunch profession. Paul now had to reconcile the voice of the risen Savior to his current persecution of Christians who held that belief. Polhill infers Paul's possible reaction:

> It would be hard to imagine how these words must have struck Paul. They were a complete refutation of all he had been. He had persecuted Christians for their "blasphemous lie" that Jesus was risen, that he was the Lord reigning in glory. Now Paul himself beheld that same Jesus and the undeniable proof that he both lived and reigned in glory.[41]

---

36. Polhill, *Acts* (NAC), 233.
37. Barrett, *Commentary on Acts*, 449.
38. Bruce, *Book of the Acts*, 183; cf. 1 Cor 9:1; 15:8; Gal 1:16.
39. Polhill, *Acts* (NAC), 235.
40. Barrett, *Commentary on Acts*, 450.
41. Polhill, *Acts* (NAC), 233.

The proof of Jesus's resurrection immediately changed his values, and Paul did not argue with the revelation. Paul immediately followed Jesus's instructions and awaited his further direction.

Jesus spoke with Ananias and gave Paul values, which included his purpose, goals, and end state. Jesus told Ananias that Paul would be his instrument to bear Jesus's name to the gentiles, kings, and sons of Israel (Acts 9:15). Barrett states, "Luke, probably with a deliberate attempt to use Pauline language, means that Saul is one whom the Lord has singled out for special service."[42] The use of a chosen instrument provided a clear depiction of God's purpose for Paul's life. Paul's divine call as an instrument of God was to exercise a specific function.[43] Peterson defines "instrument":

> The designation of Saul as *"my chosen instrument"* (*skeuos eklogēs moi*, "a vessel of choice for me") is significant. The terminology of election is used in Luke 18:7; Acts 13:17 for God's gracious choice of people for salvation. In Luke 6:13; Acts 1:2, 24; 6:5; 15:7, 22, 25, however, the choice is for a special role or mission that not all disciples share. The "election" of Saul in 9:15 refers to his ministry, not to his conversion. His role was "apostle to the Gentiles."[44]

God called Paul to bear the same name he denounced to the gentiles, kings, and sons of Israel. "The expression of bearing one's witness 'before' is the language of giving one's testimony in a legal setting and is a fulfillment of Jesus' words."[45]

The audience of Paul's calling to the gentiles, kings, and sons of Israel was fulfilled throughout Paul's ministry as he taught in synagogues, defended the gospel before kings, and traveled to gentiles as a missionary.[46] Toussaint summarizes Paul's mission in fulfillment of Jesus's call:

> Saul was to become Paul, the apostle to the uncircumcised (Rom. 11:13; Gal. 2:2, 7–8; Eph. 3:8), including kings (cf. Governor Felix [Acts 24:1–23], Governor Porcius Festus [24:27–25:12], King Herod Agrippa II [25:13–26:32], and possibly Emperor Nero [25:11]). The apostle, of course, also ministered to "the people of Israel" (cf. 9:20; 13:5, 14; 14:1; 17:2, 10, 17;

---

42. Barrett, *Commentary on Acts*, 456.
43. "σκεῦος," BDAG 927.
44. Peterson, *Acts of the Apostles*, 309.
45. Polhill, *Acts* (NAC), 237.
46. Pervo, *Acts*, 243–44.

18:4, 19; 19:8; 26:17–20; and Rom. 1:16). How amazing that the one who persecuted Christians so violently should himself be transformed into a witness of the Gospel—and such a dynamic, forceful witness at that![47]

Paul also repeats his purpose in Gal 1:15 when he explains that God set him apart, called him through grace, and revealed his Son so that Paul could preach to the gentiles.

Polhill expounds upon "chosen": "The expression is an unusual one and finds its closest New Testament parallels in Paul's own writings. The emphasis on Paul being 'chosen' recalls his own strong sense of the divine call, which set him apart from birth (Gal 1:15)."[48] Acts 13:2 repeats Paul's calling in his first missionary journey, when the Holy Spirit said that Paul and Barnabas were set apart for the work to which they were called. *Apart* means "to select one person out of a group for a purpose."[49] The Holy Spirit selected Paul out of the group to fulfill his "*call* to a special task or office."[50] Jesus confirmed Paul's calling on the road to Damascus, as well as did the Holy Spirit on the mission to Cyprus. According to Acts 9:16, however, Paul's new purpose led him to his suffering for the gospel, rather than persecuting those who believed in Jesus's resurrection. Polhill confirms the incoming suffering:

> Paul would *suffer* for the name of Christ. The one who once was the church's most vehement persecutor would now be the one who would willingly accept persecution for the sake of the name (cf. 5:41). This is the core point of the Pauline conversion narrative. It reappears at its conclusion as Paul is shown persecuted by the Jews both in Damascus (9:23) and in Jerusalem (9:29). In nothing is his conversion more clearly illustrated than in his transformation from persecutor to persecuted.[51]

Paul's conversion is a dramatic shift in his personal mission and purpose. He once was the persecutor of the church and now will suffer at the hands of those with whom he once agreed. Paul's personal transformation of his purpose dictated the rest of his ministry until his martyrdom for the gospel.

47. Toussaint, "Acts," 2:377.
48. Polhill, *Acts* (NAC), 237.
49. "ἀφορίζω," BDAG 158.
50. "προσκαλέω," BDAG 881.
51. Polhill, *Acts* (NAC), 237.

Paul's Values

Based on Paul's individual transformation, his values completely shifted. As Burns notes, "Values indicate desirable or preferred end-states or collective goals or explicit purposes, and values are standards in terms of which specific criteria may be established and choices made among alternatives."[52] Paul's conversion and God-given purpose changed his collective goals and standards. Paul's zeal for his traditional Jewish education and beliefs continued but was redirected as an instrument to the gentiles. To reach the gentiles, Paul's past wants and needs had to transform to reach his God-given purpose. Paul's values determined his boldness, zeal, and fearless defense of the gospel while addressing anyone with the gospel.

Days after Paul's conversion, his values are evident immediately as he begins to proclaim Jesus in the synagogue. Paul's past interaction in the synagogues is opposite of his current proclamation of Jesus, but his zeal remains (Acts 9:21). Bruce documents the shift in messaging:

> It was to the synagogues of Damascus that Saul had been sent with the commission from the high priest, and to the synagogues of Damascus he went. But instead of presenting his letters of credence and demanding the extradition of the disciples of Jesus, he appeared as the bearer of a very different commission, issued by a higher authority than the high priests, and as a disciple and messenger of Jesus he announced his Master's claims. No wonder that his hearers were amazed by the change that had come over him.[53]

It was completely shocking to people that Paul was now preaching the message that he had previously persecuted others for proclaiming.

The disbelief of the listeners at the complete transformation and boldness of Paul's proclamation is understandable due to Paul's recent history. However, that did not stop Paul from his new purpose and values. Polhill illustrates the reaction of others to Paul's change:

> The astonishment of his Jewish listeners in the synagogue furnishes a sort of "choral response" to the completeness of Paul's conversion. As Ananias before them (vv. 13–14), they simply could not believe that the former persecutor had made such a radical about-face. Paul simply preached all the more forcefully.

---

52. Burns, *Leadership*, 74.
53. Bruce, *Book of the Acts*, 191.

One could even say his zeal as a Christian was even stronger than his former zeal as persecutor.[54]

Paul continued to grow in strength; he troubled the Jews, while proving Jesus was the Christ and using his ability to present a logical conclusion and demonstrate strong argumentation.[55]

Barrett provides clarity: "Paul was not drawing an inference but affirming something and alleging evidence to prove it."[56] Due to Paul's change of values, his message and argumentation changed. He was convinced of his purpose and immediately and boldly changed his end state and goals. His goal was to now go to the Jews in the place where he once stood to persecute the people of "the way" (Acts 9:28–29). His zeal remained even though his purpose changed. Therefore, his zeal made him just as aggressive in his pursuit to bring the gospel to the Jews. However, now his zeal in proving Jesus Christ as the Messiah was leading him to be the one threatened with persecution (Acts 9:23–24).

Paul also maintained his boldness, proclaiming, arguing, and confronting those who challenged his new faith. While on his first mission trip, Paul confronted a false prophet (Acts 13:6). Filled with the Holy Spirit, Paul boldly declared that the prophet's sin would lead to blindness. Elwell and Comfort add, "This was the first manifestation in Paul of the signs of an apostle (2 Cor 12:12). From then on, the name Paul, not Saul, is used in Luke's record of the Acts of the Apostles (Acts 13:9), and Paul replaced Barnabas as the leader of the party."[57] Paul's leadership was beginning to take the forefront as Luke highlights his growth.[58]

Paul's boldness in his leadership continued to grow, which increased his confidence to confront opposition. Following his declaration, Paul traveled again—this time declaring to the synagogue officials that Jesus was the promised Messiah.[59] Polhill gives the background and reasoning for Paul's visit to the synagogue:

> As was their custom, Paul and Barnabas went first to the synagogue in the city. The Diaspora synagogue was more than a house of worship. It was the hub of the Jewish community—house of

---

54. Polhill, *Acts* (NAC), 239.
55. "συμβιβάζω," BDAG 957.
56. Barrett, *Commentary on Acts*, 465.
57. Elwell and Comfort, *Tyndale Bible Dictionary*, 999.
58. Barrett, *Commentary on Acts*, 622.
59. Elwell and Comfort, *Tyndale Bible Dictionary*, 998–1000.

worship, center of education, judicial center, social gathering place, general "civic center" for the Jewish community. If one wished to make contact with the Jewish community in a town, the synagogue was the natural place to begin. It was also the natural place to begin if one wished to share the Christian message. Jesus was the expected Jewish Messiah, and it was natural to share him with "the Jews first."[60]

Due to his changed purpose, Paul was traveling and boldly proclaiming the message of Jesus Christ in the synagogues to the people with whom he'd once identified. He used his Old Testament knowledge to present an accurate argumentation of the promise of Jesus.

Later in the chapter, Paul declares that he will turn his primary focus to bringing the message to the gentiles (Acts 13:44–52). Barrett confirms Paul's turning point, saying, "It would be natural to understand these words as a decisive and radical turning-point in Paul's mission."[61] His willingness to interact even with the gentile is evidence that his purpose has directly impacted his values. Paul was aware of the separation between Jew and gentile and would have been exclusive before his conversion: "This continual struggle against contamination from their neighbors led to so hard and exclusive an attitude to other nations that by the time of Christ for a Jew to stigmatize his fellow as 'Gentile.'"[62]

Paul's staunch Jewish upbringing would have limited his interaction with the gentiles, but now he was not only a missionary to them, but an advocate.[63] Acts 15:12 states further evidence of Paul's transformation of turning and defending the mission and salvation of the gentiles.[64] "All the people kept silent, and they were listening to Barnabas and Paul as they were relating what signs and wonders God had done through them among the Gentiles" (Acts 15:12). Paul's advocacy for the gentile and obedience to his calling to the gentiles provides conclusive evidence of his internal transformation from his origins.

Paul's origin of Jewish birth and upbringing created a Jewish leader who persecuted the church; but after encountering Jesus on the road to Damascus, he became an apostle, spreading to the Jews and gentiles the gospel he once opposed. He went from persecuting the church to

60. Polhill, *Acts* (NAC), 297.
61. Barrett, *Commentary on Acts*, 656–57.
62. P. A. Blair, "Gentiles," *NBD*³ 405.
63. Allen C. Myers, "Gentile," *EBD* 410.
64. Silva, *BEB* 2:1627–28.

suffering to grow the church. His internal transformation transformed his purpose, values, and end states.

Paul's Evidence of Transformational Leadership throughout Acts

The origins of Paul reveal a distinct and undeniable personal transformation in his life. However, his leadership was not limited to internal change; it shifted an entire religious institution, church, and ideologies for generations. The influence of Paul's leadership is woven into the fabric of the church. Achtemeier recounts the early leaders of the church and confirms Paul's equal authority: "Two disciples of Jesus, Peter and John, and his brother James occupied leading positions and exercised responsibility (Acts 3:1; 15:6–22; Gal 2:9). Paul, who had no connection with the historical Jesus, was eventually regarded as their equal."[65] As an apostle, Paul was not lesser in his authority, despite his not being an original disciple. Murray states, "In the present context the aorist ἔδωκεν points to a single event—Christ's appointment of Paul as an authoritative apostle at the time of his conversion. Although God was also actively involved in Paul's call into apostleship and service (1 Cor. 1:1; Gal. 1:1, 15–16; 2 Tim. 1:1)."[66] God called Paul and gave him the authority to fulfill his purpose.

Confident in his God, Paul, who was given calling and authority, stood in his own defense to the church of Corinth (2 Cor 10:8). Plummer agrees that Paul is affirming his authority: "All he says is that he can give ample evidence that he is a minister of Christ, invested with His authority."[67] Paul defends his authority but not without acknowledging Jesus Christ as the source and the purpose to fulfill his initial calling.[68] Thrall confirms, "That Paul does have his initial calling in view is probably indicated by the aorist tense of ἔδωκεν. Second, this authority was given for constructive purposes, εἰς οἰκοδομήν."[69] Since Paul's initial calling, he had been attempting to build up the church he once destroyed. God gave Paul his authority, but only according to his designated purpose.

---

65. Paul J. Achtemeier, "Church," *EBD* 168–69.
66. Harris, *Second Epistle to Corinthians*, 693.
67. Plummer, *Second Epistle to Corinthians*, 280.
68. Plummer, *Second Epistle to Corinthians*, 281.
69. Thrall, *Second Epistle of Corinthians*, 624.

However, the influence of Paul was not limited to the church of Corinth, but he planted churches throughout the nations. Robinson takes into account Paul's documentation of geographical outreach and church plants:

> Paul, however, claimed to have preached the gospel "from Jerusalem and as far round as Illyricum" (Rom. 15:19), and we know that he founded churches on the Antiochene pattern in the S provinces of Asia Minor, in Macedonia and Greece, in W Asia where he made Ephesus his base, and, by inference from the Epistle to Titus, in Crete. Whether he founded churches in Spain (Rom. 15:24) is unknown. Everywhere he made cities his centre, whence he (or his associates) reached other cities of the province (Acts 19:10; Col. 1:7.[70]

The widespread authority of Paul in the church is well documented throughout the entirety of the New Testament, especially in Paul's own letters.

Each of Paul's letters gives a clear indication of Paul's influence in each of the churches he led, planted, and oversaw, but also his authority overall for all church usage. O'Brien notes the purpose and significance of Paul's letters to the churches:

> But Paul's letters were "more than private." He wrote self-consciously as an apostle, that is, as a representative of the risen Christ (note the emphasis on apostleship in Gal 1:1, 15, 16; 5:2) in order to instruct, give advice, encourage and reprimand (note 1 Thess 5:27 and 2 Thess 3:14–15 regarding the impact on the church at Thessalonica). Most of Paul's letters were addressed to communities of Christian believers and were intended for public use within the congregations. They were occasional, contextual writings addressing particular situations (though not Ephesians), and were the substitutes for Paul's personal presence.[71]

Paul's writings are evidence of his authority as an apostle of Jesus Christ. His rebukes, corrections, and direction are a clear indication of the church's willingness to accept Paul's authority. The unquestionable leadership of Paul requires an in-depth review of his mobilization and revolutionary transformation.

---

70. Robinson, *NBD*³ 201–2.
71. Peter T. O'Brien, "Letters, Letter Forms," *DPL* 551.

Mobilization

As noted previously, at a basic level, a leader with no followers would not be considered a leader. Despite Paul's claims of influence and authority, there must be a measure to determine his transformational leadership. "And in no society are there leaders without followers or followers without leaders."[72] Paul's interpersonal transformation should lead to an active leadership that transforms followers in which he claims authority. Burns adds that a measure of transformational leadership is the stimulation of followers. "The result of transforming leadership is a relationship of mutual stimulation and elevation that converts followers into leaders and may convert leaders into moral agents."[73] Therefore, a leader's role is to activate and mobilize followers to a higher end state, morality, and goals.

"Leaders have a special role as activators, initiators, mobilizers."[74] For Paul to be considered a transformational leader, followers must be morally and motivationally activated. "Exceptional leadership may also make a difference in transforming dormant into active followers."[75] The follower's transformation is evidence of an effective leader; therefore, Paul needs to be evaluated on his ability to stimulate and elevate followers into moral agents. Therefore, there should be evidence of new and active moral agents that change to new goals among the followers in the book of Acts.

The missionary journey of Paul had considerable success. Acts 13 highlights Paul being commissioned to fulfill his calling to be set apart for God's mission (v. 2). Toussaint views Paul's being set apart in three stages: "The verb 'set apart' (*aphorizō*) is used of three separations in Saul's life—at his birth he was separated to God (Gal. 1:15); at his conversion he was set apart for the gospel (Rom. 1:1); and in Antioch he was separated for a specific service (Acts 13:2)."[76] God set apart Paul and Barnabas not only for Antioch but also to make followers for the whole church.[77] After the preaching of the message in the synagogue, many of the congregants wanted to hear more.[78]

72. Burns, *Leadership*, 4.
73. Burns, *Leadership*, 4.
74. Burns, *Leadership*, 134.
75. Burns, *Leadership*, 137.
76. Toussaint, "Acts," 2:387.
77. Bruce, *Book of the Acts*, 246.
78. Bruce, *Book of the Acts*, 263–64.

Due to Paul's complete and exegetical messaging, his declaration was well received. Bruce summarizes the results:

> Many of the hearers, however, both Jews by birth and proselytes, followed Paul and Barnabas and showed themselves favorably disposed to the message, with its proclamation of forgiveness and justification through faith in Jesus. Paul and Barnabas encouraged them to continue in this mind, to persevere in their joyful response to the grace which God extended to them in the gospel.[79]

Luke details both Jews by birth and proselytes' decisions to follow Paul. Barrett defines proselytes: "Luke here uses a noun that had come to have a precise meaning; proselytes were converts to Judaism who had fulfilled all the requirements of their new religion: they had been both circumcised and baptized and had offered (or caused to be offered) a sacrifice."[80] Defining proselytes provides background about the group of people who decided to follow Paul despite their commitment and sacrifice to become converts of Judaism. After being sent out to fulfill his calling, Paul and Barnabas had immediate success among Jews and proselytes, urging them to continue in the grace of God (Acts 13:43).

Paul concluded his message encouraging those who believed to be active as followers in their newfound grace.[81] Their mobilization of the mission continued in the following verses as the whole city gathered to hear the word (Acts 13:44). Polhill describes this event: "The word had spread like wildfire through the Gentile populace, and they were there en masse."[82] However, their popularity was not well received among all the Jews with many of them being jealous of the demand for their message with the inclusion to the gentiles (Acts 13:45). Bruce distinguishes between the receptivity of the Jews and gentiles, stating:

> The local Jews, almost invariably, gave a corporate refusal to the gospel (though in every place there were some among them who did believe it), and it was accordingly proclaimed to Gentiles, who embraced it in large numbers. It was regularly the Godfearing Gentiles who attended the synagogue that formed the nucleus of Paul's "churches of the Gentiles."[83]

79. Bruce, *Book of the Acts*, 264.
80. Barrett, *Commentary on Acts*, 654.
81. Toussaint, "Acts," 2:390.
82. Polhill, *Acts* (NAC), 308.
83. Bruce, *Book of the Acts*, 266.

Instead of celebrating the gentile and partaking in the gospel, the jealousy of the Jews led them to contradict the gospel message. Polhill adds clarity:

> The reason for their sudden change in receptivity was evident: their "jealousy" was over the presence of all these Gentiles. It was one thing to proclaim the coming of the Messiah to the Jews. It was quite another to maintain that in the Messiah God accepted the Gentiles on an equal basis.[84]

Their desire for the gentiles to become proselytes blinded their ability to recognize the message of the gospel to Jew and gentile.[85] At this point, the Jews refused to mobilize and remained stagnant in their beliefs.

Their jealousy did not deter Paul and Barnabas as they turned their attention to their calling to the gentiles. They were emboldened further despite the opposition of the Jewish leadership. Barrett provides background to their response: "Contradiction did not silence Paul and Barnabas. Παρρησιάζεσθαι is characteristic of Acts (9:27, 28; 13:46; 14:3; 18:26; 19:8; 26:26; elsewhere in the NT only twice). Παρρησιασάμενοι εἶπαν, *they boldly said*, participle and finite verb describe coincident action."[86] Their message to the Jews was clear and direct.

They were supposed to go to the Jews first, but their rejection turned them to the gentiles. Barrett clarifies Paul's remarks about turning to the gentiles: "Already before this point Paul had evangelized Gentiles (11:25f.): indeed, in his call he had been commissioned to act as missionary to the Gentiles (9:16; 22:21; 26:17)."[87] Paul was not just starting his calling to the gentiles but recognized the future rejection from the Jews and focused on the gentiles.

Barrett believes Paul and Barnabas meant they would no longer evangelize the Jews at the synagogue. "The suggestion can scarcely be that Paul had not preached to Gentiles already, but rather that he would continue to do so, without troubling about the Synagogue."[88] However, Polhill documents Paul's future trips to the synagogues:

> Paul would no longer turn to the Jews; he would now witness only to Gentiles. Such was not the case. In the very next city

84. Polhill, *Acts* (NAC), 308.
85. Bruce, *Book of the Acts*, 266.
86. Barrett, *Commentary on Acts*, 656; emphasis original.
87. Barrett, *Commentary on Acts*, 657.
88. Barrett, *Commentary on Acts*, 7.

on his missionary itinerary, he would again begin his witness in the synagogue (14:1) [see also Acts 16:13; 17:1, 10, 17; 18:4, 19; 19:8]. Again and again he experienced the rejection of the Jews and turned to the Gentiles of that town. But he never gave up on his fellow Jews. It was very much the problem he wrestled with in Rom 9–11. In spite of the overwhelming rejection of the Gospel by his own people, Paul could not bring himself to believe that the rejection was final and that God had deserted them. His great successes in witness were indeed among the Gentiles, but he never abandoned his witness to Jews. The ambiguity of the witness to the Jews persists to the very end of Acts and is never definitively settled (cf. 28:17–28).[89]

Therefore, Paul was communicating to the gentiles about the historical context of the Israelites' failure to be a light to the nations and now his intention to follow the prophecy (Isa 42:6; 49:6).

Toussaint interprets Paul's use of Isaiah: "In thus turning to the Gentiles Paul and Barnabas saw an outworking of the prophecy of Isaiah 49:6, 'I have made you a light to the Gentiles.' This Old Testament passage has at least three applications—to Israel (Isa. 49:3), to Christ (Luke 2:29–32), and to Paul, the apostle to the Gentiles."[90] Marshall agrees, saying,

> The early Christians saw the fulfilment of the prophecy in Jesus (cf. the citation of Isa. 42:1–4 in Matt. 12:17–21, and of Isa. 53:7f. in Acts 8:32–35), but the present passage asserts that the mission of the Servant is also the task of the followers of Jesus. Thus, the task of Israel, which she failed to carry out, has passed to Jesus and then to his people as the new Israel; it is the task of bringing the light of revelation and salvation to all the peoples of the world (cf. the clear allusion to Isa. 49:6 in Luke 2:29–32).[91]

This pivotal moment and bold statement declared the intent of Paul's mission. Despite Israel's contradiction and opposition, he was determined to fulfill the calling and prophecy to the gentiles.[92] Paul's decision not to allow the opposition to stop him from proclaiming, even if the Jews declined their calling, created a joyous response with immense success (Acts 13:48).

---

89. Polhill, *Acts* (NAC), 308.
90. Toussaint, "Acts," 2: 390.
91. Marshall, *Acts*, 245.
92. Bruce, *Book of the Acts*, 267.

Not only did a joyous response occur among the gentiles, but they also became the beginning of mobilization, as many of them made the decision to believe.[93] Bruce recounts the following events: "Distasteful as this announcement was to the synagogue leaders, it was joyful news to the Gentiles who heard it, and many of them believed the gospel."[94] The Jews attempted to contradict the gospel message of Paul, but the gentiles glorified God for the gift of eternal life. Barrett expounds on the plausible reason for joy: "The Gentiles hearing this rejoiced; a way of salvation had been opened to them, and it was not fenced with the unwelcome rite of circumcision."[95]

The conversion of the gentiles is the beginning of mobilization of the mission. Although a numerical number is not given, "many" can be defined as "all those who" God appointed. Polhill concurs, adding, "On their part these Gentiles took an active role in believing, in committing themselves to Christ; but it was in response to God's Spirit moving in them, convicting them, appointing them for life. All salvation is ultimately only by the grace of God."[96] Through God's predetermined plan to convict the gentiles of salvation, Paul successfully converted many to eternal life.

The spread of the word was not limited to those who heard, but it also began to spread through the entire region (Acts 13:49). Barrett believes the translation was quite literal, that "here one could translate quite literally, the word was carried through the whole region."[97] The excitement and receptivity continued to grow and is well documented.[98] Toussaint provides scriptural support: "The good news was shared so that the Word of the Lord spread through the whole region (cf. 6:7; 12:24; 19:20)."[99] This is the beginning of the gentile mobilization of the gospel. The morality and motivation began to increase the moment the gentiles converted. The gentiles awakened to their participation in the gospel and their shared morality as Christians.

Acts 14 repeats the pattern of Paul's ministry with his teaching in the synagogues and a decisive number of people believing (Acts 14:1).

93. Polhill, *Acts* (NAC), 308.
94. Bruce, *Book of the Acts*, 267.
95. Barrett, *Commentary on Acts*, 658.
96. Polhill, *Acts* (NAC), 308.
97. Barrett, *Commentary on Acts*, 659.
98. Polhill, *Acts* (NAC), 308.
99. Toussaint, "Acts," 2:391.

Toussaint summarizes Acts 14, stating, "The Spirit of God was clearly prospering the apostles' ministry, as evidenced by their preaching so effectively that a great number of Jews and Gentiles believed, But again there was opposition."[100] However, this time the number of people is more definitive. BDAG defines it as "being a large number, many, a great number of."[101] A large number of people believed, but later in the chapter, Luke accounts that disciples were made as well (Acts 14:21). Even after opposition in Lystra, Iconium, and Pisidian Antioch, Paul and Barnabas proceeded to Derbe with more communal success.[102]

Paul's journey did not limit his geographical reach when he traveled to Derbe. Polhill provides geographical details: "Derbe was the easternmost church established on the mission of Paul and Barnabas."[103] The establishment of the church required active participation and communal development. Polhill elaborates on the structure used by Paul and Barnabas:

> The two apostles returned the way they had come, revisiting the newly established churches along the route—first Lystra, then Iconium, and finally Pisidian Antioch. In each congregation they performed three essential ministries. First, they strengthened the disciples (v. 22a). This probably refers to their further instructing the Christians in their new faith [Acts 15:36].[104]

In support of the communal focus of Paul and Barnabas, BDAG defines the word "disciples" as "almost exclusively to denote the members of the new community of believers, or followers."[105] However, these new disciples of the community needed encouragement to continue in their faith. Barrett affirms that "new disciples need to be strengthened, confirmed, established in the faith."[106]

Making new converts alone is not enough without also encouraging them, exhorting them to endure suffering, and building community. Barrett concurs: "The process of strengthening is described in the next lines; it includes exhortation, the warning that suffering must

---

100. Toussaint, "Acts," 2:391.
101. "πολυπλήθεια," BDAG 847.
102. Barrett, *Commentary on Acts*, 685.
103. Polhill, *Acts* (NAC), 318.
104. Polhill, *Acts* (NAC), 319.
105. "μαθητής," BDAG 610.
106. Barrett, *Commentary on Acts*, 686.

come but leads to the kingdom, the appointment of ministers, and committal to the Lord."[107] The focus of Paul and Barnabas to build an active community was intentional and strategic. They encouraged new believers, exhorted them to continue despite challenges, and structured the church for continual growth.

In Acts 15, Paul and Barnabas continued their mission but this time returned to the places where they had proclaimed the gospel. Paul and Barnabas wanted to assess the Christian community at each location.[108] According to Barrett, the word "visit" is not limited to a physical encounter, but "the word means visit in the sense of review."[109] Paul's intention to review was not simply to report but to strengthen each place accordingly (Acts 15:41). BDAG defines "strengthen" as "to cause someone to become stronger or more firm, *strengthen,* in our of believers in connection with their commitment and resolve to remain true, esp. in the face of troubles."[110] Therefore, Paul's review of the places in which he had proclaimed the gospel was to assess new Christians and their communities' commitments and to help secure their faith in the face of possible trouble. Paul's mobilization continued despite opposition and conflict. His determination to continue the mission to create active followers is evident in his willingness to return to new believers to affirm their faith.

Leader Transformation

Paul was intentional not only in his mission and community development but also in his discipleship of leaders for the cause. Burns addresses a leader's ability to elevate followers to leaders: "Transcending leadership is dynamic leadership in the sense that the leaders throw themselves into a relationship with followers who will feel 'elevated' by it and often become more active themselves, thereby creating new cadres of leaders."[111] Acts 16 highlights Paul's decision to mobilize and transform individuals for leadership (v. 3). Paul decided to take Timothy, a young disciple, with him as he continued his mission. Barrett summarizes v. 3, saying, "Paul wished him [Timothy] to go with him. 1 Thess. 1:1; 3:2, 6 are sufficient to show

---

107. Barrett, *Commentary on Acts,* 686.
108. Barrett, *Commentary on Acts,* 753.
109. Barrett, *Commentary on Acts,* 753.
110. "ἐπιστηρίζω," BDAG 381; emphasis original.
111. Burns, *Leadership,* 20.

that a man called Timothy accompanied Paul on the 'second missionary journey' and assisted in a mission that included Macedonia."[112]

"Paul's decision to take Timothy along on the mission exposed him to the mission and development of Christian communities."[113] Their relationship was well documented, as well as Timothy's mobilization as an active disciple of the mission. Kvidahl details the development of the relationship between Paul and Timothy, stating that "Timothy became a vital member of Paul's inner circle, as seen in the number of references to him in a number of Pauline prescripts (2 Cor 1:1; Phil 1:1; Col 1:1; 1 Thess 1:1; 2 Thess 1:1; Phlm 1)."[114]

Paul created and fostered healthy discipleship and allowed Timothy the experience necessary to be a leader in the church.[115] Gillman describes Timothy:

> A missionary associate, fellow worker, and trusted emissary of Paul over an extended period of time. Timothy is mentioned after Paul in the prescript of various Pauline letters as a cosender of those letters (1 Thess 1:1; 2 Cor 1:1; Phil 1:1; Philemon 1; cf. also 2 Thess 1:1; Col 1:1). He is variously identified as "our brother" (1 Thess 3:2; 2 Cor 1:1; Philemon 1), as "fellow worker" (1 Thess 3:2; Rom 16:21), and as Paul's "beloved and faithful child in the Lord" (1 Cor 4:17; cf. 1 Tim 1:2) who enjoys a special relationship with this apostle (Phil 2:20–22; cf. 1 Tim 1:2, 18; 2 Tim 1:2; 2:1).[116]

It is clear that Paul intentionally mobilized future leaders who would create more active followers within the Christian community. Elwell and Comfort describe the future role of Timothy: "In 2 Corinthians 1:19, Timothy is named, along with Paul and Silas, as men who were proclaiming the good news about Jesus Christ. Paul put Timothy in charge of the church at Ephesus and wrote him two pastoral letters to help him perform that responsible task."[117] Timothy's discipleship led to his future leadership in the church, resulting in continual mobilization.

Three stages of mobilization are obvious in Paul's transformational leadership. This pattern repeated itself throughout the book of Acts in

112. Barrett, *Commentary on Acts*, 760.
113. Polhill, *Acts* (NAC), 343.
114. Cliff Kvidahl, "Timothy," *LBD*, para. 4.
115. John Gillman, "Timothy (Person)," *ABD* 558.
116. Gillman, *ABD* 558.
117. Elwell and Comfort, *Tyndale Bible Dictionary*, 1259.

Athens, Corinth, Berea, Thessalonica, and many other geographical locations (Acts 16–21). He led people to conversion, community, and leadership development. He was never content with people deciding to believe, and so he made a conscious effort to make active participants in their faith and communities. His willingness and intentionality to strengthen individuals is clear in his return to locations of the new followers to encourage, strengthen, and affirm their faith. Additionally, he recognized the need to develop more leaders for the community, which became clear in his discipleship of Timothy. Paul completed Burns's definition of the mobilization of a transformational leader: "The result of transforming leadership is a relationship of mutual stimulation and elevation that converts followers into leaders and may convert leaders into moral agents."[118] A survey of Paul's leadership in the book of Acts reveals his intentionality in developing a community of dedicated believers and leaders.

Paul's Revolutionary Leadership

Unquestionably, sufficient evidence exists to support Paul as a revolutionary transformational leader. Revolution "in its broadest meaning is a complete and pervasive transformation of an entire social system. It means the birth of a radical new ideology; the rise of a movement bent on transforming society on the basis of that ideology."[119] The transformation of a society demands a revolutionary leader that is willing to be characteristically different. Burns highlights a successful revolutionary leader's dedication, ability to addressing needs, pursue conflict, and being missional:

> But we know some of the requirements for success. The leaders must be absolutely dedicated to the cause and able to demonstrate that commitment by giving time and effort to it, risking their lives, undergoing imprisonment, exile, persecution, and continual hardship. Thus, Castro and his small band experienced constant privation. This commitment, which may end in martyrdom, must survive all defeats and setbacks. Too, the revolution, like all genuine leadership, must address the wants and needs and aspirations of the populace—motives that may not be felt by followers at the time but can be mobilized through propaganda and political action. Further, a revolution requires conflict, as does all leadership. But revolutionary conflict is

118. Burns, *Leadership*, 4.
119. Burns, *Leadership*, 202.

more extreme; it is dramatized in the characters of saints and devils, heroes, and villains. As the lines become more sharply drawn between the establishment or elite and the poor and the rebelling, doctrine and purpose are hardened in the crucible. Finally, there must be a powerful sense of mission, of end-values, of transcending purpose. These processes can be summarized in a phrase: the raising of social and political consciousness on the part of both leaders and followers.[120]

Although the characteristics are similar, revolutionary leaders are extreme, resolute in their purpose, undauntedly committed to the cause, and immovable in mobilization. It is vital to survey Paul's leadership in the book of Acts to investigate whether his leadership aligns with Burns's definition of a revolutionary leader. A careful review of Acts proves Paul's willingness to be committed fully despite risking his life, imprisonments, exile, persecution, and continual hardship. In addition, his dedication to the mission, values, and transcending purpose will become evident with a complete review of Acts following Paul's internal transformation and proclamation of the gospel.

The life of Paul was in juxtaposition from being a person that put believers' lives at risk, imprisonments, exile, and persecution to suffering the same fate for Christianity. Toussaint draws the distinction, stating, "Saul had left Jerusalem an inveterate enemy of Christianity to persecute the church in Damascus; but in God's sovereign grace he joined the believers and preached the gospel in that very city."[121] The book of Acts documents Paul's shift from persecutor of the church to his continual suffering, risks, imprisonments, and exiles.

Paul was continually at risk, even to the point of his own documented martyrdom. However, the book of Acts does not encompass the totality of Paul's suffering on behalf of the mobilization of the gospel. Brown suggests that comparing Paul's account of his tribulations with what one can read about him in Acts "shows that, if anything, Acts might lead us to underestimate the apostle's extraordinary career."[122] Outside of the book of Acts, in Paul's epistles, he lists his own suffering and his viewpoint on his continual distress.

Second Corinthians 11:23–28 lists Paul's suffering in detail. Lowery addresses Paul's summarization in view of Luke's account in Acts:

120. Burns, *Leadership*, 202–3.
121. Toussaint, "Acts," 2:378.
122. Brown, *Introduction to New Testament*, 557.

> The details concerning his ministry which Paul disclosed in this verse reveal how fragmentary is his biographical information in the Book of Acts. The writing of this letter coincided with the events mentioned by Luke in Acts 20:2. At this point in Luke's narrative he mentioned only one imprisonment (in Philippi), one beating (also in Philippi; Acts 16:22), and one brush with *death* (the stoning in Lystra; Acts 14:19). Yet, in 2 Corinthians, Paul referred to numerous incidents of this kind. Perhaps they occurred before his formal missionary journeys (Acts 13–20), or maybe Luke did not find it necessary to record them.[123]

Garland summarizes Paul's account in his writing: "Next, he claims that he has far greater hardships, more imprisonments, more beatings, more scrapes with death. His language reveals that these were typical, recurring situations."[124] Paul's own accounts detail his outlook on suffering and the validation to his ministry.[125] His leadership and effectiveness as a leader were not in the number of churches he planted, but the amount of suffering he partook on behalf of the gospel. Paul's validation of his ministry in 2 Corinthians concurs with Burns's definition of a revolutionary leader. Paul's definition of his leadership is identical to Burns's description of a transforming leader's willingness to risk his life to the point of martyrdom.

The persistent threat and risk to Paul's life came early in his ministry. Paul's immediate start to preaching the gospel of Jesus in the synagogues after his conversion created a simultaneous and abrupt opposing reaction (Acts 9:20). Pervo summarizes the persistent conflict: "The prediction of suffering in v. 16 is a common feature. In short, if you want to be a narrative hero, be prepared to suffer."[126] His ability to communicate the gospel continued to grow, frustrating Jews who then "plotted to do away with him" (Acts 9:23–24). The Jews' plan was to wait on him day and night for an opportunity to put him to death. However, Paul's associates thwarted their plan by putting him down through an opening in the wall. Paul gives his own account in 2 Cor 11:32–33, detailing how they let him down in a basket through a window in the wall.

"In any case, Paul saw the incident as being particularly humiliating, listing it as the crowning event of his trials as an apostle (2 Cor 11:23–33).

---

123. Lowery, "2 Corinthians," 2:581.
124. Garland, *2 Corinthians*, 495.
125. Harris, *Second Epistle to Corinthians*, 798.
126. Pervo, *Acts*, 244.

Acts pictures the same—Paul under trial, Paul the persecuted."[127] The Jews were persistent in their desire to stop Paul's proclamation of the gospel of Jesus Christ. Toussaint argued that the Jewish opposition is thematic in the book of Acts: "One of the themes in Acts, underscored in this paragraph is the Jewish leaders' opposition to the gospel."[128] Acts 9 establishes the premise and repetition of Luke's account of Paul's continual suffering on behalf of the gospel.

In the midst of external pressures, internal apprehension was revealed within the disciples (Acts 9:26). Paul wanted to associate with the disciples, but they were afraid of him.[129] According to BDAG, the definition of associate is to "*join oneself to, join, cling to.*"[130] Paul had a genuine desire to join the disciples but, due to his history, he met apprehension and fear. Barrett describes the disciples' natural inclination of distrust: "It was equally natural for the disciples not to trust him; would he not prove to be a surreptitious infiltrator, perhaps an agent provocateur? It was impossible to believe that a man who recently was organizing the persecution of Christians was now himself a disciple."[131]

Despite Paul's internal transformation, he still faced rejection within the leadership. Barnabas had to stand up to the disciples to testify to Paul's transformation:

> In any event, Barnabas fulfilled his mediating role, securing Paul's acceptance in the apostolic circle. Paul was now "with them" (v. 28). The Greek text says literally that he was "going in and out among them" in Jerusalem. The expression is familiar from Acts 1:21, where it refers to the circle of apostles. That meaning may well be intended here. Paul was fully accepted into the apostolic circle. He too was a "witness" for Christ.[132]

Without Barnabas's allegiance, internal conflict could have hindered Paul's future affiliation and leadership. The inclusion within the inner circle of the apostles secured his ability to go in and out among them.

Acts 13 addresses another account of Paul's suffering. Conflict arose again due to Paul's bold proclamation of the gospel. However, Luke

---

127. Polhill, *Acts* (NAC), 242.
128. Toussaint, "Acts," 2:377.
129. Polhill, *Acts* (NAC), 243.
130. "κολλάω," BDAG 556; emphasis original.
131. Barrett, *Commentary on Acts*, 467.
132. Polhill, *Acts* (NAC), 243.

provides the motivation of the Jews' distaste for Paul's missional success. They were filled with jealousy after seeing the crowds and began to contradict and blaspheme (Acts 13:45). The Jews' jealousy led them to speak against Paul, slandering him.[133] Paul retorted that he would turn to the gentiles. However, when words did not stop Paul's calling, they resorted to instigating persecution (Acts 13:48). Barrett defines the Jews' actions: "The Jews now went beyond the verbal opposition of v. 45. Παροτρύνειν, like the simple verb, means to incite."[134]

The Jews were strategic in their persecution, recruiting others to expel Paul and Barnabas from the city. Bruce summarizes the events:

> The Jewish leaders could not prevent the Gentiles from accepting the gospel, but they could make the place too hot to hold the missionaries. This they did by prejudicing the civic authorities of Pisidian Antioch against them. The wives of many of these authorities—like well-to-do women in many other cities of the Roman world—were attracted to the Jewish religion and were found among the God-fearing Gentiles who frequented the synagogue, and it was evidently through them that their husbands were influenced, to the disadvantage of Paul and Barnabas. Luke is at pains to represent the Jewish leaders as foremost in stirring up opposition to Paul in one place after another, rather than civic or provincial authorities acting on their own initiative.[135]

The recruitment of God-fearing gentiles, civic leaders, and prominent women reveals the extreme measures the Jews were willing to use for persecution.[136] Pervo confirms the success of the persecution: "The Jews launch a persecution, that is, they demand legal action that results in the expulsion of the missionaries."[137] However, this did not discourage Paul and Barnabas, for they dusted off their feet, left the city, and continued their mission.[138]

When expulsion would not stop Paul's mobilization, the risk increased with every visit and proclamation of the gospel. Acts 14 repeats the pattern of Paul entering the synagogue and gaining momentum with both Jews and Greeks. Again the Jews stirred and instigated the

---

133. "ἀντιλέγω," BDAG 89.
134. Barrett, *Commentary on Acts*, 659.
135. Bruce, *Book of the Acts*, 268.
136. Polhill, *Acts* (NAC), 308–9.
137. Pervo, *Acts*, 344.
138. Polhill, *Acts* (NAC), 309.

gentiles to think badly and be angry at Paul.¹³⁹ Paul persisted boldly to proclaim the gospel, but the city was divided. According to BDAG, *divided* means "to tear apart a group through conflicting aims."¹⁴⁰ With this definition in mind, the city was not divided peaceably; rather, it was torn apart due to the conflict. Bruce describes the torn city: "At last a riot broke out, and the city mob was incited to assault and stone the two men."¹⁴¹ The opposition led an attempt to mistreat and stone Paul and Barnabas. Barrett does not separate the words "mistreat" and "stone": "The content of the move against the missionaries is expressed in two infinitives (BDR §393. 5, n. 7), ὑβρίσαι (a general term, *to insult* or *to injure*, or both) and λιθοβολῆσαι."¹⁴²

Both terms distinguish the opposition's desire to injure Paul and Barnabas. Polhill summarizes the events:

> The opposition to the two grew to such a point that a plot was hatched to stone them (v. 5). It does not seem to have been a question of official synagogue stoning since the Gentile populace was equally involved with the Jews. The whole picture seems to have been one of mob violence rather than expulsion by the city officials, as was the case in Pisidian Antioch.¹⁴³

Again, Paul and Barnabas suffered at the hands of the Jews, gentiles, and city officials. This time, however, it was no longer expulsion but a clear intent to harm or injure. The mob mentality of the divided city pushed Paul and Barnabas out of the city as they fled to Lycaonia, Lystra, and Derbe, and the surrounding region (Acts 14:6). As they continued their journey to Lystra, the conflict followed (Acts 14:8–19).

The people of Lystra confused the healing of a lame man by Paul as indicating a divine visitation of the Greek gods Zeus and Hermes.¹⁴⁴ When Paul and Barnabas heard the crowd's conclusion, they tore their robes and rushed into the crowd to contradict their beliefs (Acts 14:14). They questioned the crowd, asking why, after the proclamation of the gospel, they credited vain things. Their reasoning stopped the crowd from sacrificing to them, but the Jews from Antioch and Iconium won over the crowd against

139. "κακόω," BDAG 502.
140. "σχίζω," BDAG 981.
141. Bruce, *Book of the Acts*, 271.
142. Barrett, *Commentary on Acts*, 672; see also Blass et al., *Grammatik des neutestamentlichen Griechisch*, 271.
143. Polhill, *Acts* (NAC), 311–12.
144. Bruce, *Book of the Acts*, 274.

them (Acts 14:19). Polhill explains the distance the opposition had to travel to stir the crowd: "In any event, they were turned against Paul and Barnabas by a group of Paul's former Jewish opponents who had come from Iconium and even the 100 miles from Pisidian Antioch."[145]

This time, the mob succeeded in stoning Paul before dragging him out of the city supposing him to be dead. Paul recounts this stoning in his own words. Bruce correlates Paul's writing and Luke's account:

> When, some years later, he recalled the hardships he had endured for the gospel's sake, he says, "once I was stoned" (2 Cor. 11:25), referring necessarily to this occasion. And when, writing to Christians in the cities which figure in the present narrative, he says, "I bear on my body the marks of Jesus" (Gal. 6:17), those marks or *stigmata* certainly included the indelible scars left by the stones at Lystra.[146]

Despite Paul's unwillingness to receive divine, the people still pursued him for his persecution. His opponents were determined to persecute Paul and Barnabas, even if they must travel one hundred miles to accomplish their plan.[147] This time, they achieved violence, with the culmination of Paul's perceived death. Again, this did not stop Paul; as soon as he could get up the next day, he continued his mission (Acts 14:20).

The next conflict arose when some men came down from Judea preaching circumcision as a part of salvation. However, this conflict deserves a critical review. In order to understand this fundamental conflict, a discovery of the correlation of Gal 2 and the identity of the men from Judea has to take place.[148] Polhill describes the possible correlation:

> In Gal 2 Paul told of a conference in Jerusalem that had many similarities to Acts 15:1–35. Although the two accounts contain significant differences, the similarities seem to outweigh these, and it is probable that they relate to the same event. Both dealt with the issue of circumcision, Paul and Barnabas defended their views against the more conservative Jewish Christians in both accounts, and the final agreement was reached in both that the Gentiles would not be required to submit to Jewish proselyte circumcision. In Gal 2:1–10, Paul did not go into the question of table fellowship between Jewish and Gentile

145. Polhill, *Acts* (NAC), 317.
146. Bruce, *Book of the Acts*, 279.
147. Barrett, *Commentary on Acts*, 683.
148. Barrett, *Commentary on Acts*, 698.

Christians (though Gal 2:11–14 clearly concerns table fellowship between Gentile and Jewish Christians), but that issue was a natural outgrowth of the decision not to require Gentiles to live by the Torah. That it comprised part of the agenda at the Jerusalem Conference is highly plausible. In any event, it will be assumed in the commentary that follows that Paul and Luke were referring to the same conference, and where appropriate Paul's account will be cited to supplement that of Acts.[149]

Polhill describes the similarities of Paul's account with circumcision and conservative Jews. However, the differences of the time line of the table fellowship and whether the men are from Jerusalem remain significant.

Bruce suggests two options for the men from Judea: "The people who came down from Judaea may have been those who, in Paul's narrative, came to Antioch 'from James' (Gal 2:12). Whether they were so or not, they exceeded the terms of their commission, according to the apostolic letter in verse 24. Another possibility is that they were the 'false brothers secretly brought in' of Gal 2:4."[150] However, the time line for the men coming to the table fellowship follows the initial conflict with the men from Judea. Conzelmann reconciles the differences:

> This verse is reminiscent of Gal 2:12; however, the conflict described there takes place *after* the conference (we find an echo of that conflict in Acts 15:39). Luke avoids saying that these Jewish Christians come from "Jerusalem." Instead he uses the general term "Judea" to indicate that they were not agitating under orders from the Jerusalem church.[151]

Bruce agrees that the men in the initial conflict correlate with Gal 2:4 and the table conflict follows the conflict in Gal 2:11–21.

According to the similarities, the men from Judea were not the same as the men who came from James. Barrett adds possible reasoning for Luke's inclusion of Judea: "Judaea may be intended in an ethnic rather than a strictly geographical sense; they came from Jewish territory and may therefore be expected to represent a Jewish point of view."[152] Luke's emphasis of their origin draws attention to the possible reasoning for their staunch views. In addition, Luke's geographical location provides

---

149. Polhill, *Acts* (NAC), 322.
150. Bruce, *Book of the Acts*, 286.
151. Conzelmann, *Acts of the Apostles*, 114–15; emphasis original.
152. Barrett, *Commentary on Acts*, 698.

evidence that the men were not from James but were conservative Jews who began teaching the custom of Moses on circumcision.[153]

Their main concern was the rapid growth of the gentiles being saved without evidence of circumcision. No indication suggests that they had been circumcised when they joined the Christian fellowship. Polhill agrees that "they had laid no such requirements on the Gentiles converted in their recent mission. It is altogether likely that the large number of such converts in their successful mission had attracted the attention of this Judaizing group in the first place."[154] Bruce provides another motivation for the Jewish believers: "The rapid progress of Gentile evangelization in Antioch and farther afield presented the more conservative Jewish believers with a serious problem."[155]

The Jews were willing to accept gentiles, but only if they complied with the Jews' conditions of circumcisions. Their teaching created great dissension and debate with Paul and Barnabas. Luke used two words to describe Paul and Barnabas's reaction to their false teaching. According to BDAG, dissension means lack of agreement respecting policy, strife, discord, and disunion.[156] Myers adds, "While Gk. *schísma* carries the connotation of severe disagreement, it may also refer to a discussion in which various opinions are aired."[157] Paul would not agree with their policy and was willing to disunify and engage in severe disagreement. However, Paul did not just disunify, but he also engaged in a controversial discussion and argument to prove their teaching was inaccurate.[158] Barrett concurs, adding that "Luke does not mean to suggest that the conflict ended in murder, but sharp contention (not merely discussion) is clearly indicated."[159]

Paul and Barnabas were very willing to engage in conflict for the truth of the gospel. Barrett notes the position of Paul and Barnabas: "Paul and Barnabas, leaders in the church of Antioch (11:26) and pioneer missionaries on its behalf (13:1–3) are named as leading contenders on the non-circumcision side; cf. Gal. 2:4f."[160] Paul stood amid conflict willing

---

153. Barrett, *Commentary on Acts*, 698.
154. Polhill, *Acts* (NAC), 323.
155. Bruce, *Book of the Acts*, 286.
156. "στάσις," BDAG 940.
157. Allen C. Myers, "Dissension," *EBD* 287.
158. "ζήτησις," BDAG 429.
159. Barrett, *Commentary on Acts*, 700.
160. Barrett, *Commentary on Acts*, 700.

to challenge anyone over the unification of Jew and gentile through the gospel of Jesus Christ. This conflict remained unsolved but traveled with Paul and Barnabas to Jerusalem with the apostles and elders.

Paul's willingness to engage in conflict was not limited to the opposition but also arose within his fellow believers, including other apostles. Following the Council of Jerusalem, Paul and Peter engaged in a confrontation (Gal 2:11–17). Longenecker carefully compares Paul's willingness to withstand conflict while Peter submitted to the pressure.

> Just as Paul withstood the pressures of the "false brothers" at Jerusalem, so Peter should have withstood those exerted by the delegation from James. There may have been a common practical concern behind such pressures. But to turn that concern into a theologically based call for Gentile Christians to practice a Jewish lifestyle was tantamount to a denial of the Christian gospel. Paul saw this clearly at Jerusalem; Peter should have seen it as well at Antioch. And the same is true for Gentile believers of Galatia.[161]

After the decision of the council, it was clear the gentiles were saved without circumcision, therefore eliminating any physical (circumcision) reason for dissension. However, the harmonic decision did not result in table fellowship, and this conflict revealed the still-present reality of failure of unity for table fellowship.[162]

As a result, Paul fearlessly confronted Peter in his wrong and was willing to stand for his values despite the mounting pressure from the men from James. Polhill states, "What Peter lacked, Paul possessed in full measure: the courage of his convictions."[163] This conflict is covered in ch. 3, and the comparison will happen in ch. 5. Paul's rebuke restated the values and goals of the gospel for both Jew and gentile. Amid confronting Peter, Barnabas—Paul's co-laborer in ministry—was carried away by Peter's hypocrisy (Gal 2:13). Burton notes "that even Barnabas, who shared with Paul the apostleship to the Gentiles, yielded to the pressure exerted by the brethren from Jerusalem shows again how strong was the influence exerted by the latter."[164]

Paul's willingness to stand firm, despite losing a travel companion, loyal apostle, and co-laborer in the mission reveals his fortitude and

---

161. Longenecker, *Galatians*, 80.
162. Burton, *Epistle to the Galatians*, 106.
163. George, *Galatians*, 179.
164. Burton, *Epistle to the Galatians*, 109.

resolve.[165] George addresses Paul's fortitude: "Still, the fact that "even Barnabas" could be pressured to yield over the issue of table fellowship indicates both the strong influence exerted by the legalistic Jewish Christians and the loneliness of Paul's resistance to their demands."[166] Paul's revolutionary leadership on behalf of the values and mission was evident in his willingness to risk close relationships and confront his fellow leaders. Paul states his defense that both Jew and gentile are justified by faith in Jesus Christ. God's justification declares both Jew and gentile righteous, which is to *"be acquitted, be pronounced and treated as righteous* and thereby become."[167]

Campbell paraphrases Paul's defense: "Paul's argument was addressed to those who were Jews by birth, including Peter and himself, who, in spite of their superior advantages, were saved by faith. Why then bind the Law on Gentile sinners (said in irony because of Peter's actions), who likewise were saved by faith in Christ?"[168] According to Paul's argument, both Jew and gentile need to have faith, despite the Jews' privileged heritage. The mission of Paul for the salvation of Jew and gentile directed his cause, even if he risked being cast out by his fellow apostles.

Following the internal conflict with Peter, Paul continued his mission with Silas. Acts 16 follows a similar pattern of Acts 14 as the crowd turned against Paul. However, this time Paul turned the crowd against him after commanding a spirit of divination out of a slave girl who followed Paul around repeating that Paul was a bondservant of the Most High God (Acts 16:16–17). The master, recognizing the loss of profit with the spirit of divination being removed from the slave girl, dragged Paul in front of the magistrates. Bruce summarizes the events: "The good deed done to the slave girl was not at all to the liking of her owners; when Paul exorcized the spirit that possessed her, he exorcized their means of income: she could no longer tell fortunes."[169]

Paul and Silas were placed in front of the authorities for their judgment on the matter. The magistrates of the Roman colony were municipal or dignified praetors used to settle judicial or legal matters concerning disturbances in the city.[170] They declared Paul and Silas as Jews causing

165. A. F. Walls, "Barnabas," *NBD*³ 123.
166. George, *Galatians*, 176–77.
167. "δικαιόω," BDAG 249; emphasis original.
168. Campbell, "Galatians," 2:595.
169. Bruce, *Book of the Acts*, 314.
170. Bruce, *Book of the Acts*, 314.

confusion by their proclamations of customs, which were unlawful as Romans. Barrett provides background: "It implies that it was illegitimate for Romans (members of a *colonia*) to adopt foreign customs, especially Jewish customs."[171] Polhill adds the motivation for the magistrates and the crowds to revolt against them, that "The appeal to anti-Jewish sentiments and to nationalistic Roman pride won over the crowd (v. 22). The insinuation of a threat to civil order evidently won over the magistrates."[172]

With the crowd now aroused, the magistrates tore their robes in horror and ordered that Paul and Silas be stripped, beaten with rods, and thrown in prison.[173] Their punishment had no judicial proceedings; the magistrates used their authority pre-trial to beat foreigners with their rods.[174] The magistrates carried a bundle of rods with an axe inserted to inflict corporal punishment.[175] According to Keener, this would discourage any followers of the accused of following in the disorder: "Sometimes, as here, the accused were stripped first. Public beatings served not only to secure evidence but also to humiliate those beaten and to discourage their followers."[176]

Luke's account of the scourging corresponds with one of three beatings in Paul's account in 2 Cor 11:25.[177] Toussaint agrees: "This was one of the three beatings Paul referred to in 2 Corinthians 11:25, the only other place where this verb occurs in the New Testament."[178] Luke accounts for the numerous blows Paul and Silas received before being thrown in prison with tight security. The jailer placed them in the inner prison while having their feet fastened in stocks (Acts 16:23–24). The specific mention of the inner prison and stocks highlights the lengths the jailor took to secure Paul and Silas in prison and their immense discomfort.[179]

Bruce details the possible pain the stocks could have caused: "These stocks had more than two holes for the legs, which could thus be forced apart in such a way as to cause the utmost discomfort and cramping

---

171. Barrett, *Commentary on Acts*, 790.
172. Polhill, *Acts* (NAC), 353.
173. Barrett, *Commentary on Acts*, 791.
174. Keener, *New Testament*, Acts 16:22, "Exorcism and Economics," para. 7.
175. Bruce, *Book of the Acts*, 315.
176. Keener, *New Testament*, Acts 16:22, "Exorcism and Economics," para. 7.
177. Bruce, *Book of the Acts*, 315.
178. Toussaint, "Acts," 2:400.
179. Polhill, *Acts* (NAC), 353.

pain."[180] The inner prison often was described as a dungeon.[181] This pain did not stop Paul and Silas from praising God through hymns, and after a miraculous escape, they even stopped to share the gospel with the jailor. Paul was unhindered by his persistent opposition, beating, and imprisonment; rather, he was emboldened to continue. Although they experienced rejection by the crowds and city leadership, Paul and Silas still had the courage to lead the jailor and his family to salvation.

In both Acts 17 and Thessalonica, Berea repeats the pattern of opposition and risk Paul encountered while successfully sharing the gospel.[182] Again in jealousy, the Jews raised up the crowds and authorities against Paul. "Once again Jewish unbelievers (from Thessalonica) forced the expulsion of Paul. Stirring is from the same Greek word used in verse 8 to speak of being 'in turmoil.'"[183] Again, they used the laws to ban them from the city, so Paul had to escape with the help of the brethren.

After leaving Athens, Paul entered Corinth in ch. 18. A similar pattern of teaching in the synagogue took place, and he was testifying to the Jews, but they again resisted and blasphemed. Polhill addresses this pattern: "The pattern was the same as in the synagogue of Pisidian Antioch (13:44–47), and it would be repeated again, right up to the end of Acts (28:23–28; cf. 19:8–9)."[184] Toussaint also documents the constant opposition: "Once again is seen the pattern of Jewish opposition to the gospel, followed by Paul's subsequent turning *to the Gentiles* (cf. 13:7–11, 46; 14:2–6; 17:5; 19:8–9; 28:23–28)."[185] The blaspheming and resistance are not new in the narrative of Paul's efforts and his subsequent return to the gentiles. However, Paul adds an additional statement: "Your blood be on your own heads! I am clean. From now on I will go to the Gentiles" (Acts 18:6).

After shaking off his garments, he declared the Jews were responsible for their own destruction.[186] Bruce explains Paul's statement, that "He had discharged his responsibility to them, he assured them; if they would not accept the news of salvation which he brought, he was now

---

180. Bruce, *Book of the Acts*, 315.
181. Polhill, *Acts* (NAC), 353.
182. Polhill, *Acts* (NAC), 360.
183. Toussaint, "Acts," 2:402.
184. Polhill, *Acts* (NAC), 384.
185. Toussaint, "Acts," 2:405; emphasis original.
186. Toussaint, "Acts," 2:405–07.

free of blame."[187] His efforts to spread the gospel despite their consistent resistance and opposition is no longer his responsibility.[188] Polhill summarizes Paul's actions: "We find the same language in Ezekiel's picture of the prophet as a watchman over Israel (33:1–7; cf. 3:18). So, Paul always fulfilled his role of witness to his fellow Jews. When it was no longer possible to bear that witness, he moved to the Gentiles."[189]

The Lord recognized Paul's consistent risk and came to him in a vision telling him not to be afraid and to continue to speak. The Lord assured him, "For I am with you, and no man will attack you in order to harm you, for I have many people in this city" (Acts 18:10). This vision predicated the upcoming civil opposition and God's desire for Paul to maintain his mission in Corinth. Polhill provides the background:

> In the present instance Paul's vision fortified him for the extensive witness in Corinth. Corinth was the first city where Paul settled for an *extensive* period of missionary activity. The pattern heretofore had been for such strong opposition to arise against Paul and his companions in cities where they witnessed as to force their departure. He had no reason to expect otherwise in Corinth. In 1 Cor 2:3, he even stated the fear and misgivings he had at first.[190]

In every other city after the opposition, Paul had to escape due to the impending danger. However, the Lord wanted Paul to stay, promising that he would not suffer harm despite the same Jewish and civil opposition. The Lord knew the work that had to be done in Corinth, and that reassurance helped Paul endure. Barrett concludes that "Paul is to continue his ministry without fear of opposition, for, as will appear, there are in Corinth many who are, potentially and by predestination (cf. 13:48), the Lord's people, and it is therefore impossible that Paul's work should be in vain."[191]

Luke forecasted Paul's long-term work of teaching for a year and a half in the following verse (Acts 18:11). Although no one harmed Paul, that did not stop the Jews from stirring up legal opposition. The Jews brought Paul before Gallio, accusing him of misleading men to worship

---

187. Bruce, *Book of the Acts*, 349.
188. Barrett, *Commentary on Acts*, 867.
189. Polhill, *Acts* (NAC), 384–85.
190. Polhill, *Acts* (NAC), 386; emphasis original.
191. Barrett, *Commentary on Acts*, 870.

PAUL'S TRANSFORMATIONAL LEADERSHIP AFTER PENTECOST   149

God outside of the law. But Gallio rejected Paul's opportunity to defend himself and told the Jews to handle this matter in an internal manner.[192] Paul again was willing to face exile, but God's promise prevailed. Paul remained in the city before departing of his own will.

The beginning of Acts 19 follows Paul's missionary journey and documents another repetitious incident of opposition (Acts 19:8–9). Paul repeats his pattern in the synagogue but then removes himself due to the hardness and disobedience. Later in the chapter, however, Paul encountered an abnormal conflict with the gentiles, this time in Ephesus (Acts 19:11–41). Toussaint recognizes the similarities: "In only two incidents recorded in Acts did Gentiles oppose Paul: (a) here and (b) in the case of the Philippian fortune-teller (16:16–24). In both cases, the opposition was because of vested monetary interests."[193]

This time, Paul confronted the idols—two goddesses. Polhill describes the idol worship:

> The whole incident was instigated by one of the silversmiths of Ephesus named Demetrius. His own trade consisted of fabricating silver shrines of Artemis, i.e., silver replicas of the temple of Artemis for which Ephesus was renowned. The manufacture of such shrines was a common practice. Pilgrims would purchase them for use in their own home altars or as a votive offering to be presented to the temple.[194]

According to Demetrius, Paul's opposition to idol worship and preaching of "the way" was leading the crowds away from the temple. Paul's preaching was changing Demetrius's economic growth and the purchasing of idols. However, the charges were dropped and the assembly dismissed, despite the outcry; the town clerk declared that Paul was not profaning the gods or robbing the temple.[195] Paul was in constant defense despite his persistence in sharing "the way." Again, this did not stop Paul as he continued the mission to Macedonia.

In ch. 19, Paul decided to head to Rome. "While in Ephesus, toward the end of his ministry there, Paul made a major decision. He determined to conclude his mission in the east and to move farther westward to

---

192. Polhill, *Acts* (NAC), 388.
193. Toussaint, "Acts," 2:411.
194. Polhill, *Acts* (NAC), 408.
195. Barrett, *Commentary on Acts*, 936.

Rome."[196] Toussaint concludes that the remainder of the book focuses on Paul's trajectory toward Rome and his ministry there: "Paul's sights were now set on *Rome* (via *Jerusalem*) with the ultimate goal of reaching Spain (Rom. 1:15; 15:22–24)."[197] On the way to Rome, Paul again encountered the plot of the Jews (Acts 20:3). However, Luke briefly addressed this encounter now that his focus was on Paul's preparation for Jerusalem.[198] Paul himself states his intent to go to Jerusalem despite the unknown and unforeseen future circumstances (Acts 20:22).

Barrett addresses Luke's brief account: "The visit to Corinth seems to have been a difficult one, difficult and stormy even if in the end triumphant. Problems and success are alike passed over in Acts."[199] Despite Luke's brief account, Acts 20:3 reveals the Jews' persistence and presence even on Paul's journeys. Paul addressed their efforts to prevent him from traveling to Spain (Rom 15:22–24). The success of Paul's missionary travels was not predicated on the opposition, but rather, on the mobilization of the gospel. Later in Acts 20, in his farewell to Ephesus, Paul gives an account of his suffering for the gospel to the elders of the church (Acts 20:22).

Bruce expands on the reasoning for Paul's farewell speech: "The speech which follows is not only his farewell speech to them (and to the church which they represented) but (so far as the perspective of Acts is concerned) his last will and testament to the churches which he had planted both east and west of the Aegean."[200] His farewell account is a testimony of persistent opposition, exiles, beatings, and imprisonments on behalf of the gospel (Acts 20:19). Paul has resolved that no matter what his upcoming suffering in Jerusalem, he cannot hold his life dear; his mission is more important than his possible suffering (Acts 20:24). Larkin summarizes:

> Paul's obedience includes an ability to live with uncertainty even when what he does know about the future is not encouraging. Whether by prophet or direct revelation, the Holy Spirit testifies to him in every city that *prison and hardships* (better "afflictions" born of persecution, *thlipsis*) await him in Jerusalem [Acts 20:18–27].[201]

---

196. Polhill, *Acts* (NAC), 406.
197. Toussaint, "Acts," 2:411; emphasis original.
198. Bruce, *Book of the Acts*, 381–82.
199. Barrett, *Commentary on Acts*, 946.
200. Bruce, *Book of the Acts*, 387.
201. Larkin, *Acts*, "An Apostle's Model Work" (20:18–27), para. 7.

Paul no longer valued his life above his God-given purpose.

Bruce addresses Paul's outlook: "Self-preservation was not a motive which he esteemed highly: his main concern was to fulfil the course which Christ had marked for him to run, preaching in the Spirit's power the good news of God's free grace in Christ."[202] Paul repeated his determination to live his God-given purpose despite consistent opposition. "For I did not shrink from declaring to you the whole purpose of God" (Acts 20:27). According to BDAG, to shrink away means "to be hesitant in regard or avoid with fear."[203] Paul is stating that despite his opposition, trials, and suffering, he never avoided his purpose. In his goal to mobilize the church and the leadership, he encouraged the elders to have the same attitude for the purpose of the gospel (Acts 20:28–31). Chapter 20 highlighted Paul's missionary outlook and revealed how purposeful and determined he was for the gospel. His definition of his leadership mimics Burns's definition of a revolutionary leader. However, Paul was not finished with his calling; he continued his journey to Jerusalem.

Despite continual warning and impending dangers in Paul's travel to Jerusalem, his determination led him to his mission. As Paul continued to travel, the disciples of Tyre tried to warn Paul not to set foot in Jerusalem (Acts 21:4). The Spirit led them to warn Paul in hopes that they could dissuade him from continuing his journey for his safety.[204] Again, in v. 11 a prophet illustrated what he foresaw of Paul being bound and handed over to the gentiles in Jerusalem. The people of the town began to beg Paul not to go to Jerusalem. Despite these two warnings, Paul's response reflected his earlier statements of his willingness to die in his dedication to his calling.[205] Bruce summarizes the encounter:

> He could not turn aside from the path of obedience and sacrifice, and he was prepared, if necessary, to suffer death as well as imprisonment for his Master's sake. He was not unmoved by his friends' tearful pleas and begged them to desist from attempting to soften his determination.[206]

The crowd recognized Paul's unquestionable commitment and submitted to the will of God for Paul's mission to Jerusalem. Again, Paul mirrored

---

202. Bruce, *Book of the Acts*, 390.
203. "ὑποστέλλω," BDAG 1041.
204. Toussaint, "Acts," 2:415.
205. Barrett, *Commentary on Acts*, 997.
206. Bruce, *Book of the Acts*, 402.

the definition of Burns's revolutionary leader with his willingness to risk his life to challenge existing social, religious, or political systems.

Paul finally reached his destination in Jerusalem, and the warnings of the disciples and prophets came to fruition. In only seven days of Paul's presence in the temple, the Jews stirred the crowd, laid hands on Paul, and falsely accused him again. This attack was not from a new opponent:

> He was spotted there by some Asian Jews, who immediately began to stir up a crowd against him. Not surprisingly, the opposition to Paul came from Asian Jews, probably some from Ephesus. Paul had spent three years in Ephesus and part of the time in their synagogue (19:8). They knew him well. In his Miletus address, Paul alluded to plots the Ephesian Jews had already directed against him.[207]

They had prior knowledge of Paul's teaching and disturbance to their strict adherence to the Jewish rituals. This time, the Jews wanted effective opposition and were determined to stop Paul from further disruption.[208]

They hurled serious accusations and charges against Paul, hoping for a severe penalty. Polhill summarizes the charges levied against Paul:

> The accusations they began to make against Paul were very serious. Two were the same charges leveled against Stephen (cf. 6:13): He speaks against "our law and this place"; i.e., against Torah and temple. The third charge was less specific but perhaps the most valid—that Paul taught "against our people." In a sense, Paul did. His leveling gospel of oneness of all in Jesus Christ, Greek as well as Jew, could ultimately do nothing other than reduce the significance of the Jews as God's chosen people. In this instance they charged him with temple violation. They accused Paul of having violated the temple by taking a Gentile beyond the court of the Gentiles into the sacred precincts that were open to Jews only; i.e., into the area of the temple proper. The large outer courtyard, known as the court of the Gentiles, was open to all. The temple proper was not. In fact, there was a stone barrier that separated the court of the Gentiles from the first courtyard of the temple proper, the court of the women.[209]

They were determined to accuse Paul and punish him according to their laws, which were similar to their accusations of Stephen.

207. Polhill, *Acts* (NAC), 451.
208. Bruce, *Book of the Acts*, 409.
209. Polhill, *Acts* (NAC), 451–52.

They were upset with Paul's interaction with the Greeks and his willingness to include the Greeks into the gospel and oneness of Jesus Christ. However, their charges were sure to upset the Jews by stating Paul's decision to bring Greeks into the sacred areas of the temple.[210] The Jews stirred the crowd to the point that Luke states the whole city was provoked (Acts 22:30). Polhill elaborates: "But one must recall that the temple area was very much the 'town square.' The court of the Gentiles was a large area, and great crowds would gather there. When all the hubbub started, people came running from every direction."[211]

They rushed Paul, grabbed him, and dragged him out of the temple, shutting the doors behind them. The commander bound him while the crowd shouted so loudly that the commander could not hear the accusations. The violence was so great that they took Paul to the barracks. Barrett describes the scene of violence: "He was carried up the steps (ἀναβαθμοί) by the soldiers to protect him from the crowd."[212] Their accusations confirm Paul's continual challenges to their existing religious systems. Their violence toward Paul reveals the immense challenges Paul provided to the Jews and their cultural restrictions.

The following chapters detail Paul's defense before varying audiences as he stood accused. In ch. 22, Paul used his Roman citizenship to stand before the Jews and defend his ministry. Despite Paul's defense, the commander recognized the great dissension stirred and decided to lock Paul up for his own safety (Acts 22:10). The possible violence against Paul was evident that it was safer to lock Paul away from the crowd. Polhill confirms the events, stating, "Whereas Lysias's original seizing of Paul could be seen as an arrest (21:33), this time there is no doubt the tribune served as his protector."[213]

Following his defense, the Lord comforted Paul and encouraged him to continue his witness to Jerusalem and to Rome (Acts 23:11). That did not stop the Jews from planning future violence against Paul. Forty Jews vowed not to eat or drink until they had killed Paul (Acts 23:12). They conspired to bring Paul before the Sanhedrin, but the plan was thwarted when Paul's nephew heard about the plan (Acts 23:16). The commander ordered Paul put under the protection of soldiers to be moved to Caesarea before Felix the governor (Acts 23:23).

210. Bruce, *Book of the Acts*, 409–10.
211. Polhill, *Acts* (NAC), 453.
212. Barrett, *Commentary on Acts*, 1023.
213. Polhill, *Acts* (NAC), 471.

Chapters 24–27 review Paul's travel and appearances before Felix, Festus, and Agrippa. As the Lord stated, ch. 27 highlights Paul's travel on the way to Rome. However, his travel was not without risk: he was shipwrecked and snake-bitten on his journey to Rome. Polhill summarizes the shipwreck narrative:

> The overarching theme of the shipwreck narrative is the providence of God. The central verse is 27:24: God delivered Paul and all who sailed with him for the ultimate purpose of the apostle's witness before Caesar. Paul's witness in Rome has been a central focus since he first conceived of it in Ephesus (19:21). While imprisoned in Jerusalem, the Lord assured him in a vision that he would surely witness in that city (23:11). Now, in the midst of the howling storm, Paul was given a final assurance that in God's providence the testimony before Caesar would take place. It is perhaps the major theme of Acts—the triumph of the witness to Christ.[214]

Paul's journey to Rome reiterates his determination to fulfill his purpose.

Luke's detailed account of the unfortunate travel events at the end of Acts is unique and gives the reader a view of Paul's determination. Bruce provides insight into Luke's motivation:

> Luke's devoting so much of his narrative to the details of those few weeks at sea is best explained by his desire to emphasize the divine determination that Paul's purpose of seeing Rome must be fulfilled, despite all the factors that rendered his ever getting there unlikely in the extreme.[215]

Paul's determination to reach God's chosen destination would not be deterred, even when everyone else was without hope. Paul recounts the shipwreck—days in the deep water and days hungry—in 2 Cor 11:23–27.

His complete dedication was not thwarted by shipwreck or snakebite. God was still faithful to Paul and the mission while Paul was a prisoner and under duress.

> Nowhere is this clearer than in the shipwreck narrative. Paul was delivered, but he was delivered to bear witness. He was still a prisoner in chains when he bore his witness in Rome. The book closes with his bold, unrestricted proclamation in the capital city. The gospel had reached its ultimate destination as set forth

---

214. Polhill, *Acts* (NAC), 512.
215. Bruce, *Book of the Acts*, 475.

in Jesus' commission to the apostles (1:8). It had reached the "ends of the earth."[216]

The Lord's purpose that Paul be a witness before Caesar motivated Paul to complete the mission. God's intention was for the gospel to be preached even to the remotest parts of the earth. God used a revolutionary leader to complete his mission to mobilize the church and the gospel of Jesus Christ.

A revolutionary leader confronts the existing social system despite impending opposition and risk, imprisonments, and exile. The survey of Acts reveals Paul's repetitious opposition to the religious system. With every opportunity from one city to the next, he was constantly challenging the existing religious system and his reputation followed all the way to Jerusalem. Multiple times he was beaten, exiled, threatened, and accused. However, his determination to complete his purpose of spreading the gospel to Jew and gentile could not be altered to the point of his death. Spreading "the way" and unifying Jew and gentile created persistent and undeniable opposition. Paul's suffering came from all sides, including the government, numerous attempts of the Jews, and two encounters with gentiles. Paul was the image of a revolutionary leader who was necessary to mobilize the values of the gospel and equip others to do the same to the remotest parts of the earth.

Conclusion

The book of Acts highlights the leadership of Paul from chs. 9 to 28, giving clear insight into Paul's transformational leadership. Like Peter, Paul was instrumental in the mobilization of the gospel to Jew and gentile. Luke's historical account of Paul's leadership aligns with Burns's definition of transforming leadership. Paul's origins expose his complete shift in needs, purpose, and values. His biographical account reveals his Jewish upbringing and staunch Jewish education, leading to his complete opposition of the mobilization of the gospel. However, his encounter with Jesus on the road to Damascus transformed his values, ideology, mission, and goals.

Jesus gave Paul his calling and directed him toward his mission. Despite Paul's initial fierce opposition, he eventually led the mobilization of the gospel he once severely threatened. Paul's mobilization was

216. Polhill, *Acts* (NAC), 512.

completely evident—not only in the leaders and followers that were developed under his leadership—but also in church plants. The book of Acts gives a glimpse of Paul's influence as many people became converts and began following "the way." But clearly Paul was not satisfied with conversion alone; he also desired the growth of followers, leaders, and churches. He revisited mission sites to support the growth of the health of the leaders and churches. Paul was intentional in creating disciples who would continue the mission and lead churches in his absence. Paul's efforts were consistent with Burns's definition of mobilization of a transforming leader. Paul replicated Burns's belief that a transforming leader needs to stimulate followers to become moral agents and active participants in the mission.

The task of going to the gentiles did not excuse his work with Jews. However, as Paul persistently pursued his calling of the gospel, he met Jewish opposition. The Jews with whom he'd once stood against "the way" were now arrayed against him. On Paul's missionary journeys, the consistent opposition grew from threats to physical harm, exiles, and imprisonments. In the survey of Acts, in each city and journey, Paul was in conflict from all sides, including from Jew, gentiles, and city leaders. Paul's persistent conflict was consistent with Burns's definition of a revolutionary leader. Burns believes that significant transformation in existing social systems require a leader's extreme dedication, to the point of exile, imprisonment, persecution, and continual hardship.

Based on the evidence presented in Acts, it is obvious that Paul exhibited leadership that resembles Burns's transformational and revolutionary leadership. Before Paul transformed others, he experienced his own transformation from his origins. His revolutionary leadership had its desired effect of conflicting the existing religious structure while mobilizing the gospel. Every city Paul encountered was transformed and challenged to unify both Jew and gentile. Paul would not allow the opposition to deter his mission to the gentiles.

5

The Transformational Leadership of Peter and Paul and the Principles Applied to the Current Church

Since God did not create anyone the same, every person should be evaluated for their individual calling. Aside from Jesus, there are no perfect leaders. Therefore, leaders need to be evaluated individually for their successes and failures. The comparison between the leadership of Peter and Paul in the book of Acts should detail their choices, successes, and mistakes in response to the diversity of the church. Osborne recognizes that both Paul and Peter were representatives to the church. He states, "Again Peter is seen in a representative role (note the fact that in Acts, Paul also has this representative role)."[1] One should review the outcome of their leadership to evaluate effectiveness in their roles, mission, and purpose in the church. Unity, growth, mobilization, doctrinal establishment, and leadership development of the church are outcomes that play integral roles in leadership evaluation.

Evaluation of Paul and Peter in the early church can be useful to apply to modern-day leadership and diversity issues. In addition, the twenty-first-century North American church would benefit from an evaluation of the successes and failures of the early church while dealing with ethnic diversity and unity. This chapter will review and compare the transforming leadership of Peter and Paul from the previous chapters and its effect on the ethnic diversity of the early church. These

---

1. Osborne, *BEB* 2:1665.

findings will then be applied to the current church and its issues with diversity and unity.

Comparison of Transformational Leadership and Responses to the Diversity of Peter and Paul

Contrasting the differences without having a discussion of the similarities of Paul and Peter is a disservice to this current research. Since both leaders had success, a study of their similarities reveals common principles for future leaders. The evaluation of their differences will also discern whether their failures were indicative of their leadership decisions or skills. Following previous chapters, it would be advantageous to continue the same structure in comparing the origins, purposes, mobilizations, and leadership styles.

When reviewing the origins of Paul and Peter, it is important to recognize the similarities of their religious backgrounds. First, they both grew up with similar origins, coming from Jewish cities and families. However, a primary difference is Paul's account of his strict upbringing, including detailing his heritage, education, and family. Throughout Paul's life, he maintained devoted to his religious wants, needs, and values. However, historical support exists that Peter, a Galilean, was receptive to Jesus's ministry without heavy resistance. Therefore, the wellspring wants of Paul and Peter were quite distinct.

Paul strictly opposed Jesus and those who followed him, while Peter readily wanted acceptance by Jesus. While following Jesus and listening to his teaching, Peter was able to transform some of his wants. However, Peter's transmutation of needs created tension while following Jesus, as he questioned Jesus's death (Matt 16:21–23). As noted in chapter 3, Peter desired Jewish reign through Jesus on earth and struggled with the belief of Jesus's death. Despite Peter's struggle, he remained loyal to Jesus throughout his discipleship, and his love remained for Jesus even after his denial (John 21:16). Dissimilar to Peter, Paul never accepted Jesus until his experience on the Road to Damascus.

According to chapter 4, Paul's needs and wants were loyal to his strict upbringing, heritage, and education. His socialization developed a staunch religious identity to the point of him becoming a feared enemy of the church. Despite the difficulty to review historical figures, a brief psychological analysis of Paul and Peter reveals the difference in opposition to Jesus. The review of Paul's origins exposes his extreme origins, which dramatically affected his values, purpose, goals, and morals, while Peter's analysis reveals his tension with his Jewish heritage and his interpretation of Jesus as the Messiah.

Second, due to the origins of Paul and Peter, it was necessary for both to encounter Jesus to transform individually their wants, values, purpose, and morals. The similarities are not limited to their Jewish origins, but rather the necessity for personal transformation. Paul had to experience Jesus on the road to Damascus, and Peter had to be restored after his denial. Despite Peter walking with Jesus, the Messiah, when Jesus declared his purpose, Peter had to transform his values as a leader and unifier of the church. Peter had to relinquish his values of the Jewish heritage and dietary restrictions to unify the church. Jesus provided Peter with a vision removing dietary restrictions that hindered the fellowship of Jew and gentile.

Peter also had to speak at the Council of Jerusalem to lead the debate for gentile salvation without circumcision. In both instances, Peter chose the higher morality of the gospel despite his heritage and previous origins. Distinct from Peter, Paul had a complete transformation from opposing the church to leading the growth and unification of the church. Paul's encounter with Jesus dramatically shifted his perception of Christ and the church. As a strict Jew, Paul vehemently rejected Jesus as the Messiah, but after his conversion, he became the main proponent of spreading the gospel to Jew and gentile to the remotest parts of the earth.

God had to call both individuals from their earlier wants and needs to reorient them to their God-given purpose. As addressed in chapters 3 and 4, Jesus predestined Paul and Peter as instruments for his purpose. Their calling redefined their values and morals as they sought to fulfill God's directions. Both individuals had to reorient their views of the gentiles and their proper place in the church. The purpose of uniting Jews and gentiles required both Paul and Peter to lead the church to its end goals. To lead the church to a higher morality, Paul and Peter both had to transform their own values, morality, and purposes.

After their individual transformations, Paul and Peter had to assert their authority as apostles for the unification of Jew and gentile. Throughout the book of Acts, both Paul and Peter were involved in using their leadership to make dramatic changes to the landscape of the growth of the church. Peter was critical in changing the landscape of the church, starting with preaching at Pentecost, opening dietary restrictions, and removing the Jewish mandate of circumcision. As the Jews struggled with the practices, culture, and traditions, Peter had to challenge the existing religious leadership to accept the gospel for all without the restrictions of circumcision and diet, while standing among his peers to declare the truth of the gospel for the betterment of the church.

Peter was not alone in his leadership. Paul also exerted his transformative leadership to unify the church. Paul persistently stood among his fellow Jews, declaring the gospel despite their consistent rejections. Their denials led Paul to his calling as an instrument to the gentiles. He also had to stand defiantly, declaring both Jew and gentile free from circumcision and unified under the gospel of Jesus Christ (Acts 15:2). That both leaders were willing to lead among their peers, existing religious leadership, and followers is undeniable.

In addition to their similarities, both leaders were unsatisfied with their leadership if the gospel was not mobilized. Both leaders were responsible for leading large numbers of people to the gospel of Jesus. Also, Paul and Peter were satisfied not only with conversion, but also making active followers and equipping leaders. Their transcending leadership developed leaders, churches, and active followers to continue the higher calling of the gospel. In one instance notated in chapter 3, Peter initiated finding disciples to help in the Jerusalem church due to the growth and increasing need for charity (Acts 15:19).

Although Peter actively engaged in the church, more documentation exists of Paul's intentionality with the churches and their followers. As reviewed in chapter 4, Paul was intentional with the followers of "the way." He spent months in many of his missionary journeys with people of the cities and even returned to cities where the gospel was proclaimed to strengthen their faith (Acts 15:36). As noted in chapter 4, Paul spent time in conversion, community, and leadership development. Last, Paul was intentional to make a disciple in Timothy to lead in the local church in his absence. Although Paul and Peter led in mobilization, Luke provided a detailed account of Paul's intentionality of community and leadership development.

In the midst of mobilizing followers, those who object and oppose the transformation of values, morals, and purpose will always be present. A transforming leader has to be willing to take risks to challenge existing social and religious systems.[2] According to the defining terms in chapters

---

2. Burns, *Leadership*, 202–3.

3 and 4, Burns provides terminology that fits both leaders. The fundamental difference in the transforming leadership of Peter and Paul was Peter's practice of reformed leadership. As addressed in chapter 3, Peter receded under religious pressure rather than oppose failed receptivity to new morality. George addresses Peter's attitude "that Peter's vacillating and expedient behavior was a denial of this basic gospel truth."[3]

As documented, Peter's decision hindered the mobilization of the gospel as many, including Barnabas, followed Peter's decision to withdraw. His use of reformed leadership hindered the progress of the unification of Jew and gentile among the church of Antioch. In stark opposition to Peter, Paul confronted Peter for his hypocrisy. Paul's willingness to confront Peter revealed the consistent difference in leadership. Paul's confrontation of Peter is indicative of Paul's revolutionary leadership. As defined in chapter 3, a revolutionary leader is dedicated and able to demonstrate commitment with time, risking life, imprisonment, exile, persecution, and continual hardship to confront existing systems even at the risk of the leader's life.[4]

A complete survey of the book of Acts in chs. 3 and 4 reveals that both Peter and Paul displayed revolutionary leadership.[5] One area in which that is evident is their willingness to conflict with existing political and religious institutions for their higher values and end goals. Peter and Paul were both willing to confront existing religious institutions, whether it was the Sanhedrin or current government powers. Both Paul and Peter were imprisoned and persecuted for the mobilization of the gospel. However, in Acts and in Paul's own accounts in 2 Corinthians, numerous details exist of Paul's suffering and near-death experiences. According to 2 Cor 11:22–33, Paul felt validated as an apostle through his suffering and persistent risk. Despite the repetition of Paul's risk, it is evident that both apostles were willing to suffer and exhibit dedication to the gospel.

Church Transformation of Diversity under Peter's Leadership

The measure of a leader's success is not just his followers, but the influence and desired outcome of his purpose. Peter was not seeking popularity, but

3. George, *Galatians*, 181.
4. Burns, *Leadership*, 202–3.
5. Chs. 3 and 4.

rather, the conversion of Jew and gentile and the unification of the church. As Burns notes, leadership is not about power, but about the ability to have influential relationships. He writes, "This is not to exorcise power from its pervasive influence in our daily lives; recognizing this kind of power is absolutely indispensable to understanding leadership. But we must recognize the limited reach of 'total' or 'coercive' power. We must see power—and leadership—as not things but as relationships."[6]

The review of leadership is not the analysis of power; instead, it is the relationship that shares motivation and purpose.[7] Therefore, the analysis of Peter's leadership is not his coercive power, but the relationship with leaders, churches, and followers. A survey of the book of Acts will reveal Peter's ability to transform relationships between Jews and gentiles in the church. The church's growth is unlimited to numerical growth, but also unity in shared motivations and purpose between Jew and gentile. It is also critical to review the problems within the followers, leaders, and churches to analyze any possible failures of Peter's leadership.

Growth of the Church

The book of Acts documents the birth and growth of the church.[8] In a broader sense, Luke documents the entire spread of Christianity. Brauch describes Acts in this way: "Luke grounds his documentary of the rapid expansion of Christianity in the history of the Roman Empire and Palestine during the three decades from AD 30 to 60. Some brief historical and geographical considerations will aid in understanding Luke's history."[9] Since Peter is a major part of the growth of Christianity, there are benefits to correlating Peter's leadership with the mobilization.[10] Elwell and Comfort separate the book of Acts into sections, stating that "Acts falls naturally into two parts, chs. 1–12 and 13–28. Roughly speaking, the first part contains the "acts of Peter."[11] Osborne summarizes the first part of Acts with Peter's leadership:

---

6. Burns, *Leadership*, 202–3.
7. Burns, *Leadership*, 12.
8. Elwell and Comfort, *Tyndale Bible Dictionary*, 10.
9. Brauch, *BEB* 1:19.
10. Elwell and Comfort, *Tyndale Bible Dictionary*, 14.
11. Elwell and Comfort, *Tyndale Bible Dictionary*, 14.

It is he who proposes the choice of the 12th disciple (1:15–17), who proclaims the gospel at Pentecost (2:14–40), who utters the healing word (3:6), who defends the gospel before the Sanhedrin (4:8–12, 19, 20; 5:29–32). The episode regarding Ananias and Sapphira is particularly poignant, for here Peter functions as the avenging angel of Yahweh; nowhere is his authority more evident. This authority also surfaces in the scene at Samaria concerning the attempt of Simon the Sorcerer to buy the charismatic power (8:18–24). Again, it is Peter whose influence commands the situation. In these two incidents we certainly see the "binding and loosing" jurisdiction (cf. Mt 16:19) exhibited in Peter.[12]

A survey of chs. 1–12 reveals Peter's leadership in the beginning of the Christian movement from the province of Syria.[13]

Peter's leadership is critical in the birth and initial spread of Christianity. Bruce separates the first section of Acts: "The coming of the Holy Spirit and the rise and early progress of the church of Jerusalem (1–5). Then it describes the dispersal of the Hellenistic members of that church."[14] As discussed in chapter 3, Peter's leadership in the birth of the church begins at Pentecost. Robinson captures the time line and formulation of the church: "The church in the Christian sense appeared first in Jerusalem after the ascension of Jesus. It was made up of the predominantly Galilean band of Jesus's disciples together with those who responded to the preaching of the apostles in Jerusalem."[15]

Mangum summarizes Peter's involvement in the beginning of the Jerusalem church at Pentecost: "In 1:1–2:47 the promised Spirit is poured out at Pentecost, and Peter preaches the Pentecost sermon: God raised Jesus, whom Israel crucified. Many Israelites repent, are baptized, and receive the Spirit, and the Jerusalem church grows" (Acts 1:1—8:3).[16] Peter had an instrumental role in preaching the gospel of Jesus Christ, beginning the growth of the Jerusalem church.

Initial growth was just the beginning of the Jerusalem church, but Peter's leadership continued as the church continued to grow and formulate structure. Donfried presents Peter's involvement. He writes, "The second significant matter which needs to be examined is

12. Osborne, *BEB* 2:1664–65.
13. Elwell and Comfort, *Tyndale Bible Dictionary*, 12.
14. F. F. Bruce, "Acts," *NBD*³ 11.
15. Robinson, *NBD*³ 200.
16. Mangum, *New Testament*, "The Beginnings of the Jerusalem Church," para. 1.

the relationship of Peter to the Jerusalem church. In Acts 8:14, 9:32, and 15:6–7, 22–23, Peter and the Jerusalem apostles are mentioned at significant points in the development of the Christian missionary strategy."[17] Following the structure of Acts 1:8, the witness of the apostles was supposed to begin in Jerusalem.

Although debate ensues about the structure of leadership in the Jerusalem church, Peter's vital role in the development is undeniable. Paul refers to Peter as one of the pillars of the Jerusalem church in Gal 2:8–9.[18] Peter was a part of developing the church and continued the mission; however, at some point, he transitioned his leadership to James.[19] Robinson defines early church leadership: "The first leadership of the church was by the twelve (Galilean) apostles, especially PETER and JOHN, but soon gave way to that of ELDERS in the regular Jewish manner, with JAMES the brother of Jesus as president (Gal. 2:9; Acts 15:6ff)."[20] Whether Peter was just a foundational or a continual leader, he was fundamental in the leadership structure and theological development. Osborne regards Peter's role as "the dominant director of church policy."[21]

Peter led the process of creating policy for the church. This is evidenced following Pentecost when the new believers began to create community. The first step in the formation of the Christian church was for people to receive the gospel of Jesus Christ. Acts 2:37–47 documents the ingathering in which Peter directed the new believers to repent, be baptized in the name of Jesus Christ for the forgiveness of sins, and receive the Holy Spirit. Peter led the Jews in their recognition of their sin of the rejection of the Messiah Jesus Christ to repentance.[22] After presenting the gospel at Pentecost, he set the precedent for the community and their reception of the gospel message.[23]

After Peter's message, over three thousand souls were saved. They formed a community in Jerusalem and dedicated themselves to four elements of communal growth. Fitzmyer summarizes the community's commitment:

---

17. Karl P. Donfried, "Peter (Person)," *ABD* 254.
18. Bruce, *Book of the Acts*, 283.
19. Donfried, *ABD* 254.
20. Robinson, *NBD*³ 200.
21. Osborne, *BEB* 2:1664–65.
22. Polhill, *Acts* (NAC), 116.
23. Fitzmyer, *Acts of the Apostles*, 264.

> Four things are noted as characteristic of Jerusalem Christians: their adherence to "the teaching of the apostles," "communal form of life," "the breaking of bread," and "prayers." The "teaching" of the apostles means more than the *kērygma*, "the proclamation" about the death, resurrection, and significance of Christ. What the apostles taught was the basis for what the church of Luke's own day was still teaching. *Koinōnia*, "communal form of life," is the first way that Luke names the Christian church in Acts.[24]

Along with the apostles, Peter's teaching was critical in the development of the community, beginning with their understanding of the death and resurrection of Jesus Christ. The apostles' authority helped establish the community and future generations of Christians. Bruce writes about the influence of apostles on future generations:

> The community, the apostolic fellowship, was constituted on the basis of the apostolic teaching. This teaching was authoritative because it was the teaching of the Lord communicated through the apostles in the power of the Spirit. For believers of later generations, the New Testament scriptures form the written deposit of the apostolic teaching.[25]

It's undeniable that the apostles, including Peter, dramatically affected the practices of the community. Doctrine and policy were set by the teaching of the apostles. Their healthy community was united through sincere fellowship, serving the needs of the community, and breaking bread at each other's homes. The Lord continued to add to their number and continued to grow (Acts 2:47). Robinson confirms that "the church became large (Acts 21:20) and included even priests and Pharisees in its membership (6:7; 15:5)."[26]

Despite the initial development of the Jerusalem church, intentionality existed for the community to spread.[27] Bruce agrees: "As the old Israel had its dispersion among the Gentiles, so must the new people of God be dispersed."[28] To review Peter's involvement in the spread of the gospel to other communities past his leadership in Jerusalem is advantageous. Elwell and Comfort described the mobilization of the

---

24. Fitzmyer, *Acts of the Apostles*, 269.
25. Bruce, *Book of the Acts*, 73.
26. Robinson, *NBD*³ 200.
27. Barrett, *Commentary on Acts*, 413.
28. Bruce, *Book of the Acts*, 163.

gospel through Peter. They write, "Peter and John came to Samaria (8:14), the next significant step toward the gentile mission. Thus ended the centrality of Jerusalem in the unfolding story."[29] The significance is the movement not only toward the gentiles but also to the Samaritans, whom the Jews despised. Their acceptance required the supervision and approval of Peter and John. Bruce discusses Peter's role:

> News of Philip's evangelistic enterprise in Samaria was brought to Jerusalem, and the apostles sent two of their number to Samaria to inspect this work. In the earlier years of the Christian mission, the Jerusalem apostles seem to have regarded it as their duty to exercise a general supervision over the progress of the Gospel wherever it might be carried (cf. 11:22). Peter and John, the two leaders of the apostolate, carried out this mission.[30]

Peter came to ensure the salvation of the Samaritans into the community. The divide among Jew and Samaritans was so immense that it was necessary for the apostle's authoritative involvement. Polhill adds, "Through Peter and John's participation, the Samaritan mission was given the stamp of approval of the mother church in Jerusalem."[31] Peter's laying hands on the people who accepted the gospel can be interpreted as the Samaritans' evidence of their incorporation into the new community.[32] Bruce again describes the significance of Peter's actions:

> In the present instance, some special evidence may have been necessary to assure the Samaritans, so accustomed to being despised as outsiders by the people of Jerusalem, that they were fully incorporated into the new community of the people of God. It was one thing for them to be baptized by a free-lance evangelist like Philip, but not until they had been acknowledged and welcomed by the leaders of the Jerusalem church did they experience the signs which confirmed and attested their membership in the Spirit-possessed society.[33]

Peter played an integral role in the acceptance of the Samaritans in the community of Christianity. The apostle's presence solidified the solidarity

---

29. Elwell and Comfort, *Tyndale Bible Dictionary*, 1023–24.
30. Bruce, *Book of the Acts*, 168.
31. Polhill, *Acts* (NAC), 218.
32. Barrett, *Commentary on Acts*, 412.
33. Bruce, *Book of the Acts*, 170.

and fellowship with the Samaritans.³⁴ Despite initial success, evidence suggests that Samaritans did not form a large community.³⁵

Peter's mission continued throughout all regions like Lydda, Joppa, and Caesarea (Acts 9:32). However, in the city of Caesarea, a significant encounter changed the landscape of mobilization of the gospel. Bruce confirms:

> The range of the apostolic message has been steadily broadened. Already it has begun to cross the barrier which separated Jews from Gentiles; now the time has come for that barrier to be crossed authoritatively by an apostle. The apostle who crossed it was Peter, the leader of the Twelve; the place where he crossed it was the largely Gentile city of Caesarea. The Gentiles who first heard the gospel from his lips were the family and friends of Cornelius, a centurion in the Roman army, belonging to one of the auxiliary cohorts stationed in Judaea.³⁶

The encounter with Cornelius set the precedent for the spread of the gospel to the gentiles. As defined in chapter 3, Peter's vision about dietary restrictions opened the opportunity for the gospel to spread to the gentiles with genuine fellowship.

Additionally, Peter's leadership in meeting with Cornelius established the impartiality of the gospel. Bruce summarizes the introduction of the encounter between Peter and Cornelius:

> Then, talking with him in a friendly manner, Peter accompanied him indoors, and there was the whole group of Cornelius's friends, full of eager expectation. Two or three days previously, Peter would not have believed it possible that he could find himself in such company, under a Gentile roof; but much had happened since then. "You know very well," he said to Cornelius and the others, "that to mix in Gentile society is taboo for a pious Jew; but God has taught me not to regard any person as unfit to associate with." Actually, the terms of his vision on the housetop at Joppa taught him to call no *food* profane or unclean if God pronounced it clean; but he was quick to grasp the analogy between ceremonial food laws and the conventions affecting intercourse with non-Jews.³⁷

---

34. Polhill, *Acts* (NAC), 218.
35. Elwell and Comfort, *Tyndale Bible Dictionary*, 1155.
36. Bruce, *Book of the Acts*, 201.
37. Bruce, *Book of the Acts*, 209; emphasis original.

After their introduction, Peter indiscriminately preached the gospel to everyone present (Acts 10:34–38).

Toussaint says, "These words of Peter were revolutionary. They swept away the prejudice and indoctrination of generations of Judaism."[38] He declared Jesus's impartiality to every nation and peace to all who believe. Louw and Nida define *partiality* as "one who unjustly treats one person better than another—'one who shows favoritism, a respecter of persons.'"[39] The gospel does not show favoritism or treat people unfairly. Peter also states that every nation who fears him and does what is right is welcome. The definition of nation is vital to the expansion of the gospel.

BDAG defines *nation* as "a body of persons united by kinship, culture, and common traditions."[40] Christensen adds that nation includes "'Gentiles' is used in reference to non-Jewish nations in contrast to the Jews."[41] Therefore, Peter is telling his gentile former counterparts that they are now welcome or accepted by God.[42] The gentiles are now at peace under the messianic salvation of Jesus Christ.[43]

Peter's sermon at Cornelius's home followed the basic pattern of his prior sermons to the Jews but with several significant differences. One is found at the very outset, where he stressed that God shows no favoritism, accepts people from every nation, and Jesus is "Lord of all." This emphasis on the universal gospel is particularly suited to a message to gentiles. Peter's vision had led him to this basic insight that God does not discriminate between persons, that there are no divisions between "clean" and "unclean" people from the divine perspective. The Greek word used for favoritism (v. 34) is constructed on a Hebrew idiom meaning "to lift a face." Peter saw that God does not discriminate on the basis of race or ethnic background, looking up to some and down on others. But God does discriminate between those whose behavior is acceptable and those whose attitude is not acceptable. Those who reverence God and practice what is right are acceptable to him (v. 35; cf. Luke 8:21).[44]

Peter shifted his sermon to express the universality of the gospel and God's desire for every nation to be at peace with him through Jesus Christ.

38. Toussaint, "Acts," 2:381.
39. "προσωπολημπτέω," L&N 767.
40. BDAG 276.
41. Duane L. Christensen, "Nations," *ABD* 4:1037.
42. "δεκτός," BDAG 217.
43. "εἰρήνη," BDAG 288.
44. Polhill, *Acts* (NAC), 260.

Peter's willingness to follow God's vision, despite his previous understanding, provided leadership that led to the initial unification of Jew and gentile. Mathew clearly highlights this monumental leadership display of Peter that was pivotal in the unification of Jew and gentile:

> The reformist response from Peter in amending the societal protocol, "unlawful for a Jew to associate or visit a Gentile" (Acts 10:28), is an example of cross-cultural leadership. After receiving supernatural insight from the angel, Peter did not consult with the leaders of his community but stepped out into obedience to the divine instructions. As a member of the Jewish community, Peter had adhered to the expectations and norms of the Jewish community up to that point. Peter modeled cross-cultural leadership through his spontaneous alteration to the established social structure, which brought forth the reformist response.[45]

Peter's leadership and speech directed the church toward the unification of Jew and gentile.

The circumcised witnessing the Holy Spirit pour out on the gentiles provides evidence of the universality of the gospel (Acts 10:45). Fitzmyer expands on the Jews' amazement, writing, "The bewilderment stems from the fact that up to this time in Acts, only Jewish converts have received it. The reception of it by Gentiles shows that the preaching of the Word among Gentiles has the same effect as it had among Jews earlier."[46] Polhill agrees: "It has often been described as the 'Gentile Pentecost,' and that designation is appropriate. In v. 47 Peter practically gave it that designation when he described the Gentiles as having received the Holy Spirit 'just as we have.' Like the Pentecost of Acts, it was a unique, unrepeatable event."[47]

This event is clearly more significant than a visit to Cornelius, but it denotes the inclusion of the gentiles into the gospel. The gentiles now have the same evidence of the Holy Spirit as the Jews. Peter concluded by stating the undeniability of the events and the conversion of the uncircumcised gentiles. Despite their cultural and religious differences, this meeting solidified the gentiles' acceptance into the Christian community according to the confession.

---

45. Mathew, "Apostle Peter's Cross-Cultural Leadership," 107.
46. Fitzmyer, *Acts of the Apostles*, 467.
47. Polhill, *Acts* (NAC), 264.

Peter modeled significant leadership in the formation of the church. He preached the foundational principles in the Jerusalem church and set the structure of a healthy community. He also cemented the mobilization of the gospel to the Samaritans and set the precedent for the mission to the gentiles with the events at Cornelius.

Problems in the Church

Despite the growth of the church and the inclusion of the gentiles, many difficulties still existed. The initial spread of the gospel focused on the Jews in the Jerusalem church, and Peter led the new Christian community to the doctrine of the gospel.[48] With the news of God's impartiality and inclusion of the gentiles, however, the Jerusalem church would now have to confront the differences between Jew and gentile. Since the Jerusalem community shared religious practices and the people assimilated to their heritage, conflict arose when confronted with cultural differences. Therefore, it is helpful to review Peter's leadership in the midst of conflict and his role in the unification of Jew and gentile. Following the events in Acts 10 with the conversion of gentiles, a necessary conflict occurred in the following chapter.

The conflict did not originate in Acts 11 but with the Jerusalem church's limited understanding of the gospel. A historical review of the Jerusalem church will provide clarity in their issue with Peter's declaration of gentile inclusion. Jews who responded to the gospel preached in Jerusalem after the ascension of Jesus Christ formed the Jerusalem church. Robinson describes the Jerusalem church:

> The church in the Christian sense appeared first in Jerusalem after the ascension of Jesus. It was made up of the predominantly Galilean band of Jesus' disciples together with those who responded to the preaching of the apostles in Jerusalem. Its members saw themselves as the elect remnant of Israel destined to find salvation in Zion (Joel 2:32; Acts 2:17ff) and as the restored tabernacle of David which Jesus himself had promised to build (Acts 15:16; Mt. 16:18). Jerusalem was thus the divinely appointed locale for those who awaited the final fulfilment of all God's promises (Acts 3:21).[49]

---

48. Bruce, *Peter, Stephen, James*.
49. Robinson, *NBD*³ 200.

Their seclusion of the Jerusalem church was formulated in their belief in the fulfillment of the salvation promised in the Old Testament. They were distinct in their beliefs differing from their heritage.

Robinson says, "Their distinctive practices included a baptism in the name of Jesus, regular attendance at instruction given by the apostles, and 'fellowship' on a household basis, which Luke described as being 'the breaking of bread and the prayers' (Acts 2:41–46)."[50] However, their heritage remained entrenched in their faith. The Jerusalem church maintained its obligations of the law, circumcision, and worship in the temple. Their faith in Jesus Christ and Jewish heritage created a unified community. Their unification of heritage and Christian community created inclusivity that made others outside of their heritage assimilate to their culture and practices.

The definition of a *proselyte* is "one who has come over from polytheism to Judean religion and practice, convert."[51] More specifically, it is a gentile converted to Judaism.[52] Therefore, gentiles had to convert to Jewish practices if they decided to convert to Christianity. Elwell and Comfort write:

> Yet Peter and the church still came under the strictures of their Jewish heritage. The evidence points to a Jewish proselyte self-consciousness on the part of the early church. They viewed themselves as the righteous remnant, living in the age of Messianic fulfillment, but still interpreted themselves in a Jewish sense and conducted their evangelism in the proselyte form of Jewish particularism (i.e., Gentiles could only be converted through Judaism).[53]

This limited view of conversion was challenged later in the book Acts and created conflict as the mission of Christianity began to mobilize. The need to convert to Judaism faced challenges as the apostles began to bring the gospel to the nations.[54]

The conflict came to fruition after the reports of the conversion of the gentiles, spread to Jerusalem. Bruce discusses the events, writing, "The news of Peter's revolutionary behavior, in entering a Gentile

---

50. Robinson, *NBD*³ 200.
51. "προσηλόω," BDAG 880.
52. "προσήλυτος," L&N 129.
53. Elwell and Comfort, *Tyndale Bible Dictionary*, 1023–24.
54. Robinson, *NBD*³ 200–201.

house at Caesarea, reached Jerusalem before he himself did."[55] The news that fraternization existed with the gentiles created issues among the circumcised (Acts 11:2). Robinson notes the initial conflict: "It was more or less tolerated by Judaism throughout the 30-odd years of its life in Judaea, except when the Jewish authorities were disturbed by its fraternization with Gentile churches abroad."[56] They heard and had firm opposition with Peter for assembling and fellowshipping on gentile property.[57] Luke distinguished the circumcised to highlight the conflict of the perspective of some of the Jewish contingency. Polhill summarizes the Jewish perspective:

> Evidently they represented a strongly Jewish perspective and felt that any Gentile who became a Christian would have to do so by converting to Judaism and undergoing full Jewish proselyte procedure, which included circumcision. Hence, they were known as the circumcision group, since they would require it of all Gentile converts.[58]

The dissension was evident in their firm opposition to and requirement for gentiles to adhere to their Jewish heritage practices. This conflict was not reactionary but deeply entrenched into their heritage and belief at the Jerusalem church.

Peter's response to these problems requires attention and thorough investigation. Acts 11 and 15 tie Peter's response to the conflict and disunity of the church in the mobilization of the gospel. The inevitable conflict between Jew and gentile created an opportunity for leadership to mend the divide. Pervo summarizes the events, stating that "The scene intimates Peter's declining authority: he is called on the carpet, as it were, by the entire community. This loss of prestige is associated with the gentile mission."[59] Peter's first response to being adamantly opposed by the circumcised was to relay the events in an organized explanation (Acts 11:4). Pervo concludes, "Peter's defense is a detailed summary of chap. 10. Repetition again serves the object of emphasis."[60] Peter sequentially outlined the events of his vision and the Spirit leading them

---

55. Bruce, *Book of the Acts*, 219.
56. Robinson, *NBD*³ 200.
57. Barrett, *Commentary on Acts*, 533.
58. Polhill, *Acts* (NAC), 266.
59. Pervo, *Acts*, 283.
60. Pervo, *Acts*, 283.

to Cornelius's house, where he spoke to them about the gospel, and the Holy Spirit fell on them like at Pentecost.[61]

Toussaint confirms that "In recounting what happened next, Peter made an important identification of the day of Pentecost with the Lord's prediction of Spirit baptism."[62] He remembered God's promise of the Holy Spirit to those who believe in Jesus Christ (Acts 11:16). Peter concluded with a pointed statement: "Who was I that I could stand in God's way?" (Acts 11:17). Barrett writes, "The general sense however is clear: God had made plain his intention; who was I to act in a contrary fashion?"[63] This statement from Peter finalized his argument, and the people quieted down and glorified God. Fitzmyer says,

> Words coming from the leader of Jewish Christians of Jerusalem are enough to put an end to all further criticism, especially since Peter has shown how the authority of God has been involved.... The reaction of the Jewish Christians of Jerusalem is one of praise, glorifying God for such an inauguration of the mission to the Gentiles.[64]

If Peter was unwilling to oppose God's authority, then the Jerusalem Christians should accept God's plan for the gentiles. The silence was not complicit, but rather their approval of Peter's message. Barrett says, "Their objection was silenced by the spontaneous action of God who thereby showed that he approved of what Peter had done."[65] Also, glorifying God was a total reversal of their earlier disposition of opposition. According to BDAG, *glorifying* means to praise, honor, and extol.[66]

Peter successfully presented the plan and authority of God, changing the minds of the people to accept the gentiles into the faith. Pervo agrees, stating, "The gift of life has burst the fence of Torah and the boundaries of Israelite observance."[67] Peter's first response to lead the church to unity between Jew and gentile was to report structurally and submit to God's plan. However, Peter's leadership through conflict was

---

61. Polhill, *Acts* (NAC), 267.
62. Toussaint, "Acts," 2:382.
63. Barrett, *Commentary on Acts*, 543.
64. Fitzmyer, *Acts of the Apostles*, 472.
65. Barrett, *Commentary on Acts*, 543.
66. "δόμα," BDAG 258.
67. Pervo, *Acts*, 288.

just beginning. Additionally, Peter's leadership was just beginning to be called into question.

Conflict over the gentiles' acceptance of the gospel seemingly subsided, but opposition over the practices arose in ch. 15. Pervo concludes the initial opposition by alluding to the future conflict, writing, "This fine ending does not lead the reader to ask what decisions were taken. The issue of circumcision, mentioned here only in the context of the purity regulations, will appear in chap. 15."[68] Due to mobilization to the gentiles and their inclusion into the gospel, the issue over regulations was necessary. Boa and Kruidenier address the unification: "The Jerusalem Council was pivotal in the development of the earlier church in terms of doctrine and practically in terms of uniting the Jewish and Gentile portions of the church. The early church was predominantly Jewish."[69] Their inclusion highlighted conflicting practical and cultural issues that leadership needed to determine. Bruce summarizes:

> The Council of Jerusalem is an event to which Luke attaches the highest importance; it is as epoch-making, in his eyes, as the conversion of Paul or the preaching of the gospel to Cornelius and his household. As he reports it, the Council was a meeting of the apostles and elders of the Jerusalem church convened to consider, primarily, the terms on which Gentile believers might be admitted to church membership (with special attention to the question whether they should be circumcised or not); in the second place, the means by which social intercourse, and especially table fellowship, might be promoted between Jewish and Gentile believers. Paul and Barnabas, with some representatives of the church of Antioch on the Orontes, were present at the meeting, where they were given an opportunity to relate their recent experiences in Cyprus and Asia Minor, but they took no part in making the decision; that was the responsibility of the Jerusalem leaders.[70]

The growth of the church of Antioch and the inclusion of gentiles into the church created dissension in religious practice.[71] Issues of community, fellowship, and religious practices were now the crux of Christianity's development. Barrett highlights the shift:

68. Pervo, *Acts*, 288.
69. Boa and Kruidenier, *Romans*, 437.
70. Bruce, *Book of the Acts*, 282–83.
71. Fitzmyer, *Acts of the Apostles*, 552.

> One view is that Luke allows the theme to shift in the course of ch. 15 from this fundamental problem of theology to the practical question of the terms on which Jewish Christians and Gentile Christians might have fellowship, especially at the common Christian meal, within one society.[72]

The issue at hand was circumcision of the gentiles and their inclusion due to their faith in the gospel (Acts 15:1–6). This debate was so tenuous that Paul and Barnabas were sent to report to the Jerusalem church (Acts 15:2).

The believing Pharisees brought their questioning forward. Luke purposefully identified the believing Pharisees. Bruce states, "Dissatisfaction was voiced in particular by those members of the Jerusalem church who were associated with the Pharisaic party. Pharisees, as believers in the doctrine of the resurrection, could become Christians without relinquishing their distinctive beliefs."[73] The Pharisees wanted to maintain the law of Moses and legalistic patterns of faith. The law of Moses signified the gentiles' responsibility to maintain the demands of the law given to Moses in Deut 5:28–33.[74] Polhill discusses the Pharisees and the implications of their demands:

> They must live by the entire Jewish law. It was not the moral aspects of the law that presented the problem but its ritual provisions. The moral law, such as embodied in the Ten Commandments, was never in question. Paul, for instance, constantly reminded his churches of God's moral standards in his letters. The ritual aspects of the law presented a problem. These were the provisions that marked Jews off from other people—circumcision, the food laws, scrupulous ritual purity. They were what made the Jews and seemed strange and arbitrary to most Gentiles. To have required these of Gentiles would in essence have made them into Jews and cut them off from the rest of the Gentiles. It would have severely restricted, perhaps even killed any effective Gentile mission. The stakes were high in the Jerusalem Conference.[75]

The ramifications of the Pharisees' demands restricted genuine fellowship unless gentiles fully converted to Judaism. Such restrictions would

---

72. Barrett, *Commentary on Acts*, 696.
73. Bruce, *Book of the Acts*, 288.
74. Fitzmyer, *Acts of the Apostles*, 545–46.
75. Polhill, *Acts* (NAC), 324.

have limited the mission. Therefore, the Jerusalem Council was necessary to set the foundation for religious practices. Leadership recognized the importance of this conflict and met to debate the issues (Acts 15:7). According to BDAG, the Greek word used for *debate* is "engagement in a controversial discussion, debate, argument."[76] Based on the original language, this debate was based on controversy; therefore, the leaders had varying opinions within the leadership of the council.[77]

As discussed in chapter 3, Peter assumed leadership and testified of God's decision to give the Holy Spirit with no distinction between Jew and gentile. His speech was brief, with the possible assumption of his previous conclusion of his confirmation of Cornelius's salvation.[78] Despite the brevity, Peter concludes that Jews should not put a yoke on the neck of the gentiles (Acts 15:10). Peter also stood to proclaim that enforcing the law of Moses, including circumcision, would put God to the test. Putting God to the test is challenging or doubting what God has already made clear to the gentiles.[79] Fitzmyer agrees: "To 'put God to the test' would mean to approach God in a spirit of unbelief and mistrust; those who would so test him show that they cannot trust a deity who would free Gentiles from such Jewish obligations."[80]

Peter's statement communicated that the persistent compulsion of the law of Moses and circumcision for the gentiles was questioning God's plan, confirmed through the Holy Spirit. Those concluding statements summarized Peter's experience with Cornelius and current belief in God's plan for the gentiles. However, Peter's words were not the last as Paul and Barnabas continued to relate their experience of God's signs and wonders among the gentiles. Following Peter, Paul, and Barnabas's relating of God's work among the gentiles, James spoke to expand upon Peter's experience.[81] However, James's speech was definitive in the decisions of the council. Fitzmyer explains James's role:

> Luke has just depicted Peter as the one whose voice has prevailed in the debate about circumcision and the Mosaic law; in effect, this is what Peter learned from his experience at the conversion of Cornelius. Now Luke presents James, another influential

76. BDAG 429.
77. Polhill, *Acts* (NAC), 326.
78. Polhill, *Acts* (NAC), 326.
79. "πειράζω," BDAG 793.
80. Fitzmyer, *Acts of the Apostles*, 547.
81. Polhill, *Acts* (NAC), 329.

figure in the Jerusalem church, who basically supports Peter, but who qualifies the assembly's decision in some details, about dietary problems and illicit marital unions.[82]

James's detailed declaration pinpoints the judgments of the council and provides clarification about religious practices. After providing evidence from the gentiles, he pronounced no more trouble for the gentiles turning to God (Acts 15:19).

James's decisive and detailed conclusion differed from Peter's experiential testimony. As a leader and spokesperson of the Jerusalem Council, James delivered four obligations for the gentiles to follow, but he eliminated circumcision and dietary restrictions (Acts 15:6–21).[83] Polhill highlights James's leadership as "one of the 'pillars' of the church, along with Peter and John. . . . James had evidently become the leading elder of the Jerusalem congregation. His leadership of the church had already been indicated in 12:17."[84] James's emergence highlighted Peter's concluding role in the unification of Jew and gentile:

> While Peter recommended to the "council" no circumcision or law based on the precedent of his conversion of Cornelius, James urges a few regulations to be observed by the gentiles. Not only did James concede less than Peter did on this issue, the apostles and elders followed James in their decision to enforce these regulations in a letter to those "who are of the gentiles in Antioch and Syria and Cilicia" (15:23). Thus, in Luke's presentation, all play a decisive role: Peter through his witness; James in his judgment; and, the apostles and elders in their letter of enforcement.[85]

Although Peter was a part of the council's decision-making, he was not the only voice for unification of Jew and gentile. Following the decree, the leadership selected leaders, including Judas (Barsabbas) and Silas, to accompany Paul and Barnabas to spread the decree and continue the mission to the gentiles (Acts 15:22–29).[86] As noted, Peter is not mentioned among the missionaries sent to declare the message decided at the council. Bruce highlights Peter's diminishing role, stating that "Peter now

---

82. Fitzmyer, *Acts of the Apostles*, 552.
83. Mangum, *New Testament*, "The Jerusalem Council" (15:6–21), para. 17.
84. Polhill, *Acts* (NAC), 328.
85. Donfried, *ABD* 254.
86. Mangum, *New Testament*, "The Jerusalem Decree" (15:22–29), para. 2.

disappears from the narrative of Acts; so far as Luke is concerned, says Martin Hengel; 'the legitimation of the mission to the Gentiles is virtually Peter's last work.'"[87] Peter initiated the foundation of the Jerusalem church and the unification of Jew and gentile in the book of Acts, but his activity was not highlighted in the remaining portion of Acts.

Peter's last work highlighted his leadership role in the unification of Jew and gentile. Although he began the work and confirmed God's plan for the gentiles, he slowly faded, in the book of Acts, in his continual activity of the unification. Peter receives no further mention in Acts. However, we cannot overlook that his role in the formation of the church was pivotal in the gentiles' understanding of the gospel. He played a pivotal role in the Jerusalem church and their doctrinal foundation of Jesus as the Messiah. He initiated the work among the gentiles with his experience with Cornelius.

Later, he confirmed the plan and work of God among the gentiles at the Jerusalem Council but was no longer highlighted for the remainder of the book of Acts. Peter was integral in setting the polity of the church and was willing to suffer for the gospel, but his failure in reformed leadership reveals his limitations in transformational leadership in the book of Acts. However, Peter's failure did not stop his dedication to his missional calling of unifying Jew and gentile. Although Luke shifted his historical accounts to Paul and the spread of the gospel to the remotest parts of the earth, Peter maintained his leadership in the unification of Jew and gentile.[88]

J. D. G. Dunn poignantly states, "It was Peter who became the focal point of unity in the great Church, since Peter was probably in fact and effect the bridge man who did more than any other to hold together the diversity of first-century Christianity."[89] It is important not to minimize Peter's continual influence in the unity of Jew and gentile for the remainder of the New Testament. Bruce summarizes and details Peter's possible continual involvement in at least three areas of the Mediterranean world. He supports his claim that Peter remained influential and authoritative in Antioch, Corinth, and Rome. In three places in the Mediterranean world, Peter's name is specially associated. Antioch and Corinth already have been mentioned; the third is Rome.[90] Despite his

87. Bruce, *Book of the Acts*, 291.
88. Bruce, *Peter, Stephen, James*.
89. Dunn, *Unity and Diversity*, 385.
90. Bruce, *Peter, Stephen, James*, 425.

failure and contribution and the problems in the early church, Peter remained persistent in his pursuit of the unity of the church.

Church Transformation of Diversity under the Leadership of Paul

The second portion of Acts highlights Paul's leadership in the growth and mobilization of the church. Paul played a pivotal role in the spread of the gospel, especially to the gentiles. Johnson affirms, "Luke thereby makes two points essential to his overall purpose. First, Paul's mission to the gentiles is not idiosyncratic but part of the Spirit-guided mission of the whole church."[91] After Peter's role concluded in Acts, Luke turned his attention to Paul's leadership and missionary efforts. Elwell and Comfort discuss the theme in the second portion of Acts, stating, "Proclamation of the gospel to the Gentiles through Paul's ministry is the theme of part two of Acts (chaps 13–28). The story primarily concerns three major missionary tours, each of which moved the gospel into yet untouched territory and expanded earlier missionary efforts."[92] Paul's missionary work expanded the gospel to the remotest parts of the earth. He was pivotal not only in the spread of the gospel but also in the planting and growth of the church. However, while growing and stabilizing the church, conflict and opposition existed in the unification of Jew and gentile. Therefore, it's important to analyze Paul's transformational leadership in the growth, stabilization, and problems in the church.

Growth of the Church

The formation and growth of the church is evidence of Paul's leadership and influence in the spread of the gospel. Ample evidence exists to support Paul's leadership in planting churches and continual influence throughout the New Testament. The book of Acts centers on his missionary journeys, which result in the development of churches and later his leadership.[93] The rest of the New Testament confirms Paul's authority and role in the development of the church. Robinson writes:

---

91. Luke Timothy Johnson, "Luke-Acts, Book of," *ABD* 416.
92. Elwell and Comfort, *Tyndale Bible Dictionary*, 14.
93. Johnson, *ABD* 415–17.

> The fullest evidence for what took place when a church actually assembled is 1 Cor. 11–14. There was no organizational link between Paul's churches, though there were natural affinities between churches in the same province (Col. 4:15–16; 1 Thes. 4:10). All were expected to submit to Paul's authority in matters of the faith hence the role of Paul's letters and of the visits of TIMOTHY—but this authority was spiritual and admonitory, not coercive (2 Cor. 10:8; 13:10). Local administration and discipline were autonomous (2 Cor. 2:5–10). No church had superiority over any other, though all acknowledged Jerusalem as the source of "spiritual blessings" (Rom. 15:27), and the collection for the saints there was a token of this acknowledgment.[94]

The epistles of Paul authenticate his authority and ability to lead the churches as they grew. Paul helped transform the church in his missionary efforts to share the gospel with Jew and gentile and founded churches on his journeys. Betz summarizes Paul's journeys and initial success in the foundation of churches, writing,

> They met their first success in Philippi, where they founded the first church in Macedonia (16:11–40). From Philippi they went to Thessalonica, establishing a church there as well (17:1–9). The next stations were Beroea (17:10–15), Athens (17:16–34; 1 Thess 3:1–2), and Corinth (18:1–17; 1 Cor 1:1–2, 14, 16; 3:5–15; 16:15, 17); in all these cities, churches were established.[95]

Betz discusses the successful journeys and the mobilization of the gospel through the foundation of churches. Paul founded the churches and also maintained contact and leadership, even as he continued his missionary travels.

In his discourse with the church of Ephesus, Paul maintained his authority in his letters and farewell address. In addition, in the churches in Galatia, Paul maintained pastoral leadership as he addressed their issues in his epistle. He continually led the church as it grew and dealt with issues of people drifting away from the church.[96] Romans critically illustrates Paul's persistence in unifying Jew and gentile, highlighting Paul's leadership in unifying Jew and gentile.[97] Mounce summarizes the purpose of Romans: "They needed to have a systematic statement of the

---

94. Robinson, *NBD*³ 201–2.
95. Betz, *ABD* 189.
96. Betz, *ABD* 189.
97. Dunn, *Romans 1–8*, lxxi.

gospel as Paul understood it as well as his position on the relationship between the Gentiles and the Jewish community."[98]

Despite the book of Acts declaring the unity of Jew and gentile doctrinally, problems in ethnic and cultural practices persisted. Dunn agrees and adds that Paul's desire "was to free both promise and law for a wider range of recipients, freed from the ethnic constraints, which he saw to be narrowing the grace of God and diverting the saving purpose of God out of its main channel—Christ."[99] Paul recognized the need to explain doctrinally the gospel's effect on the relationship between Jew and gentile.

His letters in the New Testament provide ample proof of his sustained role within the churches he founded. As noted, Paul revisited the churches he helped establish to strengthen and encourage the people, leaders, and churches. Ample evidence exists in the book of Acts and his continual writing in the New Testament to support his leadership and development of the church.

Problems in the Church

During the birth and development of the church, significant issues arose under Paul's leadership and influence. Each church presented unique problems as Jew and gentile navigated relationships and unification under the gospel. Paul played an integral role in the resolution of the church's internal problems, often writing letters or visiting churches amid turmoil. Due to the limitations of the research, a quick summary is given of Paul's consistent involvement within the problems of the church.

As noted previously, one of the initial conflicts was Paul's willingness to engage in conflict, even as the Jerusalem church challenged the unification of Jew and gentile. Paul documented his conflict with Peter and certain men of James as they fellowshipped with the gentiles.[100] Paul refrained from joining the delegation from Jerusalem, Peter and Barnabas, and continued his mission to the gentiles. Paul persistently pursued his calling to the gentiles despite the problems that continued in the unification of the church. Betz describes the continual conflict between Jew and gentile:

---

98. Mounce, *Romans*, 26–27.
99. Dunn, *Romans 1-8*, lxxi–xxvii.
100. Silva, *BEB* 2:1628.

Henceforth Paul and the gentile churches founded by him were on their own, though plagued by contrary Jewish-Christian missionaries. To the end, however, Paul never lost hope that a reconciliation with the Jerusalem church might be accomplished, pinning this hope to the collection for the poor (1 Cor 16:1-4; 2 Corinthians 8 and 9; see Betz, *2 Corinthians 8-9*); and intercession by the church of Rome (Rom 15:30-32).[101]

Paul maintained hope for unification of the churches of Jew and gentile.

Despite his persistence and hope, problems continued externally in the universal church and internally in the local churches. However, the book of Acts has limited notes on internal conflict evident in the churches. Betz confirms:

> These scarce notes, which are based on some sources known to Luke, can be correlated only roughly with what we know from Paul's letters, esp. 1 Cor 16:1-11; 2 Cor 1:8-11, 15-18; 2:12-13; 7:5-7, 13-16; Rom 15:22-31. The main differences were (1) the situation was much more complicated than Acts leads us to believe; (2) Paul had to change his travel plans several times; and (3) he almost lost his Corinthian church because of internal strife and opposition.[102]

The church of Corinth had numerous issues, including moral conflict, divisions, doctrinal divisions, and disruptions in the worship service. However, Paul did not shy away from the conflict but addressed the issues within his letters and even visited after they rejected his authority. Paul persistently led the church of Corinth even as they rejected his authority. His willingness to pursue resolution within the church is evidenced in his writing, visitation, and providing leadership through Titus in his absence.[103]

The church of Corinth is not an isolated church conflict. In his epistles, Paul led the people through numerous conflicts in other local churches. The church of Ephesus also presented problems for Paul and his leadership. He was driven away by the same Jewish opposition but spent two years mobilizing the gospel and the church.[104] The opposition from the Jews was a consistent threat in numerous churches, including Galatia.

101. Betz, *ABD* 188-89.
102. Betz, *ABD* 189.
103. Silva, *BEB* 2:1630-31.
104. Silva, *BEB* 2:1630-31.

While in Ephesus, Paul was notified of severe problems in the churches of Galatia. The problem with the Jewish opposition grew as they challenged the authority of Paul, therefore inhibiting the influence Paul had on the churches of Galatia. Silva explains:

> Reports from the churches in Galatia (Iconium, Lystra, Derbe) indicated that Judaizers had visited these Christians and largely persuaded them that Paul, who had received his teaching and authority from the Jerusalem apostles (James, Peter, John), was a renegade who could not be trusted. Quite impressed by the Judaizers' arguments, the Galatians listened to their claim that Gentiles ought to be circumcised and observe the Jewish rites.[105]

Despite continual attacks on the legitimacy of Paul's authority, he defended his apostleship and the illegitimacy of his attackers. Galatians 5:10 highlights his confidence in the churches' resolve to disregard false teachers and maintain their commitment to the truth.

Paul's persistence pursuit of the churches provides insight into transformational leadership he displayed after his initial journeys and within each of the local churches. While initially mobilizing the gospel, Paul embraced the conflict and did not change as the churches developed. He encountered new problems as the church unified Jew and gentile but remained consistent in his transformational approach to conflict.

Transformational Leadership Principles of Peter and Paul Applied to the Current Church

The leadership analysis of Paul and Peter throughout Acts provides critical insight and application to the modern-day church in North America. From their origins to their leadership in the development and growth of the church, Paul and Peter provide ample evidence of the success and failure of their transformational leadership. A survey of the book of Acts reveals the success and failure of diversification in the growth of the church. Combining the birth, growth, and diversity of the church with Paul and Peter's transformational leadership revealed the necessity for leaders personally to transform, follow their calling, mobilize followers, and practice revolutionary leadership. Therefore, it is vital for leadership of the current church to apply the successful principles that Paul and Peter's transformational leadership exemplified

105. Silva, *BEB* 2:1630–31.

as they led through the challenges facing the unification of Jew and gentiles in the churches in the book of Acts.

First Principle

The first principle for current church leaders to apply from Paul and Peter is to recognize their origins and make appropriate personal transformations according to their calling. Burns defines *origins* as powerful influences of biographical data such as family, school, and adolescent experiences in a leader's life.[106] Paul's and Peter's origins conflicted with their calling to the gentiles. But their encounter with God transformed their conflicting origins to the mission God designated. Leaders must be willing to transform their family backgrounds, socialization, traditions, culture, and education according to their God-given calling or values.[107] Both leaders in the book of Acts personally transformed their wellspring of wants and transmutation of needs according to the corresponding values of their God-ordained mission.

To institute the demand for the personal transformation of values, there has to be a recognition of God's demand for diversity in the universal and local church. As discussed previously, God's demand for diversity is evident in Scripture and creation.[108] Therefore, it is mandated for church leaders to adopt God's mission for a unified church and the values that encompass God's mission for the church. Guder recognizes God's eternal purpose and mission to heal the world.[109]

Soong-Chan Rah adds that since God has been seeking the whole world, then God is not limited to the West or Western missions. Rah writes, "When we consider the work of God throughout human history, we need to acknowledge that God's plan of redemption has been at work before the church even existed, that he is present in different places even before the Western missionaries show up."[110] Even before the establishment of the church and Western missions, God had an eternal mission to heal the entire world and his creation (Eph 1:4; 2 Tim 1:9; Titus 1:2; Rom 16:25). Jesus repeats the eternal mission for everyone to be one in unity

---

106. Burns, *Leadership*, 60–61.
107. Mathew, "Apostle Peter's Cross-Cultural Leadership," 110.
108. See ch. 1.
109. Guder, *Missional Church*, 4.
110. Rah, *Many Colors*, 341.

(John 17:20–23). Since God has an eternal plan for unity and redemption for all people, it should remain the mission of the local church. The church should be the agency of seeking unity amid diversity. DeYmaz and Li address the church's mandate for multiethnic unified worship:

> We should also recognize that the multi-ethnic church, and on a broader scale, the multi-ethnic church movement, represents nothing new; rather, it is reformative in nature. It was first envisioned by Christ (John 17:20–23), then described by Luke (Acts 11:19–26; 13:1), and ultimately prescribed by the apostle Paul throughout his writings, most notably in his letter to the Ephesians. Therefore we embrace the vision not because it is politically correct but because it is spiritually correct, and while it is not necessarily an easy vision to pursue, it is a sound ecclesiology.[111]

Therefore, God demands that the church, who claims to lead his mission, practice his eternal plan and mission for the whole world. The church needs to reflect God's plan for unity, therefore demanding leaders to share the value of diversity.

To lead a diverse church, leaders must be willing to relinquish their origins to accomplish the mission for unity among the diversity in North America. Mathew correctly assesses that, "as a cross-cultural leader, the influences of your personal cultural background must never hinder you but rather equip you to be an effective cross-cultural leader."[112] Despite North American upbringing, schooling, socialization, traditions, and culture, church leaders are responsible to transform personally to the values and mission of God. Emerson agreed that a leader must first have a personal deep commitment to ethnic equity. Emerson poignantly claims, "Without this personal commitment, multiracial congregations will fall short."[113] Leaders cannot change their external systems without first challenging their origins and social norms that conflict with God's mission for ethnic diversity.

Church leaders must personally commit to learning continually about ethnic diversity, even if it contradicts their personal origins. Mathew agrees, stating, "Cross-cultural leaders are open to learning new information and, as a result, willing to amend social structures within their organizations for changing the world."[114] Leaders' willingness to

---

111. DeYmaz and Li, *Leading Healthy Multi-Ethnic Church*, 38.
112. Mathew, "Apostle Peter's Cross-Cultural Leadership," 110.
113. Emerson, *People of the Dream*, 2216.
114. Mathew, "Apostle Peter's Cross-Cultural Leadership," 110.

amend their personal upbringing and accepted social structures is critical to their abilities to diversify their cultural understanding. Rah says that personal transformation is necessary:

> Cultural intelligence is not merely changing externalities of cultural forms or recognizable external events. These changes can occur on an individual level. It is not only the changing of external behavior, but also the transformation of internal values. It is a transformation of the system that produced those values in the first place. The way a system is organized, operates, and influences the individual is more important than simply changing the individual. Cultural intelligence requires systemic change.[115]

David Livermore agrees in his writing about leadership and cultural intelligence. One area he pinpoints is the necessity for leadership to increase its cultural knowledge. A leader with cultural knowledge has a "rich, well-organized understanding of culture and how it affects the way people think or behave. They possess a repertoire of knowledge about how cultures are alike and different."[116] However, ethnocentrism hinders leaders from seeing the world outside of their own cultural backgrounds.[117] Livermore defines ethnocentrism and its detrimental effect on leading effectively in diversity:

> Ethnocentrism—evaluating other people and their culture by the standards of our own cultural preferences—is found among people everywhere. Seeing the world in light of our own cultural background and experience is inevitable. But ignoring the impact of ethnocentrism on how we lead is the single greatest obstacle to CQ Knowledge.[118]

For ethnocentric leaders, self-reflection on possible bias and closed-mindedness will frustrate their enclosed worldview.[119] "Knowledge without the critical thinking and reflection that comes from CQ Strategy leads to overconfidence and real-world ignorance."[120] Therefore, an ethnocentric leader will struggle to engage ethnicities outside of their cultural background and experience. In order to overcome ethnocentrism, a

---

115. Rah, *Many Colors*, 1072.
116. Livermore, *Leading with Cultural Intelligence*, 65.
117. Livermore, *Leading with Cultural Intelligence*, 65.
118. Livermore, *Leading with Cultural Intelligence*, 66.
119. Bock, *Cultural Intelligence*, 67.
120. Livermore, *Digital, Diverse & Divided*, 49.

leader must understand different languages, see culture's role in oneself, analyze cultural systems, and learn about cultural values.

According to Livermore, a leader with cultural intelligence knowledge will recognize another culture's values and systems. He provides ten systems to help leaders make sense of people and their situations. Hackman and Johnson agree, stating that leaders often function based on their own experiences. Hackman and Johnson write, "Most of the time, we operate mechanically without giving much conscious thought to our behaviors and to the behaviors of the other person. This mind-set, which relies on the scripts we've learned through experience."[121]

Church leaders have to be willing to hear the stories and experiences of other cultures in order to expand their knowledge past the dominant culture in the United States. They must be willing to expand their learning experience through travel, diverse friendships, and changing environments. Rah says,

> Most of our understanding of culture develops on the ground. We learn about the world around us by observing our immediate surroundings. We are justifiably preoccupied with navigating our way through our immediate cultural environs. We may not be aware how limited our worldview and how narrow our analysis of our own cultural context may be. It requires a trip to another level to see the whole panoramic view or to experience the bird's-eye perspective in order to appreciate the scope of cultural differences. Cultural intelligence requires knowledge about our own cultural framework and the immediacy of our cultural environment. But it also requires a willingness to go to another place and to reflect upon your own culture and to see the culture of others from a new angle.[122]

The willingness of church leaders to step outside of their comfort and change their environment widens their worldview and knowledge. Sadly, pastors who do not open their minds to the bird's eye perspective will be narrower in their knowledge. This limits their abilities to navigate through other cultures and appreciate differences. With cultural intelligence, leaders can understand how their culture shapes their thinking and behavior and learn about other cultures' values and structures. They must remove their ethnocentrism and value other cultures enough to desire knowledge.

121. Hackman and Johnson, *Leadership*, 317.
122. Rah, *Many Colors*, 1066.

Education without God, however, is limited to the transfer of information. Therefore, it is vital for church leaders to recognize God's call for unity and diversity and to educate themselves accordingly. Paul and Peter were both educated by God and the values according to the mission of the gospel. Paul was called to the gentiles and learned from God about his calling (Gal 1:16–24). Galatians 1:15–16 refers to Paul's unique learning and revelation from God that distinguished and educated Paul for his mission to the gentiles.[123] Paul designates God as the source of his initial education and learned role to the gentiles.[124] Similarly, Peter had a vision and revelation from God before spreading the gospel to the gentiles (Acts 10). According to the model of Paul and Peter, it is important for a personal transformation determined by God and to be educated accordingly.

For Christian leaders, their motivation for cultural knowledge is their genuine desire to lead in God's priority mission for inclusion of diversity. Paul and Peter were motivated to fulfill the values and mission of God because of their encounter of revelation with God and his demand of their mission.

Second Principle

The second principle for current church leaders to apply is to mobilize active followers who engage in the unification of the church. Christerson, Emerson, and Edwards state, "Interracial religious organizations that actively promote theological justifications for multiculturalism are more stable than those that do not."[125] Therefore, it is important for leaders to establish multicultural values within the whole organization and mobilize others to pursue actively God's mission.

Paul and Peter set the precedent for mobilization. They were missional in the calling of God and formed and developed the church to carry on the values of God for the unification of Jew and gentile. Each played integral roles in the mobilization of the church. Peter was active in the development of the values of the church. As established previously, he set the foundation of ministries to the gentiles. Bruce writes, "The great leap forward then takes place when Peter, who opened a door of faith to Jews on the day of Pentecost, now performs the same service for

---

123. George, *Galatians*, 121–22.
124. Martyn, *Galatians*, 159.
125. Christerson et al., *Against All Odds*, 177.

Gentiles (Acts 10:34–48)."[126] Peter began the great work to the gentiles forming the values for the church and mobilizing the Council of Jerusalem. Peter's work continued, and Bruce highlights his missionary efforts: "That Peter's missionary activity was not restricted to Jews is implied here and there in the New Testament. Whatever view be taken of the life setting of 1 Peter, that letter is addressed in Peter's name to Gentile converts in various provinces of Asia Minor."[127] Therefore, it is critical not to rob Peter of his significant role in unity within the church to give it to Paul.[128] Peter was formative in the mobilization of the unification of Jew and gentile and the values of the mission of God.

Paul played an integral role in the development and continuation of the mobilization of the values for the unification of the church. Chen describes Paul as the architect and coach, "functioning as a social architect for the Philippians to build their church on the foundation of agape love, Paul, the transforming leader, functioning as a coach."[129] Northouse references that Paul's ability to communicate a direction that transformed life "communicated a direction that transformed their [church's] value and norms."[130] In agreement with Northouse, Yukl says that Paul's ability "suggests specific things that could help to improve the person's performance."[131] He displayed transformative leadership that mobilized churches to higher values and performance. Paul's mobilization extended past Luke's writing to the churches in his writing of the epistles.

Chen describes Paul's transformative leadership to the church of Philippians and his ability to raise the values of the church. Chen writes,

> To strengthen the Philippians' faith to grow wise, mature, moral, and undefeatable, Paul elevated (a) Philippians' Christian values of servant leadership with accountability and responsibilities, (b) values of suffering for the sake of Christ, and (c) values of transformation. Augmenting Philippian Christian values of accountability, Paul encouraged local leaders, overseers, and deacons in the formation and nurturing of the church in Philippi.[132]

---

126. Bruce, *Peter, Stephen, James*, 226.
127. Bruce, *Peter, Stephen, James*, 304.
128. Peake, *Plain Thoughts*, 43.
129. Chen, "Transformational Leadership," 152.
130. Northouse, *Leadership*, 197.
131. Yukl, *Leadership in Organizations*, 77.
132. Chen, "Transformational Leadership," 153.

Paul was active in the development of church values in the church of Philippi, as well as other churches in his writings. DeYmaz highlights the church model Paul used by discipling Timothy intentionally to carry the vision and calling to the gentiles.[133] He set the standard for persistence in communication and actions of the mobilization of followers.

Paul and Peter played significant leadership roles in the development, growth, and structure of the church and its unification. Therefore, church leaders are responsible to mobilize the development, growth, and structure of the unified and diverse church. In addition to church development, church leaders are responsible to mobilize more leaders willing to engage in the same values. DeYmaz agrees that effective leaders should seek to plant other churches and develop leaders to engage in multiethnic churches. DeYmaz writes,

> For planters and reformers, the pursuit of Christian unity should not be limited in scope to their own multi-ethnic church. I believe we also have a responsibility to pursue it with others throughout the city as well, that is, with other local churches and their pastors. Indeed, it is long past time for local church leaders to stop competing and start cooperating for the sake of the Gospel. And with this in mind, our vision for unity demands that we encourage the greater Body of Christ throughout the city and beyond.[134]

The value of ethnic diversity should drive leaders to spread the scope of diversity to others through the city and beyond. A leader's calling for congregational diversity and unity should not be limited to their personal life or church but spread to the city and worldwide.

Emerson agrees that everyone in the congregation should have a common purpose. He says, "Racial cooperation and equity are typically best achieved not by making them the central focus, but rather a means to a common purpose."[135] Derwin Gray discusses the responsibility of pastors to disciple others in the discovery of the mystery of Christ in the local church. Gray concludes,

> Discipleship and leadership development are critical to local churches fulfilling their calling as agents of transformation. Therefore, high-definition leaders are committed to a

---

133. DeYmaz, *Building Healthy Multi-Ethnic Church*, 71.
134. DeYmaz, *Building Healthy Multi-Ethnic Church*, 125.
135. Emerson, *People of the Dream*, 2217–18.

discipleship philosophy that is rooted in creating local congregations throughout America and the world that reveal the mystery of Christ as a sign and foretaste of God's faithfulness to Abraham and of Jesus' victory.[136]

As modeled by Paul and Peter, modern-day church leadership needs to continually make more disciples who actively carry the mission of Christ. An effective leader will equip the lives of others to experience their own transformations, therefore experiencing the mystery of Christ in the churches worldwide.

As the mobilization of similar values of unification and diversity in church increases, it will result in church leaders and followers creating organizations that foster diversity. In order for a church to be truly diverse, there has to be a structure, leadership, and followers that incorporate diverse races, ethnicities, and cultural experiences into their congregation. Stallard agrees with Gushiken that North American churches need to make every effort to plant churches that are culturally relevant.[137] Stallard correctly concludes, "If God has created humans to be culture makers, and this manifests itself in a rich diversity of expressions, then it behooves the church to contextualize its message to correspond to this diversity."[138]

Research indicates that applicable strategies to church diversification exist that can assist in creating a multiethnic church. Churches that genuinely desire to have a diverse church must develop a vision, environment, and diverse leadership that incorporate and blend all cultures into the congregation. Collectively, however, Christians together in churches bear the responsibility for accepting, prioritizing, and integrating other cultures for the purpose of a diverse church. "With this in mind, a healthy multiethnic church is a place in which people are comfortable being uncomfortable. In such a place, members recognize that they are part of something much bigger than themselves."[139]

Churches can create social change, but internal change must occur inside the lives of the people in the church. However, churches have continued with the failures of history, forming congregational bodies with a homogeneous population that serves its culture's needs and

---

136. Gray, *High-Definition Leader*, 188.
137. Stallard, "Majority World Theology," 119.
138. Stallard, "Majority World Theology," 111.
139. DeYmaz, *Building Healthy Multi-Ethnic Church*, 110.

comforts. Fowler writes, "The United States, especially in urban areas, is becoming increasingly multiethnic, yet churches are failing to reach out to this mission field in their own communities. The ethnic representation in most churches does not reflect the diversity of ethnicity in the community."[140] Emerson concurs with the lack of diversity in church, but added that some lament for diversity, while others recognize and are indifferent to congregations that are racially divided.[141] Churches need to be seeking diligently for the unity of God in the church. "Where the Church denies or rejects or perverts the gift of unity the witness of the Church to the world is lost."[142]

Practical Applications of Mobilization

The models of Paul and Peter for the modern-day church are vital to ethnic unity and increasing the diversity of local congregations. Churches struggle with unity, similar to churches in the New Testament. Therefore, it is critical for considerations of practical applications to occur, although inexhaustive of the principles modeled by mobilization of the gospel by Paul and Peter. Mobilization begins with the vision evident in the diversity of leadership and environment.

VISION

A church needs to begin by having a vision that incorporates a multicultural church. As Blackaby and Blackaby affirm, "If great visions inspire great organizations, then it is imperative for leaders to develop the loftiest vision possible."[143] As evident with Paul and Peter, a vision communicates the mission, values, and calling of God. Both leaders experienced a physical vision that permeated throughout the New Testament, especially of Jew and gentile. The vision sets the direction and purpose for the church, and a leader needs to begin with having a vision for a multiracial church. Emerson correctly assesses,

> Often, the primary impetus for a congregation becoming multiracial comes from its mission—its theological, cultural, and/or

140. Fowler, "Planting, Transitioning, and Growing," 15.
141. Emerson and Smith, *Divided by Faith*, 135.
142. Stringfellow, "Unity of the Church," 524.
143. Blackaby and Blackaby, *Spiritual Leadership*, 86.

symbolic orientation. In short, its goals are the impetus. In this case, a congregation's becoming multiracial is consistent with the very purpose for its existence, either directly—"we desire to be multiracial"—or indirectly—"we wish to serve all people."[144]

The vision sets the goals for the church and the purpose of its existence. An often-scriptural quote that stresses the importance of vision is Prov 29:18, "Where there is no vision, the people perish."

Blackaby likened a vision to the North Star—it helps leaders find their way and reduces the risk of being sidetracked and failing to accomplish its purpose.[145] In his book *The Nuts and Bolts of Church Planting*, Aubrey Malphurs discusses the importance of vision:

> A good vision is compelling. The right people want to be part of it, and it serves to motivate these people. The ministry's vision inspires them to partner with what the ministry is convinced God wants it to do. A compelling vision moves people out of the pews and into the community and, most important, gives birth to ministry.[146]

Blackaby reminds us that a vision for the church is God-given, and leaders not only should seek the needs of others for direction but God for his purpose.[147] A leader needs balance, prioritizing God for vision, while remembering the needs of the people.

However, the term *vision* needs definition, as researchers and authors have tried to pinpoint an accurate explanation for vision and its results on organizations. According to Ford, vision is "the ability to see in a way that compels others to pay attention."[148] Charles Swindoll writes that vision is spawned by faith, sustained by hope, sparked by imagination, and strengthened by enthusiasm."[149] Blanchard and Hodges write, "A vision, or view of the future, is an ongoing, evolving, hopeful look into the future that stirs the hearts and minds of people who know they will never see its end or limit."[150] Each author attempts to clarify vision, but the church is sorely in need of the biblical definition of vision. Ford

---

144. Emerson, *People of the Dream*, 721.
145. Blackaby and Blackaby, *Spiritual Leadership*, 85.
146. Malphurs, *Nuts and Bolts*, 101.
147. Blackaby and Blackaby, *Spiritual Leadership*, 93.
148. Ford, *Transforming Leadership*, 99.
149. Ford, *Transforming Leadership*, 100.
150. Blanchard and Hodges, *Lead Like Jesus*, 88.

says, "Vision is commonly used of an ecstatic experience in which saintly people with an awareness of God receive a special word from Him."[151] This current research will use the biblical definition for vision, since it encompasses the direction necessary for the church.

A vision cannot impact a church unless it is communicated effectively. Leadership needs to communicate a vision to the congregation in order to mobilize congregational transformation. Fowler's research concludes that leadership has to communicate a vision clearly, effectively, and consistently. "These churches all seem to agree that vision was communicated frequently to the point that there could be no misunderstanding of what these churches were going to be, affecting the way they did ministry and lived out their vision."[152] Emerson agrees that consistent communication is necessary for congregational change, noting that the pastors he studied consistently mentioned the necessity to adjust their vision in order to adjust the direction of the church.[153]

Communication of Vision

A leader is responsible for communicating the vision effectively for the mobilization of the followers. Paul and Peter both stood among their peers and followers to communicate their God-given visions. Communication is critical in any organization, especially in the midst of any type of change. Lee and Krayer write, "Communication is not contained within the organization. Instead, communication is the organization."[154] Communication is the vehicle that transports the culture of the organization.[155] Without communication, a church will fail and change will not occur. Congregations do not change solely on the authority of a leader, but it is a leader's capability to effectively communicate the necessity of cultural shifts in the church. Hackman and Johnson state, "The goal of communication is to create a shared reality between message, sources, and receivers."[156]

---

151. Ford, *Transforming Leadership*, 101.
152. Fowler, "Planting, Transitioning, and Growing," 137.
153. Emerson and Smith, *Divided by Faith*, 100.
154. Lee and Krayer, *Organizing Change*, 203.
155. Walrath, *Leading Churches through Change*, 122.
156. Hackman and Johnson, *Leadership*, 6.

For change to occur, a leader is responsible to communicate proper messages to the followers for a new shared reality. Communication is not only necessary, but appropriate communication delivers proper messages for the intended purpose to become active. A transformational leader's communication has to be effective enough for a shared message to create behavioral change. Hackman and Johnson add, "Leadership is human (symbolic) communication that modifies the attitudes and behaviors of others in order to meet shared group goals and needs."[157] Transformational communication moves beyond the proclamation of the vision, since it is the empowerment of the followers to engage actively in the new direction of the church. Therefore, congregation cultural change can only occur through transformational communication.

A leader is responsible to communicate, but the Holy Spirit will confirm the vision with the congregations. A church cannot achieve true diversity without a clear God-given vision communicated. God clearly defines his vision for his church in Scripture, but leaders need earnestly to seek God for him to reveal the necessary changes for the church to implement in order to integrate all races into the congregation. The vision needs to incorporate the diversity that comes through God-given experiences that stretch the leader's mind. The vision's purpose is to energize followers into action. The leader's willingness to communicate the vision persistently and convincingly will transform the congregation through the conviction of the Holy Spirit.

A vision is empty without the implementation of what God has directed the church to fulfill. Kim declares, "A vision is only as effective as its strategy. In other words, a conceivable and practical strategy puts legs on a budding vision, enabling it to be achieved."[158] Michael Hackman describes this process, identifying problems as problem-finding orientation.[159] William W. Lee and Karl J. Krayer refer to this phase of planning as input. They define input as the period in the planning phase in which "there is an issue or opportunity within the organization that requires investigation."[160]

This phase or period requires intense investigation and preparation to identify problems and start creatively addressing solutions to the problem. A church has to engage in finding the problems in its church, declaring a

---

157. Hackman and Johnson, *Leadership*, 11.
158. Kim, *Preaching with Cultural Intelligence*, 13.
159. Lee and Krayer, *Organizing Change*, 106.
160. Lee and Krayer, *Organizing Change*, 60.

vision, and then with intense investigation prepare a plan to address solutions. Fowler's research indicates that a church that communicates a clear vision has to encounter a forward-thinking strategic planning to decide what methodology the church will use to create a multiethnic church. Fowler discovered that a vision without an urgent plan and leadership support leads to significant fallout. Without a vision, the church has no direction and purpose, but intentional strategic planning for the purpose to come to fruition has to occur.[161] Paul and Peter were responsible for the vision God revealed to them. However, a vision communicated ineffectively would have stifled the mobilization of the gospel. The New Testament, and especially the Epistles, highlights the necessity for persistent and effective communication to create active followers.

Environment

The vision is the beginning to creating a multiethnic church. Environments are constantly changing, and the church has to change to its surrounding community and cultures. Emerson states, "Organizations are not self-sufficient. They depend on their environments to survive. Environments, constantly changing, can serve to shape the goals and boundaries of organizations."[162] The vision should incorporate an appropriate environment that contextualizes to the congregation's diversity. A church should exemplify all the cultures that attend or desire to come, but not for the minority to assimilate to the majority culture.

Paul and Peter highlighted the ability to adjust to their surrounding culture to mobilize and share the gospel. Peter's interaction with Cornelius perfectly illustrates his adjustment after receiving the vision from God. Peter changed his dietary restrictions and created an environment for sincere fellowship between Jew and gentile. Additionally, Paul changed his interactions with his Jewish counterparts and gentile believers. Paul highlighted his ability to adjust to the environment when he addressed the church of Corinth about his desire to become "all things to all men" (1 Cor 9:22). Rah concurs:

> Genuine multicultural ministry requires understanding the potential range of responses that may arise in a particular context and scenario. Often, we assume that others will respond the way

---

161. Fowler, "Planting, Transitioning, and Growing," 137.
162. Emerson, *People of the Dream*, 643.

we ourselves would, given a particular situation. We have cultural blinders that prevent us from having cultural peripheral vision. If our perspective is solely shaped by our own immediate cultural context, then we fail to understand where a person from a different culture may be coming from and may even inadvertently denigrate the other's culture.[163]

The church has to be sensitive to the needs of all cultures and their experiences in order to create an environment suitable and accommodating.

Gushiken writes, "Within a multiethnic congregation, individuals import cultural histories, ethnic values, and racial traditions into the life of the local church. One of the primary challenges to heterogeneous churches is to give validity to ethnic stories, recognizing their place in community learning."[164] In order for the church not to remain a monoethnic environment, it must be intentional about understanding other cultures and also recognizing the possible biases. After learning other cultural experiences, history, values, and traditions, the church needs to validate and then incorporate their needs into the environment.

Part of the environment is the worship experience. DeYmaz says, "To build a healthy multiethnic church, then, it is in worship that leaders must begin to promote a spirit of inclusion."[165] For a church to be inclusive in the worship environment and willing to change to accommodate all of God's people is critical. Rah concludes,

> If one cultural expression of worship dominates, then the Sunday service does not feel welcoming. Instead, it may even strike some as being a hostile environment that undermines cultural sensitivity. If there are cultural expressions in the worship setting that are assumed to be normative or more spiritual than others, then this extolling of one becomes an inhospitable context for those coming from others.[166]

Worship is an expression extolling God, and every person, no matter their race, should be able to worship God together. Rah believes worship is the face of the church representing what the church is about.[167] Paul and Peter both demonstrated and modeled the need for the church to be

---

163. Rah, *Many Colors*, 1072.
164. Gushiken, "Spiritual Formation," 190–91.
165. DeYmaz, *Building Healthy Multi-Ethnic Church*, 109.
166. Rah, *Many Colors*, 2279.
167. Rah, *Many Colors*, 2273.

willing to adjust its environment, according to the vision of God for all ethnicities to receive the gospel without limitation. Therefore, it is critical that worship represents the diversity of the church.

Diverse Leadership

A church will be as diverse as its leadership. Leadership represents the diversity in the church. Failure to diversify the leadership of the church diminishes the opportunity to create a multiethnic church. The modeled mobilization of leadership of Paul and Peter includes men and women from different backgrounds. As noted previously, Paul's purposeful choice of Timothy perfectly illustrates the need for intentionality for the diversification of leadership according to the vision and purpose of ethnic diversity.[168] Paul's choice of Timothy, both Greek and Jew, pinpoints the need for leaders to be chosen, according to mobilization of the gospel. McIntosh and McMahan write, "Diversity of leadership communicates that the church is serious about sharing power with all ethnic groups in the church."[169] The diversity of leadership communicates to the congregation that the church values diversity and desires leadership from all places. Fowler says,

> Having diverse leaders in visible positions demonstrates the vision of the church and communicates to the guests that the church is multiethnic and that there is a place for them. Practicing diversity in leadership that is visible but also even down to the less visible positions is a statement about where the congregation is headed and what they value.[170]

The visibility of diverse leadership allows congregants to see that the vision statement is a reality, and the purpose of diversity is being implemented in the leadership. Leadership has to be careful not to communicate diversity without allowing people of different cultures to have influence in the church.

Emerson notes that a church seeking diversity has to be careful that their leadership is not monoethnic. A monoethnic leadership could lead

---

168. See ch. 4.
169. McIntosh and McMahan, *Being the Church*, 189.
170. Fowler, "Planting, Transitioning, and Growing," 130.

to the misuse of power and the prevalence of one culture over another.[171] Emerson concludes,

> Misused power is the closest thing I observed to a nightmare in multiracial congregations. Congregations that seemed able to reduce such problems had clear-cut standards that were institutionalized, such that the voices of all groups were included. Not having standards for such inclusiveness eventually led to the misuse of power that adversely affected members of some groups more than members of other groups.[172]

A monoethnic leadership can allow for the misuse of power and the continuance of an imbalance of influence from the majority cultural group. The diversity of staff allows for power to spread to diverse people groups, allowing each culture an opportunity to express their values, experiences, history, and traditions.

Mobilization of the church should increase values organizationally that foster and contribute to a diverse church. Values need to be reflected in the vision, environment, and leadership of each church. After receiving the vision, Paul and Peter communicated God's vision for ethnic unity, adjusted their environment for the mobilization of the gospel, and equipped diverse leaders to do the same. Mobilization reflects the continuity of the values of the followers who are actively engaged in the mission of ethnic unification.

Third Principle

The third principle for current church leaders to apply is to be willing to engage in conflict in the persistent pursuit of unification of the diversity of the church. However, Peter and Paul played differing roles in the transformation of the diversity of the church. Peter set the foundation and, at times, practiced reformed leadership in contrast to Paul who practiced revolutionary. Although both were transformed personally and committed to the mobilization of the church, Peter's reformed leadership helped establish the polity and doctrine of church, while Paul carried the mission of the unification forward in constant conflict. Peter initiated the unification of Jew and gentile and used his authority to confirm the mission of God. He defended God's values after confirming

---

171. Emerson, *People of the Dream*, 2019.
172. Emerson, *People of the Dream*, 2029.

the work of God with Cornelius and continued to stand for the mission at the Council of Jerusalem.

Church leaders must be prepared to engage in both reformed and revolutionary leadership. Peter's role was necessary for the advancement of the unity of both Jew and gentile in the church. Peter stood by the values of God and the morality of uniting Jew and gentile. Burns argues that a reformed leader is a moral leader: "Reform leadership by definition usually implies moral leadership, and this imposes a special burden."[173] Peter maintained morality and sought to reform the morals of others. Mathew addresses Peter's reformed leadership: "As a cross-cultural leader, one must be willing to engage and confront an insular in-group cultural mindset within one's own culture. The idea that the world is corrupt because social structures are corrupt is the reformist response view."[174] He utilized his authority to stand against any social or religious structure that objected to inclusion of the gentiles in the gospel.

Burns addresses the success of reformed leadership: "But the most powerful impulse among the reform leaders was the democratization and ultimately the purification of party."[175] Peter played a leadership role in the purification of Jewish leadership and the Council of Jerusalem for the inclusion of gentiles into the church. "All social structures are susceptible to corruption over time as they become insular. The confrontation toward change is why social structures need reformation. The supernaturally given insights in the visions to Cornelius and Peter sparked the reformist responses."[176] However, Peter's reformed leadership had limitations and inconsistencies.

Peter's documented failure when approached by the Jews while fellowshipping with gentiles created division within Jew and gentile. His reluctance to commit fully coincided with the weaknesses of Burns's reformed leadership. Burns thoughtfully expands:

> The other tendency is the failure of reform leadership to achieve the actual (real) social change proportionate to the transformations that the leaders promised, and in the name of which reform was promised. Reform leaders may act on the benevolent notion that true politics is simply morals applied to public affairs, but they find in the heat of battle that true

---

173. Burns, *Leadership*, 170.
174. Mathew, "Apostle Peter's Cross-Cultural Leadership," 110.
175. Burns, *Leadership*, 197.
176. Mathew, "Apostle Peter's Cross-Cultural Leadership," 95.

> politics is the everyday scuffling and swapping in governmental and political marketplaces. Because reform leaders typically accept the political and social structures within which they act, their reform efforts are inevitably compromised, and usually inhibited, by the tenacious inertia of existing institutions. Far-reaching change in the end is carried through less by reform leaders, vital though their role is, than by politicians who see their political ambitions entangled in the reform effort. Reform is ever poised between the transforming and the transactional—transforming in spirit and posture, transactional in process and results. Revolutionary leaders understand this.[177]

In the midst of immense pressure, Peter conformed to the social and religious structures. His concession in the heat of conflict resulted in division and compromise to the morality that he was committed to uphold.

His leadership in that moment was poised between transactional and transforming. Also, the lack of documentation of Peter's involvement in the unification of the church is not as extensive as that of Paul's, therefore limiting the ability to have extensive knowledge of his continual leadership in the churches. However, this does not mean Peter did not continue to lead in diversity. Bruce confirms,

> Equally, it is unlikely that Peter felt himself debarred from evangelizing the Jews of, say, Corinth or Rome. But since the churches eventually established in those cities comprised both Jewish and Gentile converts, some dovetailing or overlapping of the two spheres of missionary activity was inevitable. That Peter's missionary activity was not restricted to Jews is implied here and there in the New Testament.[178]

Peter continued to hold to the morality, values, and mission of God, although the details of his leadership are not exhaustive. Mathew references Peter's willingness to remain in morality: "The openness in heart and mind to the supernatural influence is the reformist response displayed by Apostle Peter."[179] Despite Peter's initiation and use of authority to establish the morality between Jew and gentile, his failure pinpoints the weakness of reformed leadership. However, enough existent evidence proves his influence between Jew and gentile remained in the church.

---

177. Burns, *Leadership*, 190.
178. Bruce, *Peter, Stephen, James*, 302.
179. Mathew, "Apostle Peter's Cross-Cultural Leadership," 95.

Peter led the church into the unification of Jew and gentile and initiated the spread of the values to all the churches. Church leaders are therefore responsible to morally lead the mission of God for unity amid diversity in the church. Their moral leadership aligns their decisions and policies with their values. A reformed church leader will initiate causes within social and religious organizations according to their morals.

Additionally, Peter modeled using the religious structure to cause permanent change within the organization. Peter's leadership within the Jerusalem Council and his willingness to engage in conflict with church leadership after his interaction with Cornelius reveal his intention to pursue God's calling. However, church leaders have to avoid any compromise to religious, political, and social structures. Due to reformed willingness to accept existing structures, they will have to reject and be willing to conflict with any external structures. Also, church leaders must avoid any tendency to practice transactional leadership within an organized system.

Although reformed leadership functions and morally purifies from within the existing structures, revolutionary leadership is willing consistently to conflict and change existing organizations. Burns's revolutionary leadership is a "complete and pervasive transformation of an entire social system."[180] Paul demonstrated revolutionary leadership that was willing to transform society with an ideology with the rise of a new movement. Coinciding with Burns, Paul modeled a complete dedication to the cause, willing to risk lives, imprisonment, exile, persecution, and continual hardship. With extensive research already dedicated to Paul's persistent conflict in the book of Acts, it is an apparent model for church leaders to model.[181]

For church leaders to practice revolutionary leadership is critical. Despite the evidence of conflict existing within cultural change, Smith determines that few leaders are willing to sacrifice for congregational diversity:

> Second, although several evangelicals discuss the personal sacrifice necessary to form friendships across race, their solutions do not require financial or cultural sacrifice. They do not advocate or support changes that might cause extensive discomfort

---

180. Burns, *Leadership*, 202.
181. Polhill, *Acts* (NAC), 512.

or change their economic and cultural lives. In short, they maintain what is for them the noncostly status quo.[182]

When a church is trying to change social and religious structures, conflict will persist. Christerson et al. state that a religious organization will have more conflict: "Interracial religious organizations have higher levels of conflict than interracial nonreligious organizations because cultural differences tend to be given absolute and transcendent meanings, making compromise more difficult."[183]

DeYmaz agrees that a pastor or church leader has to be willing to sacrifice in order to achieve a multiethnic congregation.[184] Christerson et al. conclude that cultures coming together will always be in conflict:

> As culture represents truth, when people of different cultures come together, the consequence must always be some conflict, for it is more than people coming into contact. It really means that truths come into contact and that means conflict. Each group tends to believe that its beliefs and practices are the right or more correct ones. They judge others by it and being convinced of its correctness, each group makes every effort to impose their truth on everybody else. As everybody does the same thing, cultural contact will always mean conflict.[185]

As evidenced in the book of Acts, it is impossible to bring cultures together without conflict. Therefore, a leader must be willing to lead in conflict and embrace the ongoing cultural differences.

Emerson's research also recognizes impending organizational conflict: "This research indicates that it takes more effort, and often comes with more conflict, to have an organization change from uniracial to multiracial than it is to begin multiracial."[186] It is inevitable for conflict to occur as multiple cultures clash. It is not limited to the beginning of a church but even after a church integrates cultures, remaining conflict will still exist. Christerson's research also led him to resolve that "all of the organizations we studied experienced particular conflicts between ethnic groups regarding some aspects of how the organization operated."[187] Therefore, even in

---

182. Emerson and Smith, *Divided by Faith*, 130.
183. Christerson et al., *Against All Odds*, 175.
184. DeYmaz and Li, *Leading Healthy Multi-Ethnic Church*, 56.
185. Christerson et al., *Against All Odds*, 159–60.
186. Emerson, *People of the Dream*, 2177.
187. Christerson et al., *Against All Odds*, 160.

the midst of integrating cultures, conflict will remain within organizational structure and operation. As gleaned from the book of Acts, compromise between cultures within the organization will result in cultural conflicts. Jew and gentile consistently debated cultural and religious practices including food, circumcision, and church organization.

Leaders who refuse to engage in conflict or compromise will inevitably inhibit the church from a multicultural congregation. Conflict will persist in the church that refuses to address cultural differences and unite around values that outweigh their differences. Since conflict is unavoidable, a church leader needs to prepare and be dedicated totally to the cause of diversity. They have to be willing to sacrifice financially, numerically, and personally for the mission of diversity God has called for the church. Paul perfectly modeled a revolutionary leader due to his dedication to the cause and his willingness to suffer personally according to his conviction to unite Jew and gentile in the church. Church leaders must follow Paul's revolutionary model to achieve a complete and pervasive transformation of their religious system. A church leader's unwillingness to be dedicated to the cause of diversity will lead to a monoethnic congregation and status quo.

Conclusion

With the establishment of the church, it is necessary to study the leaders who were formidable in its formation. Leadership plays an integral role in the organizational structure and is responsible for a church's vision, mobilization, doctrinal establishment, and unity. Therefore, a review of apostolic church and influence of Paul and Peter on its diversity provided applications for the modern-day church. Both apostles were instrumental in the leadership of the church in the book of Acts, therefore, requiring an in-depth review of their transformational leadership in the growth and failures in the growth and diversification of the church.

Comparing their leadership styles revealed similarities, including personal transformations and mobilization. However, the major difference remained in their leadership when under pressure and conflict. Peter performed well within the existing religious structure, while Paul independently challenged and conflicted with all opposition. Peter's failure highlighted the weaknesses of reformed leadership, along with the necessity for consistent revolutionary leadership. Paul's persistent conflict pinpointed the necessity of conflict when overhauling religious structure.

Research indicates Peter and Paul were both fundamental in the growth of the church. However, Peter was foundational in the spread of the gospel and initial introduction to the gentiles, while Paul was instrumental in its growth to the remotest parts of the earth, especially the continuation of the gospel to the gentiles. Paul and Peter both encountered problems while unifying the church. Peter used his God-given authority to correct and set the doctrinal practices for the Jew and gentiles of the church. Paul, in obedience to his divine calling, persistently confronted his Jewish heritage in an effort to unify the church. Evidence of Paul's resolutions to church conflict exist in his writing to the churches. Although Peter was foundational, Peter and Paul were both responsible for the growth of the church and resolution to church practices between Jew and gentile.

The leadership of Paul and Peter set the model for the modern-day church. They modeled leadership in growth and in reconciling the problems in the unification of the church. They also revealed principles for modern-day church leaders to practice unifying the ethnic divide into their local congregations. Three consensus principles can be supported.

First, modern-day church leaders need to have a personal transformation and willingness to learn of cultures outside of their experiences. Second, they must mobilize followers and leaders with the values of unity amid diversity. Mobilization within the church will directly affect establishing the vision, environment, and leadership. Third, modern-day church leaders must practice reformed and revolutionary leadership. They have to lead the church morally but also practice revolutionary leadership to confront existing structures that hinder God's value, vision, and mission for diversity. They have to be prepared for conflict and not to compromise or become transactional when facing the pressure of the existing religious and social systems.

Paul and Peter provided the blueprint for leading and changing a church's culture for the unity of God's church. They modeled leadership that will grow and unify a diverse church through cultural and ethnic challenges. Modern-day church leaders are responsible to mobilize God's vision, value, and mission for a diverse church, therefore modeling his gospel plan of leadership model provided in the book of Acts.

6

Leadership Themes Summary and Conclusions

Summary of the Transformational Leadership Principles of Paul and Peter

Contemporary leaders must be willing to learn from historical leaders' successes and failures, especially when dealing with the same religious structure. Review and analysis of God's ordained leaders provide proficient models in leading the church he created. The birth of the church gives us the original framework for modern-day churches to analyze doctrine, leadership structure, conflict resolution, and mission mobilization. Therefore, through Luke's historical account, study of the two primary characters in the book of Acts provides a model of leadership for current leaders, especially as they lead through issues of diversity and cultural unity. Luke tells the historical setting of the birth of the church at Pentecost and the ethnic and cultural diversity that ensued in its growth. This current study applied Burns's *Transforming Leadership* to Paul's and Peter's responses to diversity in Acts and established leadership models for the modern-day church.

Both Paul and Peter exemplified the necessity for a leader to experience personal transformation and calling before embarking on the transformation of existing structures, organizations, and followers. In agreement with Burns's transformational leadership, a personal transformation from origins is necessary to shift values, needs, and wants. In addition, it is only after personal transformation that leaders can revolutionize or reform their existing religious structures. In concurrence with

Burns's origins, Paul and Peter were staunch in the original beliefs and values established by their backgrounds, experiences, family, culture, and education. However, both had to experience Jesus and be redirected to his calling before they were able to lead their respective followers. Therefore, the first principle modeled by Paul and Peter in response to diversity is personally to transform leader origins to reproduce the values of God. God called church leaders to lead the cultural and ethnic diversity aspect of the church. The inescapability of God's diverse plan forces leaders to relinquish their personal backgrounds, experiences, political affiliations, and educations to follow the calling of God for his church.

Only after a leader's personal transformation can they lead others to be active followers of the leader's values. Without a personal transformation, the ability to transform others will fall short because the leader will not withstand the conflict and perseverance necessary to mobilize active followers. Also, "reformed" and "revolutionary leadership" is defined by Burns as leadership that changes existing systems, which requires active followers to transform their values. Both Paul and Peter demonstrated transforming leadership, which demands mobilization as evidence for successful revolutionary and reformed leadership. Peter and Paul committed their lives to the mobilization of the church including the development of followers and leaders, while persistently pursuing the unity of Jew and gentile.

Peter is documented in Acts as utilizing his authority to confirm and initiate gentile inclusion. He was willing to authenticate the work of God in the church for Jew and gentile. Called to the gentiles, Paul persistently traveled on missions with the gospel, planting churches and returning to churches to encourage their leaders and followers. As evidenced in his later epistles, he remained active in the mobilization of more followers and leaders for the continual growth of the church. Therefore, the second principle modeled requires modern-day church leaders to mobilize their followers to become active participants in the mission of God. Evidence of mobilization is when the church begins to participate in the vision and mission of God's plan for diversity.

Although multiple applications exist to the church mobilizing toward diversity, ample support also exists for a church to change its vision, environment, and leadership to reflect its active pursuit of diversity. For a church to mobilize toward God's mission of diversity, it must change or add to its organization, values, and vision. The vision provides purpose and goals for the church, therefore making it critical for a church to set a vision for diversity. The vision will directly affect the leadership and environment of the church to be inclusive and integrating for all ethnic diversity to be representative, active, and included. Churches that do not mobilize toward diversity will grow complacent and indifferent and remain monoethnic.

The most prevalent model that needs to be replicated with church leaders is Paul and Peter's reflection of conflict in Burns's *Transforming Leadership*. They were willing to confront the existing system with new values of the union of Jew and gentile in the church. Peter engaged in conflict early on against the Jewish leadership, risking his life to defend God's mission to the gentiles. He consistently stood among the leadership of the church and Jewish leadership to declare God's plan for Jew and gentile to be united in the church. He led among others at the Jerusalem Council to set the doctrine and practices of the church. However, his one failure in conforming to the pressure revealed his tendency to fall back to reformed leadership rather than revolutionary leadership.

Peter negatively modeled the failure of leadership to withstand pressure from existing structures and the detrimental effect it has on followers. Although reformed leaders create values through their morality, they can be susceptible to transactional leadership and compromise to religious, social, and political structures. Therefore, it is critical that all modern-day church leaders be willing to withstand the pressure of existing religious structure by refusing to be transactional or compromising.

Paul perfectly modeled revolutionary leadership that necessitates risk and conflict. Despite facing conflict in every city, his persistent revolutionary leadership represented the necessary leadership to create a total upheaval of an existing structure. Paul did not stop mobilizing Jew and gentile, although he was imprisoned, beaten, and exiled. The book of Acts extensively documented Paul's pattern of revolutionary leadership as he entered cities, despite threats to his life and near-death experiences. It is essential that church leaders model revolutionary leadership. They must be willing to face criticism, conflict, and risk to change an existing religious structure. They must be willing to lose membership, conflict with current leadership, and even being exiled from their organization to unify diverse cultures and ethnicities. Conflict is unavoidable when pursuing a multiethnic church; therefore, a leader's commitment to the cause is uncompromisable. Church leaders must practice the morality of reformed leadership, but when conflict presents itself from the existing church structure, they must be revolutionary to change the church.

New Learning from Historical Analysis

The book of Acts provides the proper documentation to evaluate Paul's and Peter's leadership. Their leadership in the midst of unifying Jew and gentile provides a model to modern-day leadership. The historical account of Luke creates an accurate documentation to evaluate Paul, Peter, and the church. Historical analysis provides an evaluation of the past, which can provide a model for anyone who needs to review similarities in their modern-day situations. The survey of Acts provides ample principles to provide modern-day churches the record of challenges facing the unification of ethnicities, exemplified by Jew and gentile relations in Acts. The survey of Acts reports the conflict, growth, and doctrine of the church. Luke also identifies leaders who were critical in the church's development. Therefore, Acts must be utilized to research any conflicts, growth, leadership, and doctrine, which could help church success and avoid historical failures.

Future Areas of Study

Variant Approaches

Although Burns's transforming leadership theory supports key principles in the leadership of Paul and Peter, other leadership theories could be applied to Paul and Peter to find other models to benefit the modern-day church in the pursuit of diversity. To discover whether principles related to theories, such as adaptive or servant leadership, are also prevalent in efforts toward unification of ethnic and cultural diversity in the churches of the New Testament would be advantageous. Leadership theories models applied to Paul and Peter will possibly find proper historical fits. If applicable, other leadership theories will increase the applications to the modern-day church.

Areas for Future Research

Despite Luke's historical account, a study of Paul's and Peter's epistles would have supplemented the study of the leadership of Paul and Peter and the continuation of Jew and gentile unification. Although this writing referenced their letters, extensively utilizing these documents would have provided additional support to their continual work in the church, especially the unification of Jew and gentiles. Additionally, a survey of

Paul's and Peter's epistles would supply more patterns of growth, conflict, and solutions. Peter's letters would support his continual leadership role between Jew and gentile in the church after the book of Acts. Peter's letters are more of a necessary resource because of Luke's departure from Peter's continued involvement after Acts.

In addition, the letters would supplement whether Peter and Paul continued to be transforming leaders and the results of their leadership in the church. A continual study would provide evidence of how the church responded to either reformed or revolutionary leadership and whether a preferred approach to secure long-term structural change is needed.

A potential area of future study must include an inclusive historical approach of the persisting conflicts, growth patterns, and formations in the church following the book of Acts. This exploration will reveal the initial persistent and reoccurring conflicts, which occurred while uniting ethnicities and culture. Upon identifying the challenges and conflicts in the continuation of unification of diverse cultures, modern-day leaders can evaluate whether those issues are present in their churches. If conflicts and challenges exist in the current church, then modern-day leaders should evaluate a biblical leader's model and solutions to their current unification issues. Upon discovery of a biblical model, modern-day leaders will have the correct leadership theory to apply for cultural conflicts. One church that needs continual research is the church of Antioch and its ability to handle diversity. The depth of the study into the church of Antioch will reveal leadership principles, which was successful during the diversity in Antioch.

Conclusion

The North American church has a choice whether to remain complacent or complicit in its desire to seek diversity in its local churches. History has demanded a response from the church with mixed results and detrimental effects dependent on the church's willingness to engage in ethnic and cultural problems. Leadership plays an integral role in the church's response to the challenges of diversity. Viewed through Burns's transforming leadership theory, the book of Acts frames the necessary leadership model to change existing structures and mobilize followers' values. To test transforming leadership theory properly, this current study applied the definitions, descriptions, and principles to biblical leaders. Therefore, to analyze biblical leadership's response in the birth of the church in Acts and the diversity that ensued after Pentecost was critical.

Paul and Peter provide modern-day leadership a model to follow, which transformed the existing religious structures and mobilized the church. With church leaders' immense impact on the vision, environment, and mobilization of the church, it is vital that church leaders to reevaluate their morals and leadership to transform the church toward diversity.

Use of the book of Acts reveals God's intent for mobilization of the gospel and diversity in his mission. God's plan for diversity became evident at Pentecost when Jews from different nations returned from the diaspora to the Feast of Weeks. It also highlights Peter and Paul as primary characters of God's plan for the birth and spread of the gospel. The study of Acts is perfectly situated to evaluate God's historical plan for diversity and the leaders he chose to mobilize the gospel to Jew and gentile from Jerusalem to the remotest parts of the earth. Studying the birth, growth, and challenges of the movement provided ample evidence for God's purpose, mission, leadership, and strategy for his church.

The model applied to modern-day church leaders becomes a clear guide to changing church history and amending its failure to respond to diversity. The practice of reformed and revolutionary leadership is necessary to change the values and morality of an existing system. Before church leaders can lead a church toward diversity, they first must personally transform their wants and needs to the values, morality, and calling of God. In addition, a church will not change unless the leader mobilizes followers to be active in the pursuit of the mission of God for a unified multiethnic church. Mobilization in the church should be reflected in its doctrine, vision, environment, and leadership. However, church leaders must be prepared to embrace conflict as revolutionary leaders, especially to a preestablished structure.

Reformed leadership is fundamental, especially when establishing the morality in the beginning of a movement and one critical to its foundation. Additionally, transactional leadership will never accomplish permanent change of an existing system. Both forms of transforming leadership are necessary to change the church. Paul's and Peter's leadership were both fundamental in the unification of Jew and gentile; therefore, their study is warranted to modern leaders' efforts to grow and unify a multiethnic church.

Cultivating a healthy, diverse church requires leaders who model the example provided in the Bible. The book of Acts creates a comprehensive historical setting for diversity and leadership. Paul and Peter modeled transforming leadership that sets the precedent for modern-day leadership in pursuit of God's calling to a diverse church. Burns's transforming leadership model perfectly aligns with the leadership of Paul and Peter, validating the necessity of transformation so that churches can accomplish diversity in their congregations.

Bibliography

Achtemeier, Paul J. "An Elusive Unity: Paul, Acts, and the Early Church." *CBQ* 48 (1986) 1–26.
Allbaugh, Jonathan. "Paul's Rhetorical Leadership in an Arena of Cultures: A Sociorhetorical and Content Analysis of Acts 21–26 and Romans 13:1–7 That Provides Guidance for Presidents of Christian Colleges during Challenges to Religious Liberty." PhD diss., Regent University, 2017.
Allen, Debra Harding. "Pastoral Transformational Leadership and Church Human Service Provision." PhD diss., Walden University, 2017.
Allen, Willoughby C. *A Critical and Exegetical Commentary on the Gospel According to St. Matthew*. ICC. New York: Scribner's Sons, 1907.
Bandura, Albert. "Social-Learning of Identification Processes." In *Handbook of Socialization Theory and Research*, edited by David A. Goslin, 213–62. Chicago: Rand McNally and Co., 1971.
Barak, Michal E. Mor, et al. "Organizational and Personal Dimensions in Diversity Climate: Ethnic and Gender Differences in Employee Perceptions." *Journal of Applied Behavioral Science* 1 (1998) 82–104.
Barrett, C. K. *A Critical and Exegetical Commentary on the Acts of the Apostles*. ICC. Edinburgh: T&T Clark, 2004.
Barton, Ruth. *Strengthening the Soul of Your Leadership: Seeking God in the Crucible of Ministry*. Downers Grove, IL: IVP, 1998.
Bass, Bernard M. *Leadership and Performance beyond Expectations*. New York: Free, 1985.
Beasley-Murray, George R. *John*. 2nd ed. WBC 36. Dallas: Word, 2002.
Bernard, J. H. *A Critical and Exegetical Commentary on the Gospel According to St. John*. Edited by A. H. McNeile. New York: Scribner's Sons, 1929.
Blackaby, Richard, and Henry Blackaby. *Spiritual Leadership: Moving People on to God's Agenda*. Nashville: B&H, 2011.
Blanchard, Ken, and Phil Hodges. *Lead Like Jesus: Lessons from the Greatest Leadership Role Model of All Time*. Nashville: Thomas Nelson, 2005.
Blass, Friedrich, et al. *Grammatik des neutestamentlichen Griechisch*. 14th ed. Revised by Friedrich Rehkopf. Göttingen: Vandenhoeck & Ruprecht, 1979.

Blomberg, Craig. *Matthew*. NAC 22. Nashville: Broadman & Holman, 1992.
Blum, Edwin A. "John." In *The Bible Knowledge Commentary: An Exposition of the Scriptures*, edited by John F. Walvoord and Roy B. Zuck, 2:267–348. Wheaton, IL: Victor, 1985.
Blum, Edward J., and Paul Harvey. *The Color of Christ: The Son of God and the Saga of Race in America*. Chapel Hill: University of North Carolina Press, 2012.
Boa, Kenneth, and William Kruidenier. *Romans*. Holman New Testament Commentary 6. Nashville: Broadman & Holman, 2000.
Bock, Darrell L. *Acts*. BECNT. Grand Rapids: Baker Academic, 2007.
———. *Cultural Intelligence: Living for God in a Diverse, Pluralistic World*. Nashville: B&H Academic, 2020.
Borchert, Gerald L. *John 12–21*. NAC 25B. Nashville: Broadman & Holman, 2002.
Boston, Jonathan, et al., eds. *Public Policy: Why Ethics Matters*. Canberra: ANU Press, 2010.
Breckenridge, James F., and Lillian Breckenridge. *What Color Is Your God? Multicultural Education in the Church*. Grand Rapids: Baker, 1995.
Brown, Raymond E. *Introduction to the New Testament*. New York: Doubleday, 1997.
Bruce, F. F. *The Book of the Acts*. NICOT. Grand Rapids: Eerdmans, 1988.
———. *The Epistle to the Galatians: A Commentary on the Greek Text*. NIGTC. Grand Rapids: Eerdmans, 1982.
———. *Peter, Stephen, James, and John: Non-Pauline Diversity in the Early Church*. Nashville: Kingsley, n.d.
Burns, James MacGregor. *Leadership*. Harper Perennial Political Classics. New York: Open Road, 2010. First published 1978. Kindle.
———. *Transforming Leadership*. New York: Grove/Atlantic, 2003. Kindle.
Burton, Ernest De Witt. *A Critical and Exegetical Commentary on the Epistle to the Galatians*. ICC. New York: Scribner's Sons, 1920.
Bush, Tony. "Transformational Leadership: Exploring Common Conceptions." *Educational Management Administration & Leadership* 46 (2018) 883–87.
Campbell, Donald K. "Foreword." In *Basic Bible Interpretation: A Practical Guide to Discovering Biblical Truth*, edited by Craig Bubeck Sr., 10–26. Colorado Springs: Cook, 1991.
———. "Galatians." In *The Bible Knowledge Commentary: An Exposition of the Scriptures*, edited by John F. Walvoord and Roy B. Zuck, 2:594–612. Wheaton, IL: Victor, 1985.
Carson, D. A. *The Gospel According to John*. Grand Rapids: Eerdmans, 1991.
Chen, Abraham Shinchieh. "The Transformational Leadership of the Apostle Paul: A Socio-Rhetorical Analysis of Philippians 1." PhD diss., Regent University, 2020.
Christerson, Brad, et al. *Against All Odds: The Struggle for Racial Integration in Religious Organizations*. New York: NYU Press, 2005.
Collins, Gary R. *Christian Coaching: Helping Others Turn Potential into Reality*. Colorado Springs: Navigators, 2009.
Conzelmann, Hans. *Acts of the Apostles: A Commentary on the Acts of the Apostles*. Edited by Eldon Jay Epp and Christopher R. Matthews. Translated by James Limburg et al. Hermeneia. Philadelphia: Fortress, 1987.
Cooper, Michael. "The Transformational Leadership of the Apostle Paul: A Contextual and Biblical Leadership for Contemporary Ministry." *Christian Education Journal* 2 (2005) 48–61. https://doi.org/10.1177/073989130500200103.

Davies, W. D., and Dale C. Allison Jr. *Matthew 8–18*. ICC 2. London: T&T Clark, 2004.
DeYmaz, Mark. *Building a Healthy Multi-Ethnic Church: Mandate, Commitments, and Practices of a Diverse Congregation*. Leadership Network. San Francisco: Jossey-Bass, 2007.
DeYmaz, Mark, and Harry Li. *Ethnic Blends: Mixing Diversity into Your Local Church*. Grand Rapids: Zondervan, 2010.
———. *Leading a Healthy Multi-Ethnic Church*. Leadership Network Innovation. Grand Rapids: Zondervan, 2015.
DeYoung, Curtiss Paul, et al. *United by Faith: The Multiracial Congregation as an Answer to the Problem of Race*. New York: Oxford University Press, 2004.
Dunn, James D. G. *The Acts of the Apostles*. Grand Rapids: Eerdmans, 2016.
———. *Romans 1–8*. WBC 38A. Dallas: Word, 1988.
———. *Unity and Diversity in the New Testament*. London: Trinity International, 1977.
Easton, M. G. *Easton's Bible Dictionary*. New York: Harper, 1893.
Elwell, Walter A., and Philip Wesley Comfort, eds. *Tyndale Bible Dictionary*. Tyndale Reference Library. Wheaton, IL: Tyndale, 2001.
Emerson, Michael O. *People of the Dream: Multiracial Congregations in the United States*. Princeton, NJ: Princeton University Press, 2006.
Emerson, Michael O., and Christian Smith. *Divided by Faith: Evangelical Religion and the Problem of Race in America*. New York: Oxford University Press, 2001.
Enns, Paul P. *The Moody Handbook of Theology*. Chicago: Moody, 1989.
Evans, Tony. *Oneness Embraced: Through the Eyes of Tony Evans*. Edited by Cheryl Dunlop. Chicago: Moody, 2011.
Family and Youth Services Bureau. *Guide to Enhancing the Cultural Competence of Runaway and Homeless Youth Programs*. Silver Spring, MD: Johnson, Bassin, and Shaw, 1994.
Fitzmyer, Joseph A. *The Acts of the Apostles: A New Translation with Introduction and Commentary*. AYBRL 31. London: Yale University Press, 2008.
Ford, Leighton. *Transforming Leadership: Jesus' Way of Creating Vision, Shaping Values, Empowering Change*. Downers Grove, IL: IVP, 1991.
Fowler, Gloria Young-Eun Kim. "Planting, Transitioning, and Growing Multiethnic Churches." DMin diss., Asbury Theological Seminary, 2015
Garland, David E. *2 Corinthians*. NAC 29. Nashville: Broadman & Holman, 1999.
Gauer, Laura. "A Christian Perspective on Poverty and Social Justice: Sin Is More than Just Flawed Character." *Journal of the North American Association of Christians in Social Work* 32 (2005) 354–65.
George, Timothy. *Galatians*. NAC 30. Nashville: Broadman & Holman, 1994.
Gray, Derwin L. *The High-Definition Leader: Building Multiethnic Churches in a Multiethnic World*. Nashville: Thomas Nelson, 2015.
Grunlan, Stephen. "Leadership Principles from Proverbs." *Ministry* 79 (2007) 25–27.
Guder, Darrell, ed. *Missional Church: A Vision for the Sending of the Church in North America*. Gospel and Our Culture. Grand Rapids: Eerdmans, 1998.
Gushiken, Kevin. "Spiritual Formation and Multiethnic Congregations." *Journal of Spiritual Formation and Soul Care* 4 (2011) 185–203.
Hackman, Michael Z., and Craig E. Johnson. *Leadership: A Communication Perspective*. Long Grove, IL: Waveland, 2013.
Hagner, Donald A. *Matthew 14–28*. WBC 33B. Dallas: Word, 1995.

Hansen, G. Walter. *Galatians.* IVP New Testament Commentary 9. Downers Grove, IL: IVP Academic, 1994. Ebook.

Harris, Murray J. *The Second Epistle to the Corinthians: A Commentary on the Greek Text.* NIGTC. Grand Rapids: Eerdmans, 2005.

Hawthorne, Gerald F. *Philippians.* WBC 43. Dallas: Word, 2004.

Hughes, Robert B., and J. Carl Laney. *Tyndale Concise Bible Commentary.* Tyndale Reference Library. Wheaton, IL: Tyndale, 2001.

Jackson, Ervin C. "The Impact of Ethnically Diverse Leadership upon the Culture of a Historically African American Church of Christ." PhD diss., University of Alabama, 2002.

Keener, Craig S. *New Testament.* IVP Bible Background Commentary. Downers Grove, IL: IVP Academic, 1993. Ebook.

Kidder, S. Joseph. "The Biblical Role of the Pastor." *Ministry* 81 (2009) 19–21.

Kim, Matthew D. *Preaching with Cultural Intelligence: Understanding the People Who Hear Our Sermons.* Grand Rapids: Baker Academic, 2017.

Knudsen, Donald N. "The Effect of Transformational Leadership on Growth in Specialized Non-Profit Organizations: Churches." PhD diss., Touro University International, 2006.

Kotter, John P. *Leading Change: Why Transformation Efforts Fail.* Boston: Harvard Business School Press, 1998.

Kouzes, James M., and Barry Z. Posner. *The Leadership Challenge: How to Make Extraordinary Things Happen in Organizations.* 3rd ed. San Francisco: Jossey-Bass, 2012.

Larkin, William J., Jr. *Acts.* IVP New Testament Commentary 5. Westmont, IL: IVP Academic, 1995.

Leander, A. Brian. "Intercultural Leadership: A Mixed Methods Study of Leader Cultural Intelligence and Leadership Practices in Diversity-Oriented Churches." PhD diss., Eastern University, 2014.

Lee, William W., and Karl J. Krayer. *Organizing Change: An Inclusive, Systemic Approach to Maintain Productivity and Achieve Results.* Danvers, MA: Pfeiffer, 2003.

Livermore, David. *Digital, Diverse & Divided: How to Talk to Racists, Compete with Robots, and Overcome Polarization.* Oakland, CA: Berrett-Koehler, 2022.

———. *Leading with Cultural Intelligence: The Real Secret to Success.* New York: AMACOM, 2015.

Longenecker, Richard N. *Galatians.* WBC 41. Dallas: Word, 1990.

Lowery, David K. "2 Corinthians." In *The Bible Knowledge Commentary: An Exposition of the Scriptures,* edited by John F. Walvoord and Roy B. Zuck, 2:550–81. Wheaton, IL: Victor, 1985.

Lutz, Alison. "Economic Inequality as God's Law: Considering the Nature of Economic Life." *AThR* 95 (2013) 251–74.

Malphurs, Aubrey. *The Nuts and Bolts of Church Planting: A Guide for Starting Any Kind of Church.* Grand Rapids: Baker, 2011.

Mangum, Douglas, ed. *New Testament.* Lexham Context Commentary. Bellingham, WA: Lexham, 2020. Ebook.

Marshall, I. Howard. *Acts: An Introduction and Commentary.* TNTC 5. Downers Grove, IL: Inter-Varsity, 1980.

Martyn, J. Louis. *Galatians: A New Translation with Introduction and Commentary.* AYBRL 33A. New Haven, CT: Yale University Press, 2008.

Matheson, George. *Spiritual Development of St. Paul.* New York: Thomas Whittaker, 1985.
Mathew, Sonny. "Apostle Peter's Cross-Cultural Leadership in Christian Missions to the Gentiles: A Sociorhetorical Analysis of Acts 10:1–11:18." PhD diss., Regent University, 2018.
Mathews, Kenneth A. *Genesis 1—11:26.* NAC 1A. Nashville: Broadman & Holman, 1996.
McIntosh, Gary L., and Alan McMahan. *Being the Church in a Multi-Ethnic Community: Why It Matters and How It Works.* Indianapolis: Wesleyan, 2012.
Melick, Richard R. *Philippians, Colossians, Philemon.* NAC 32. Nashville: Broadman & Holman, 1991.
Morris, Leon. *The Gospel According to Matthew.* Pillar New Testament Commentary. Grand Rapids: Eerdmans, 1992.
Mounce, Robert H. *Romans.* NAC 27. Nashville: Broadman & Holman, 1995.
Murray, Julio E. "The AGAPE Economy: The Church's Call to Action." *AThR* 98 (2015) 125–35.
Nolland, John. *The Gospel of Matthew: A Commentary on the Greek Text.* NIGTC. Grand Rapids: Eerdmans, 2005.
Northouse, Peter G. *Leadership: Theory and Practice.* Thousand Oaks, CA: Sage, 2004.
Peake, Arthur S. *Plain Thoughts on Great Subjects.* London: Allenson, 1931.
Pervo, Richard I. *Acts: A Commentary on the Book of Acts.* Edited by Harold W. Attridge. Hermeneia. Minneapolis: Fortress, 2009.
Peterson, David G. *The Acts of the Apostles.* Pillar New Testament Commentary. Grand Rapids: Eerdmans, 2009.
Phillips, Elaine A. "The Geographic Importance of Antioch on the Orontes (Acts 6:5; 11:19–30; 13:1–3; 14:26–28; 15:1–3, 22–35; 18:22–23)." In *Lexham Geographic Commentary on Acts through Revelation*, edited by Barry J. Beitzel et al., 269–77. Lexham Geographic Commentary. Bellingham, WA: Lexham, 2019.
Plummer, Alfred. *A Critical and Exegetical Commentary on the Second Epistle of St. Paul to the Corinthians.* ICC. New York: T&T Clark, 1915.
Polhill, John B. *Acts.* NAC 26. Nashville: Broadman & Holman, 1992.
———. *Acts.* Edited by David S. Dockery. Holman Concise Bible Commentary 26. Nashville: Broadman & Holman, 1998.
Porter, Stanley E. "Acts." In *CSB Study Bible: Notes*, edited by Edwin A. Blum and Trevin Wax, 1713–15. Nashville: Holman Bible, 2017.
Rah, Soong-Chan. *Many Colors: Cultural Intelligence for a Changing Church.* Chicago: Moody, 2010.
———. *The Next Evangelicalism: Releasing the Church from Western Cultural Captivity.* Downers Grove, IL: IVP, 2009.
Ramirez, Raul Martin Latoni. "Pastoral Leadership Practices in Evangelical Multiethnic Congregations: A Multi-Case Study." DEd diss., Southern Baptist Theological Seminary, 2012.
Robertson, A. T. *Word Pictures in the New Testament.* Nashville: Broadman, 1933. Ebook.
Scarborough, Thomas O. "Defining Christian Transformational Leadership." *Conspectus* 10 (2010) 58–87.
Short, Chadwick L. "Meeting the Challenge of Diversity: Ministry and Mission in a Multicultural Milieu." PhD diss., Asbury Theological Seminary, 2006.

Soupios, Michael A., and Panos Mourdoukoutas. *Ten Golden Rules of Leadership: Classical Wisdom for Modern Leaders*. New York: AMACOM, 2015.

Stallard, Stephen. "Majority World Theology in an Urban, Multiethnic North American Church Plant." *Journal of Ministry and Theology* 20 (2016) 106–24.

Stringfellow, William. "The Unity of the Church as the Witness of the Church." *AThR* 100 (2018) 523–30.

Thomas, R. Roosevelt. *Redefining Diversity*. New York: American Management Association, 1996.

Thrall, Margaret E. *A Critical and Exegetical Commentary on the Second Epistle of the Corinthians*. ICC. New York: T&T Clark, 2004.

Tisby, Jemar. *The Color of Compromise: The Truth about the American Church's Complicity in Racism*. Grand Rapids: Zondervan, 2019.

Toussaint, Stanley D. "Acts." In *The Bible Knowledge Commentary: An Exposition of the Scriptures*, edited by John F. Walvoord and Roy B. Zuck, 2:349–434. Wheaton, IL: Victor, 1985.

Vincent, Marvin Richardson. *A Critical and Exegetical Commentary on the Epistles to the Philippians and to Philemon*. ICC. New York: Scribner's Sons, 1897.

Walrath, Douglas. *Leading Churches through Change*. Creative Leadership Series. Nashville: Abingdon, 1979.

Willis, Sheilesha. "Toward a Model of Diversity Leadership: Examining Leadership's Role in Creating an Inclusive Workplace." PhD diss., Claremont Graduate University, 2014.

Winthrop, Robert H. "Ethnicity." *Dictionary of Concepts in Cultural Anthropology*. Reference Sources for the Social Sciences and Humanities. New York: Greenwood, 1991.

Yount, William R. *Created to Learn: A Christian Teacher's Introduction to Educational Psychology*. 2nd ed. Nashville: B&H Academic, 2010.

Yukl, Gary A. *Leadership in Organizations*. 8th ed. Upper Saddle River, NJ: Prentice Hall, 2012.

www.ingramcontent.com/pod-product-compliance
Lightning Source LLC
Chambersburg PA
CBHW060603230426
43670CB00011B/1945